IMAGES
of America

AROUND GREENSBORO

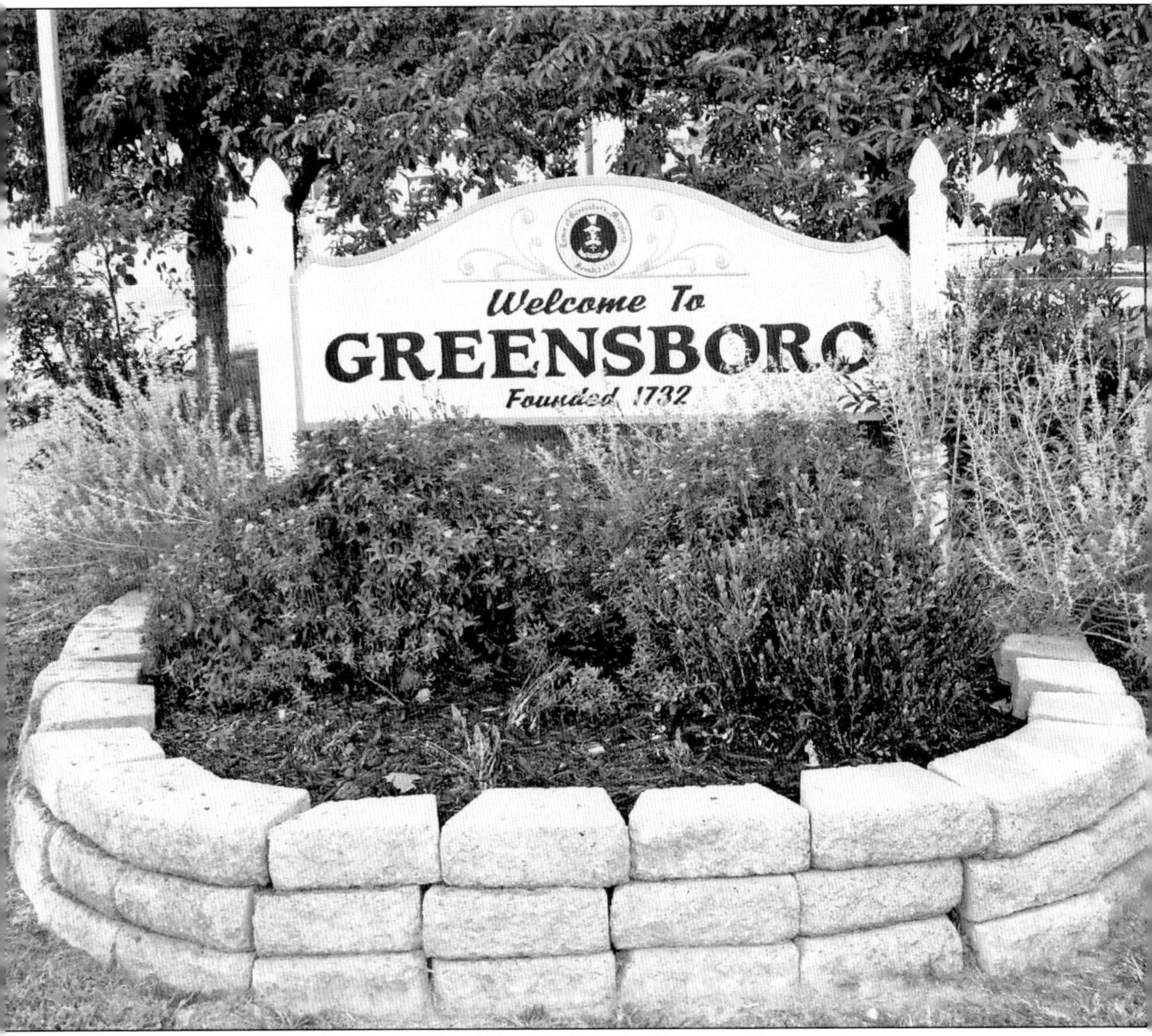

The town of Greensboro, Maryland, located on the Eastern Shore, welcomes everyone to come and enjoy its history and friendship. (Courtesy J. C. Reveal.)

ON THE COVER: The railroad was instrumental in aiding the town of Greensboro in maintaining a healthy business environment. Residents and businesspeople alike gathered at the Greensboro train depot to welcome incoming visitors and load and unload products necessary to the business community. (Courtesy Sara K. Edwards/Richard Smith.)

IMAGES
of America

AROUND GREENSBORO

Judith Reveal

ARCADIA
PUBLISHING

ISBN 978-0-7385-5372-6

Published by Arcadia Publishing
Charleston SC, Chicago IL, Portsmouth NH, San Francisco CA

Printed in the United States of America

Library of Congress Catalog Card Number: 2007939922

For all general information contact Arcadia Publishing at:
Telephone 843-853-2070
Fax 843-853-0044
E-mail sales@arcadiapublishing.com
For customer service and orders:
Toll-Free 1-888-313-2665

Visit us on the Internet at www.arcadiapublishing.com

This book is dedicated to the children of Greensboro's past, present, and future. "Today is the tomorrow we dreamed about yesterday!"

—*Anonymous*

Contents

ACKNOWLEDGMENTS

Special thanks to David Spencer, mayor, for his insightful remembrances of growing up in Greensboro. Completion of this book would not have been possible without the many contributions from people who helped gather information and photographs and brought many memories to life.

Thanks to the Library System of Caroline County and especially to Richard Smith of the North County Branch in Greensboro for encouragement regarding this project and his generous permission to use the cover photograph in memory of Sara K. Edwards. I would be remiss if I did not thank the Town of Greensboro's staff and the citizens of Greensboro and the surrounding area for their enthusiasm and contributions, including Cheryl Jones, Virginia Bishop Jones, Mary Kinnamon Jones Raughley, Joan Cesarini, Tony Gianninoto, Jean Gardner Warren, Tom and MaryLou Riddleberger, the Maryland Historical Trust, the Greensboro Baptist Church, St. Paul's Methodist Church, the Caroline County Board of Education, the Town of Denton, and the *Times Record* newspaper. And special thanks to Lauren Bobier and Maggie Bullwinkle, Southern publishers for Arcadia Publishing, for their ongoing support and encouragement.

WORKS CITED

Cochrane, Laura C., et al. *The History of Caroline County, Maryland, From Its Beginning*. Baltimore, MD: Regional Publishing Company, 1971.

Eshelman, Ralph E., and Carl W. Scheffel Jr. "Maryland's Upper Choptank River and Tuckahoe River Cultural Resource Inventory." April 1999. www.riverheritage.org/choptank_tuckahoe_inventory.pdf

Howard, Doris. *Baptist Church History*. self-published, 1984.

Jensen, Christian E., MD. *Lives of Caroline County, Maryland, Physicians, 1774–1984*. Denton, MD: self-published, 1986.

Lednum, John. *A History of the Rise of Methodism in America*. Philadelphia, PA: self-published, 1859.

McClyment, Claudine I., Paul L. Howard, and Historical Committees of St. Paul's United Methodist Church. *History of Methodism*. Greensboro, MD: St. Paul's United Methodist Church, 1959.

INTRODUCTION

I am 52 years old and have always called Greensboro "home," except for my time spent serving our country in the U.S. Army. I grew up on a quiet, dead-end street that borders the town's most economically viable resource, the Choptank River. As a young child, I walked with my friends the two miles or so every day to the old brick schoolhouse that now serves as an apartment complex. Each trip was an adventure. Townsfolk often sat on their front porches or stood outside talking with their neighbors. Everyone knew you and your family by name, and news of bad or mischievous behavior often arrived home before you. Each day, you could stop by the hardware store for conversation or any of the several "general stores" for penny candy or a cold soda in a bottle. Getting a haircut was never a problem with as many as three shops to choose from. Each visit was an educational experience for a young man as I listened and learned from the "old men" who gathered at the shops to pass the time away and to share the news of the day.

Looking back, the wisdom I learned from those conversations still guides me today. It was the way the stories and history of the town and its townsfolk were passed on to the next generation. As a child, the "uptown" had lots of busy stores where you could find almost anything you needed for your daily life. Going to Denton was considered a "trip." When giving directions to anyone, the stoplight was used as the focal point, sitting at the center of the town at Main and Sunset Streets. The whistle at the Pet Milk Plant always told you the time of the day, blowing at 8:00 a.m., at 12:00 noon, and again at the 5:00 p.m. quitting time.

The sounding of the fire siren would send everyone on our street scurrying to the top of the road near the Redman's Lodge just to see which way the fire trucks were headed. This would inevitably spark a debate over their destination since scanners and pagers weren't yet in vogue.

The changing of the seasons was always ushered in with a special event. The annual Little League parade and activities always signaled spring was upon us. In those days, young boys and girls could be found playing baseball in someone's vacant lot during the day or playing hide-and-seek at night. The Firemen's Carnival and fireworks signaled that summer had arrived, and the firemen actually worked the rides. Even if you couldn't afford the 10¢ for the ride, the firemen somehow always made sure that all the kids got to ride. Halloween would signal the arrival of fall. No one seemed to mind if you soaped their windows, and homemade treats were the best and most sought after by the kids. Of course, you had to take your mask off and tell them who you were (even though they already knew) and how your family was doing. Santa Claus always arrived in a fire truck with goodies for the kids and signaled the start of a long cold winter. In those days, the river actually froze solid enough for ice skating, and no one was afraid to use the ice from the river for homemade ice cream.

The names of townsfolk who passed on were traditionally displayed on a plaque on the outside of the funeral home. No one ever passed by without looking to see if another neighbor was lost.

Ah, the wonderful memories of childhood. Today, as I look over Greensboro as its mayor, I am proud to say I can still see the same "Old Town" amid some of the inevitable changes that we all face over time. Today many of the businesses that once populated the town have disappeared, following an unfortunate trend in all small communities. The names of townsfolk who have passed away are still displayed on a plaque on the outside of the funeral home. The Greensboro Cemetery still stands as a sentinel to the entrance to town from the south. This historic landmark is home to many of the guardians of the town, will someday serve as my final resting place with my family, and must be preserved.

Another sure sign of growth is the addition of a second stoplight at the entrance to the town from the east at the top of the new John Riffle Memorial Bridge. At the foot of the bridge is the new Curtis Harvey Memorial Park. This land was purchased by the town to help protect the river while at the same time providing an area for families to have fun by fishing, enjoying a picnic, or simply watching the ever-present waterfowl. The park, where we are creating positive memories for our little ones, is also home to new annual town activities, such as the Fishing Derby for kids, Founders' Day, and the "Lighting of the City" at Christmas. If you enter the town from the north, you are greeted by the new elementary school. On the west side of town, the Pet Milk Plant no longer operates, but the Old Greensboro Supply grain business still greets you, although it just recently changed names. The grain bins serve as a reminder of our farming heritage.

While there are many positive signs for the future, we are on the brink of a major decision regarding the future path of the town. The town is currently involved with a mixed residential and commercial development that was annexed on the south side of town and a substantial development on existing property within the town. These two developments, when completed over the next five to 10 years, will add 380 homes. Any further growth will require major upgrades to the Waste Water Treatment Plant. How the elected officials decide to address the issue of continued growth will decide our course for the future. Protecting the surrounding farm lands, the river, our quality of life as a small rural community, and our economic viability as a self-sufficient community are at the heart of this decision. It is not a question to be taken lightly or one that should be answered hastily. Speaking as your mayor, I have too many wonderful memories of a small, close-knit community to support any additional growth in the foreseeable future that would threaten our quality of life.

—Mayor David Spencer
2008

One

Greensboro's History

The convenience of this site as a point of delivery and distribution through the Delmarva Peninsula cannot be disputed. One of the earliest businesses in this area was Hughlett's Tobacco warehouse, started in 1769. Public warehouses were established for tobacco inspection and storage. The popularity of tobacco and the resulting boom in this region occurred from about 1620 to 1680. During this period, tobacco was grown and traded for a variety of other goods, such as sugar, salt, rum, and slaves. In 1736, Peter Rich purchased Ingram's Desire, a 200-acre tract at the bridge on the west side of the river. Upon his death in 1762, Rich deeded one half of his lands to his daughter, Sidney, and her husband, Nathan Harrington. In 1778, this and several other properties were passed to their son, Peter Harrington, who pursued his grandfather's dream of building a town at this location. His efforts resulted in the official founding of the town of Greensboro.

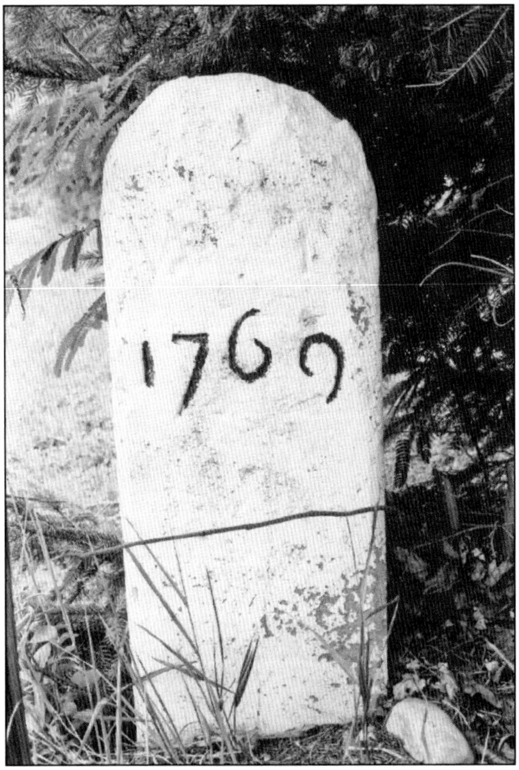

The Hughlett Marker is a property boundary marker of the area. The significance of this marker is the initials "WH" for William Hughlett and the date of 1769. William Hughlett was a well-established businessman of the area, although he and his family eventually moved to Dorchester and Talbot Counties. Several property markers such as this one can be found throughout the north and east sides of Greensboro. (Courtesy Maryland Historical Trust.)

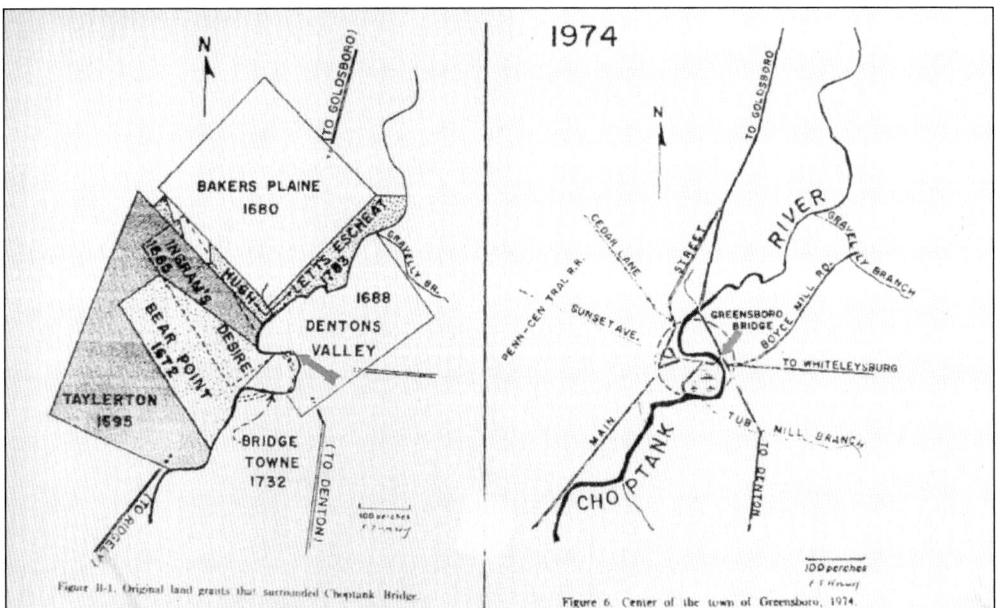

The tobacco market in Greensboro during the mid-17th century is reflected in the map above. The popularity of tobacco and the resulting boom in this area occurred from about 1620 to 1680. Tobacco was grown and traded for other products such as sugar, salt, rum, and slaves during this period. This map shows the land grants (left) of the prominent merchants in Greensboro; on the right is the map of the town as it appeared in 1974. (Courtesy J. C. Reveal.)

This plaque, placed at one of the three sites selected for a Greensboro historical marker by the Maryland Historical Society, recognizes Peter Harrington for his role in establishing the town of Greensboro. This particular marker is located at the old First Methodist church and cemetery, where Peter Harrington is buried. (Courtesy J. C. Reveal.)

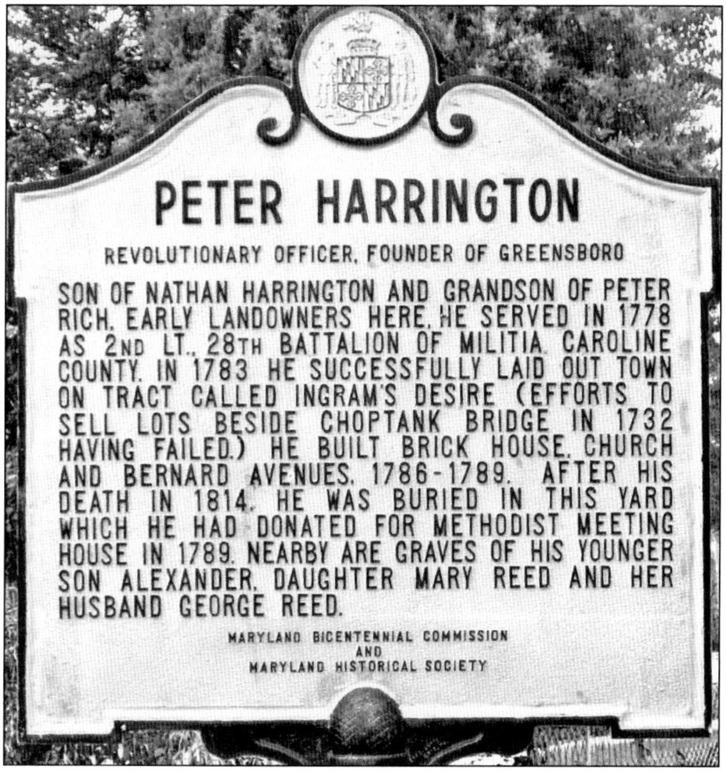

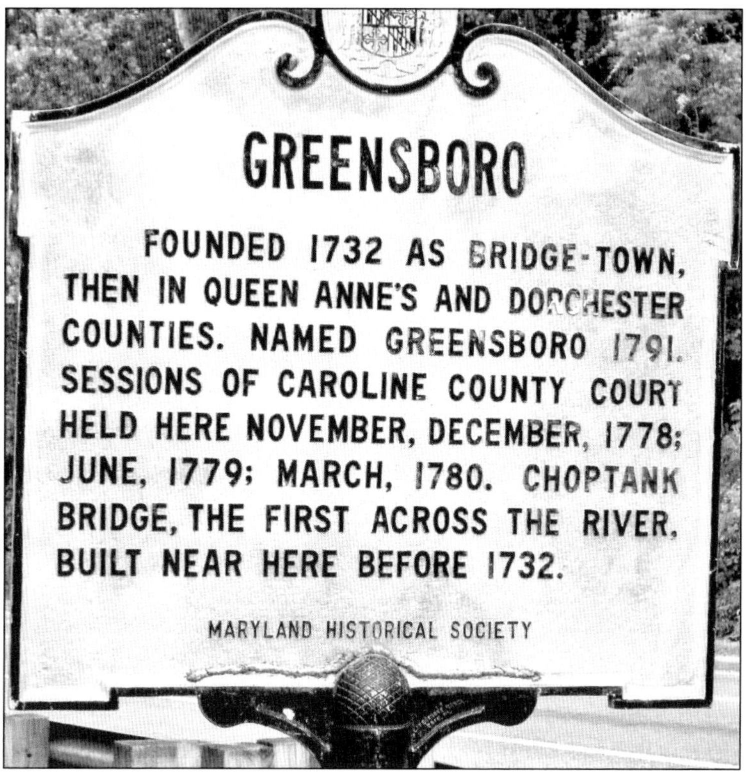

The second Maryland Historical Society plaque recognized the birth of Greensboro in 1732, with it formally being named "Greensboro" in 1791. Important dates identified by the society include 1778, 1779, and 1780, when sessions of the Caroline County Court were held in the town, and 1732, when this was the location of the first bridge across the Choptank River. (Courtesy J. C. Reveal.)

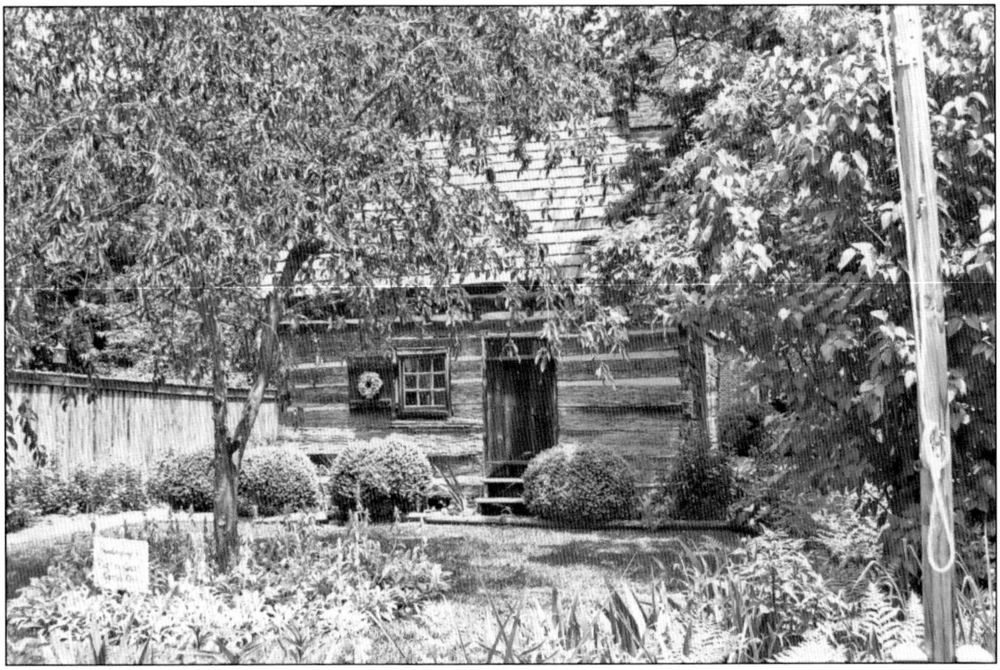

The Log Cabin Kitchen, officially known as the Comegys Log Cabin, was originally built on the Newton Hubbard farm located two miles east of Marydel, Maryland, in the late 1700s. The building and property were purchased in 1887 by Albert M. Comegys, and is where Albert and his wife, Mary, raised their family. The last known birth to occur in the building was that of Mary Emily Comegys, a granddaughter of Albert M. and Mary, in 1915. Reconstruction was completed, and the building was dedicated on June 21, 1980. (Courtesy J. C. Reveal.)

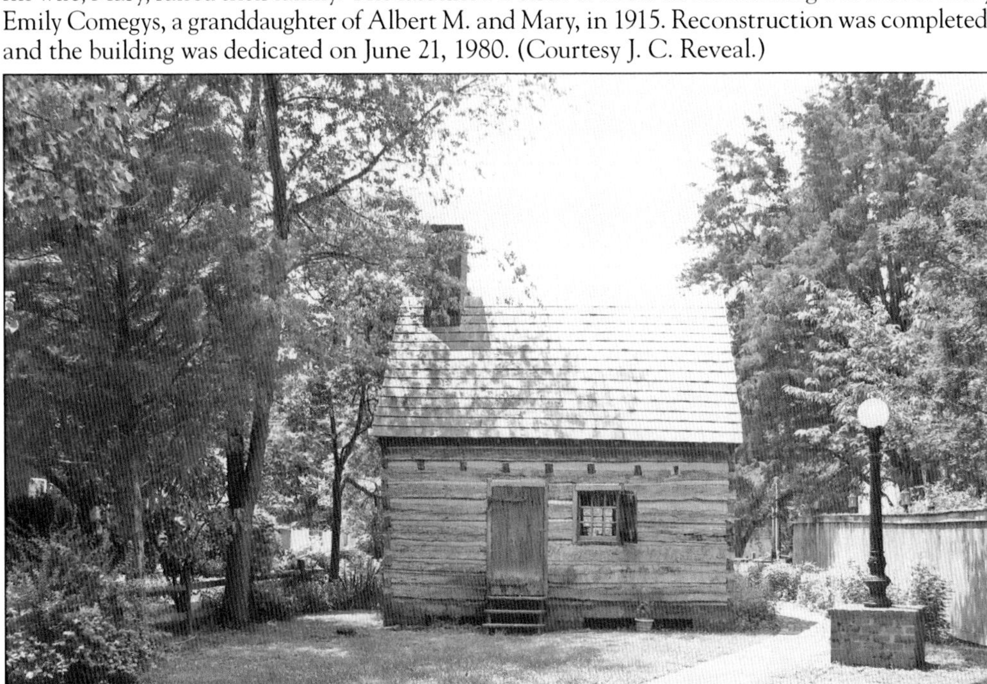

The cabin, as seen from the back, is simple in its structure; the two entryways—one in the front and one in the back—can be clearly seen in these pictures. (Courtesy J. C. Reveal.)

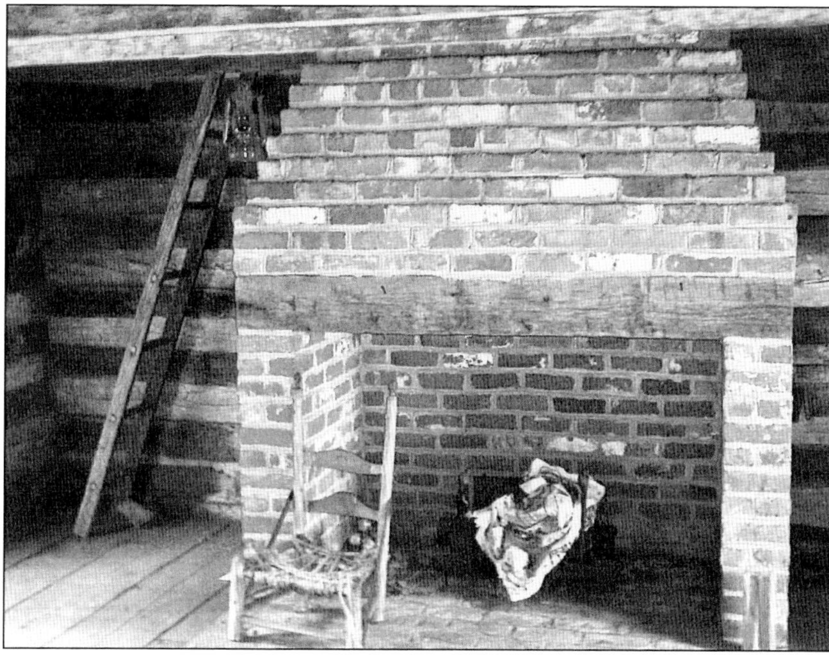

The size of the cooking fireplace in a small one-room building reflects the importance of this structure to rural life. (Courtesy J. C. Reveal.)

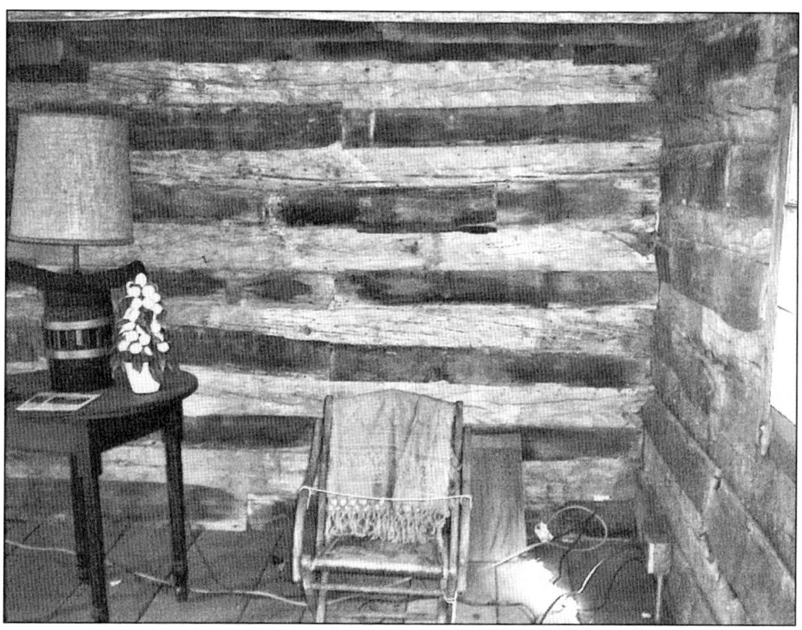

Life in agricultural Caroline County during the late-18th and 19th centuries is reflected in the simplicity of this one-room home. (Courtesy J. C. Reveal.)

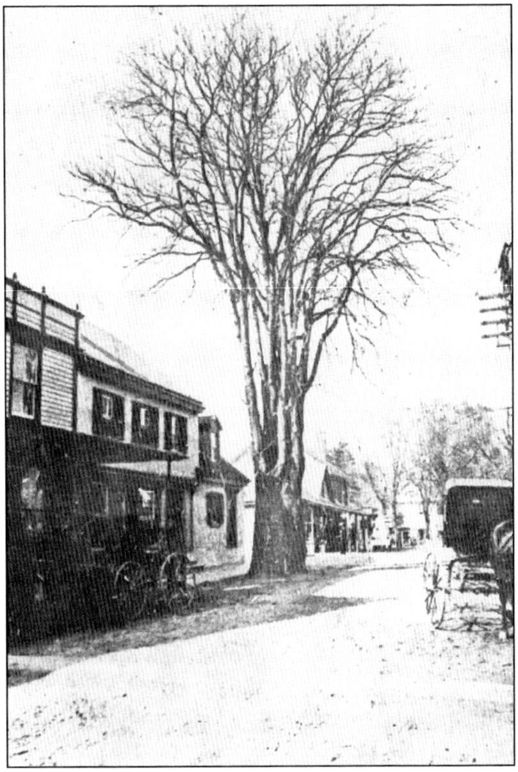

This picture of two ailanthus trees at the gateway to Greensboro dates to before 1900. The Ailanthus Gateway house was built around 1800 when the owner brought his bride to this house, and they planted these two slender trees. Over the years, the trees grew until their trunks and branches formed an archway beneath which swung a gate welcoming visitors to the home. The trees and the house have long since disappeared, and few pictures remain to remind us of Greensboro's history. (Courtesy Town of Greensboro.)

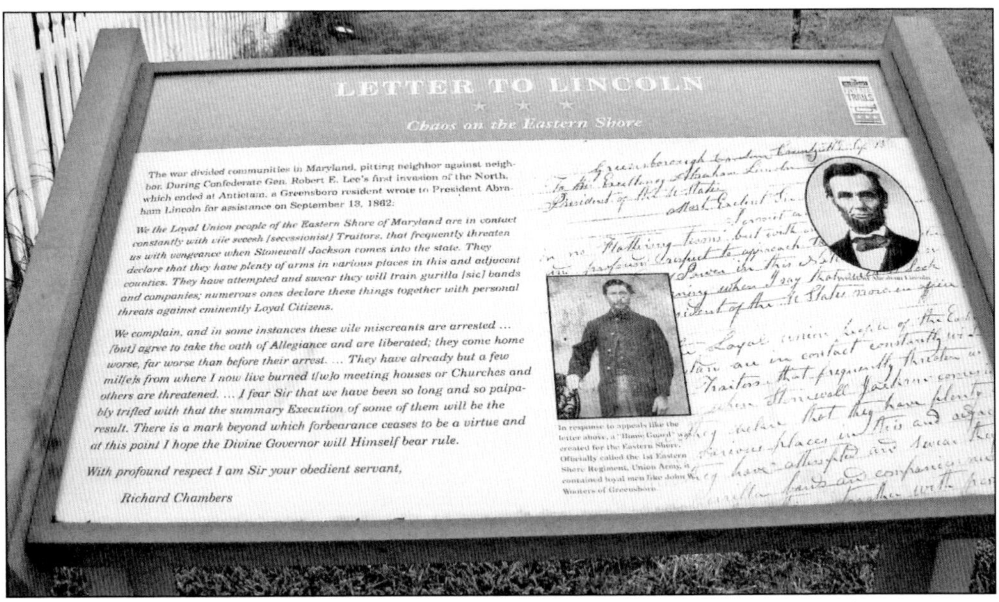

Company D represented Greensboro with 74 soldiers, many from the same family. This monument reflects the feelings of many of Greensboro's residents, like Richard Chambers and John W. Wooters, who wrote to President Lincoln expressing their concerns. As indicated on this monument, in response to appeals like the letter above, a "home Guard" was created for the Eastern Shore. Officially called the 1st Eastern Shore Regiment, Union Army, it centralized loyal men like John W. Wooters (pictured) of Greensboro. (Courtesy J. C. Reveal.)

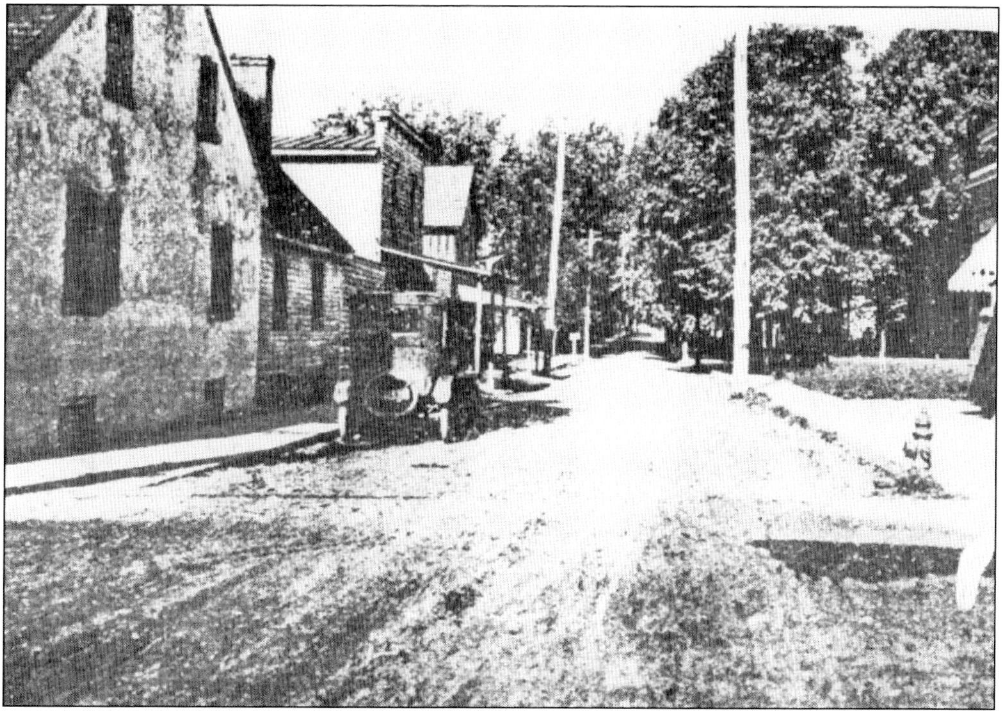

This view of "Four Corners" looks west on Railroad (Sunset) Avenue around 1925. (Courtesy Town of Greensboro.)

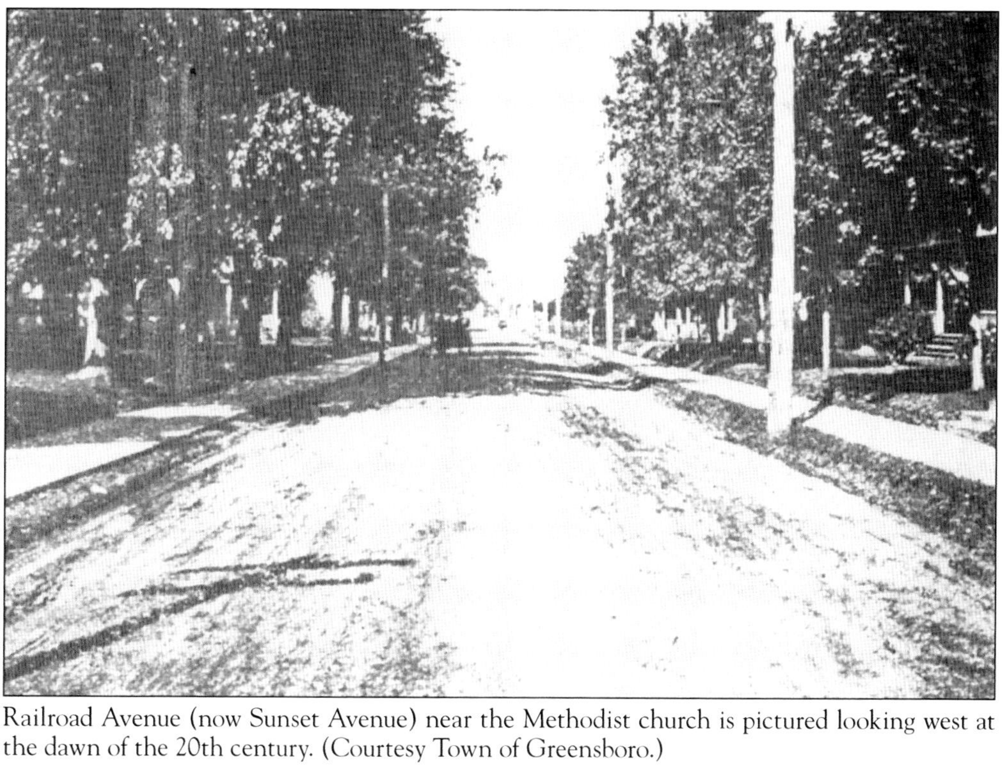

Railroad Avenue (now Sunset Avenue) near the Methodist church is pictured looking west at the dawn of the 20th century. (Courtesy Town of Greensboro.)

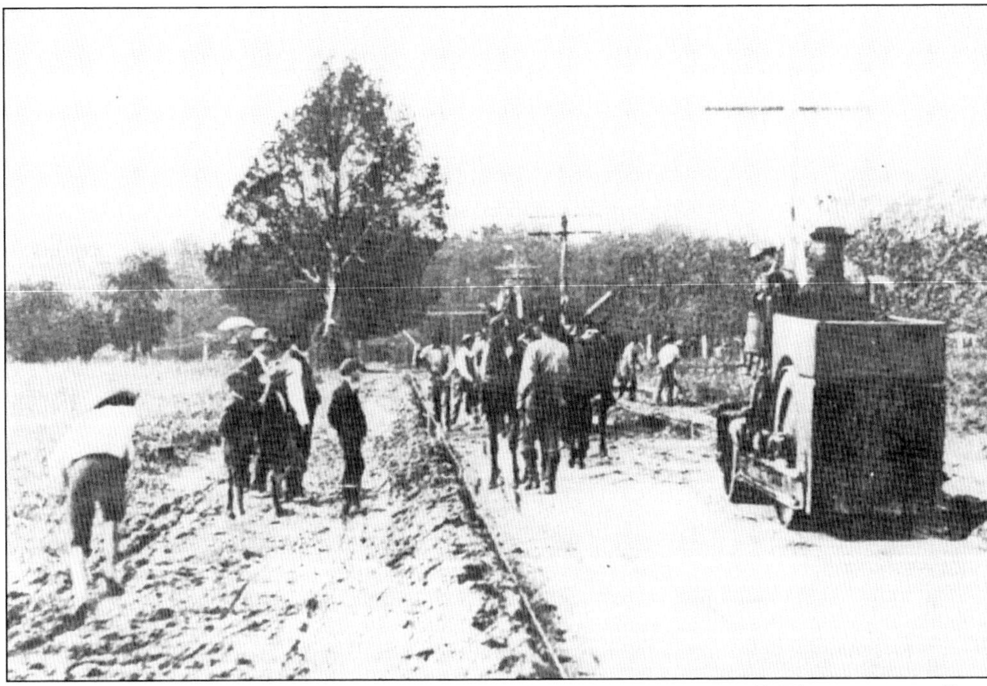

As Greensboro grew, the need for easy access to other towns arose as well. These pictures (from around 1909) show the construction of the paved road from Greensboro to Denton. (Courtesy Town of Greensboro.)

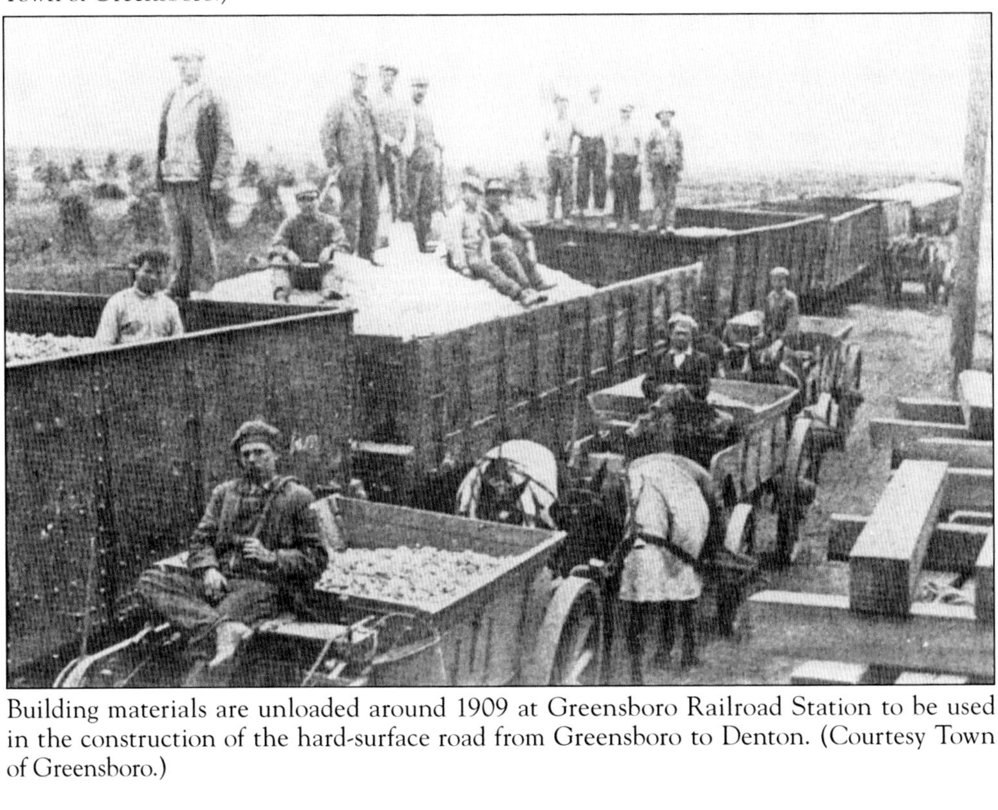

Building materials are unloaded around 1909 at Greensboro Railroad Station to be used in the construction of the hard-surface road from Greensboro to Denton. (Courtesy Town of Greensboro.)

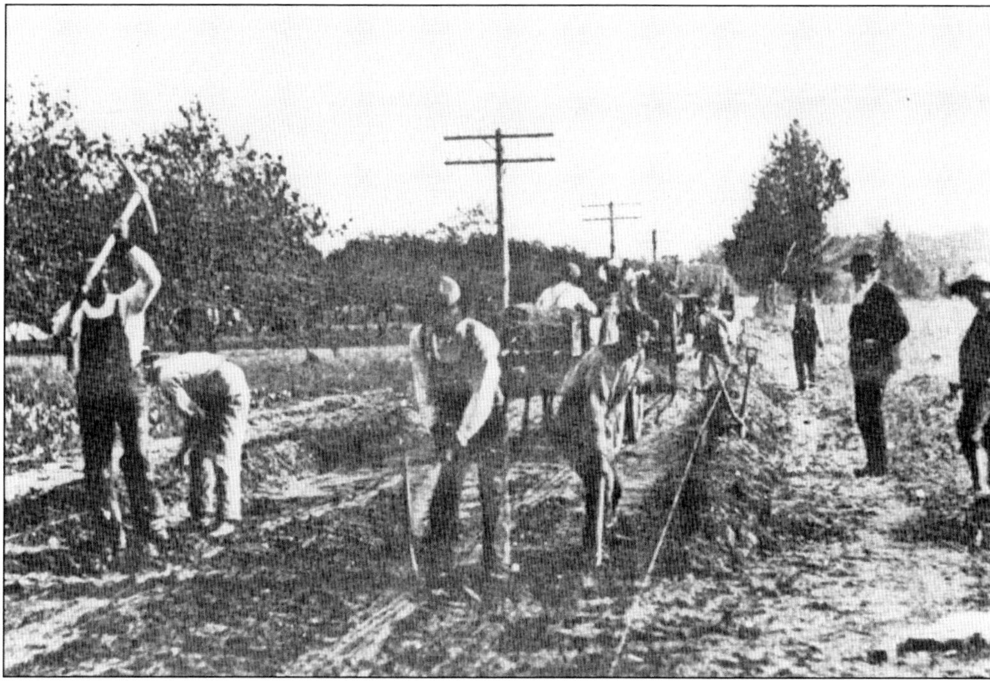

Construction of the first paved highway—from Greensboro to Denton at Knife Box Road and Route 313—defined the term "manual labor." (Courtesy Town of Greensboro.)

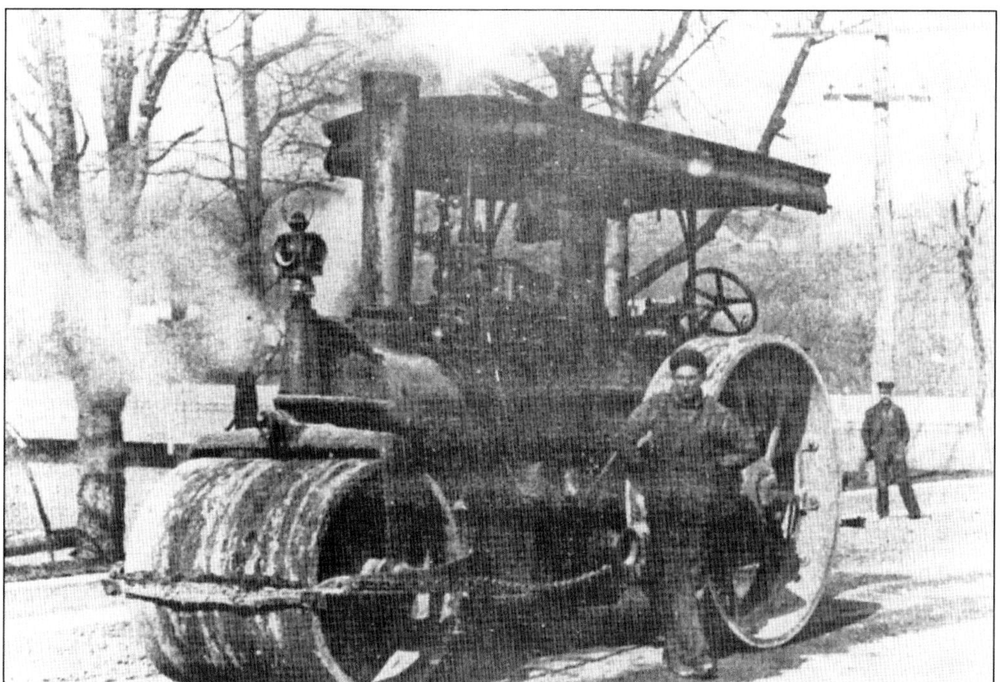

Workers performed ongoing improvements to bridges and roads. Around 1920, local resident Harry Karcher poses beside the steamroller used during the surfacing of East Sunset Avenue near the concrete bridge. (Courtesy Town of Greensboro.)

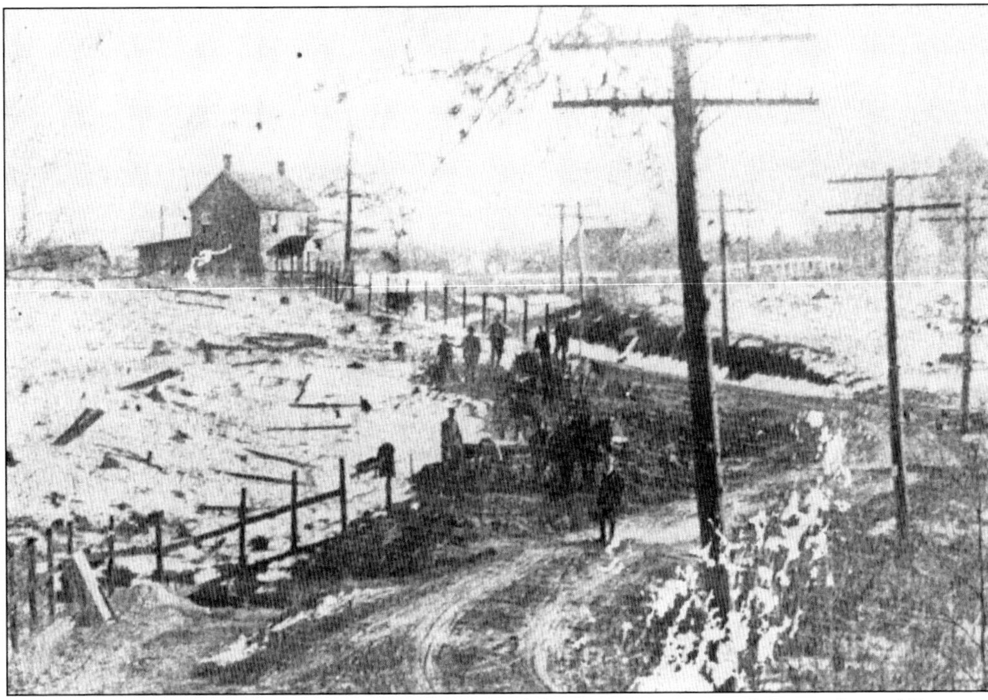

Road construction takes place on the six-mile stretch between Denton and Greensboro. (Courtesy Town of Greensboro.)

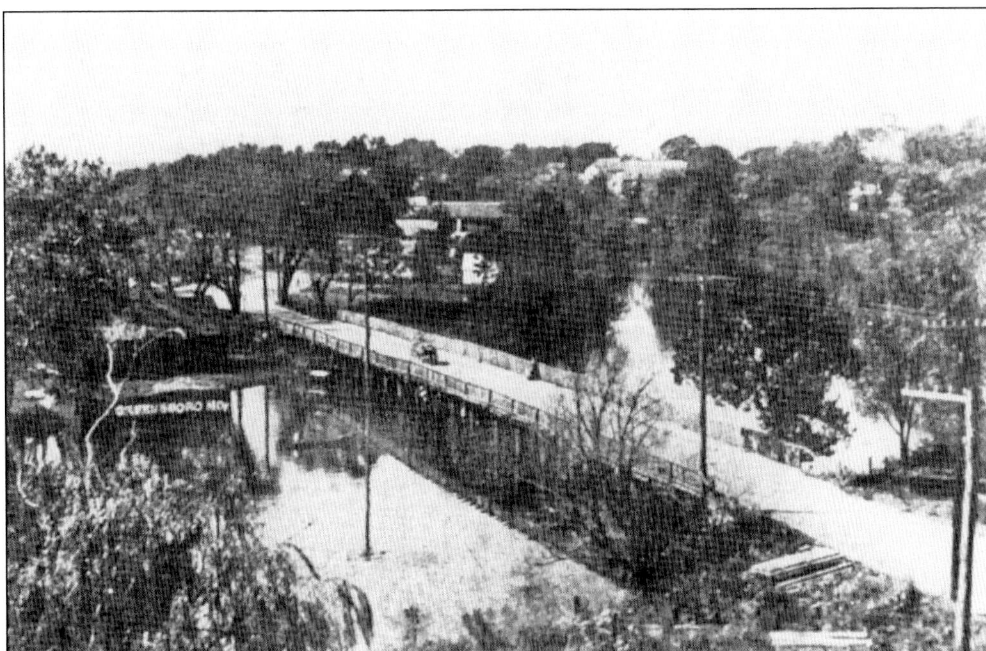

The 1891 wooden bridge at Greensboro shows the original width of the river facing west toward town. (Courtesy Town of Greensboro.)

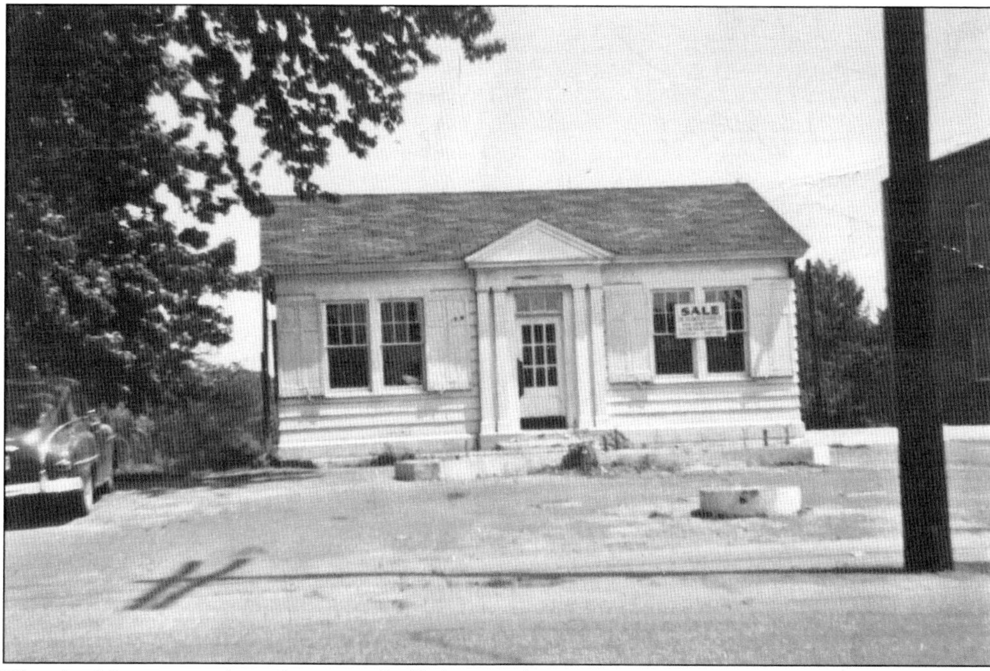

This building served as the town hall during the 1940s and into the 1970s. As the town expanded, it built a new building, and this building became the local police department. Now it is part of Greensboro's industry as it takes on the face of the town barbershop. (Courtesy Town of Greensboro.)

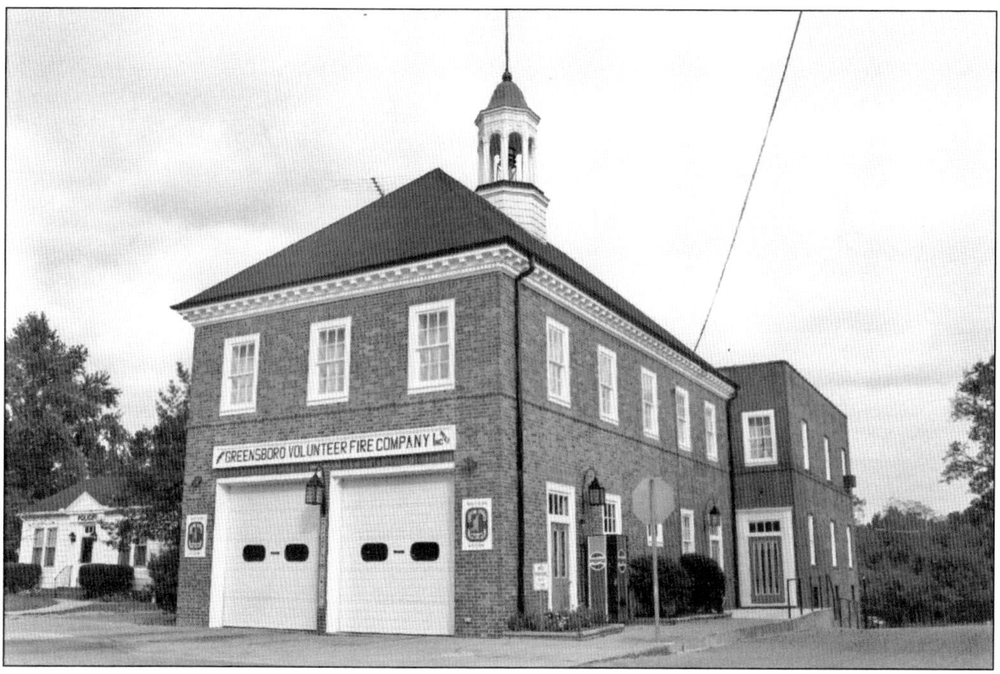

This building housed the Greensboro Volunteer Fire Department for many years until the larger, more modern building was built behind it. The building now serves as a home for EMT Emergency Services for the area. (Courtesy *Times Record* newspaper.)

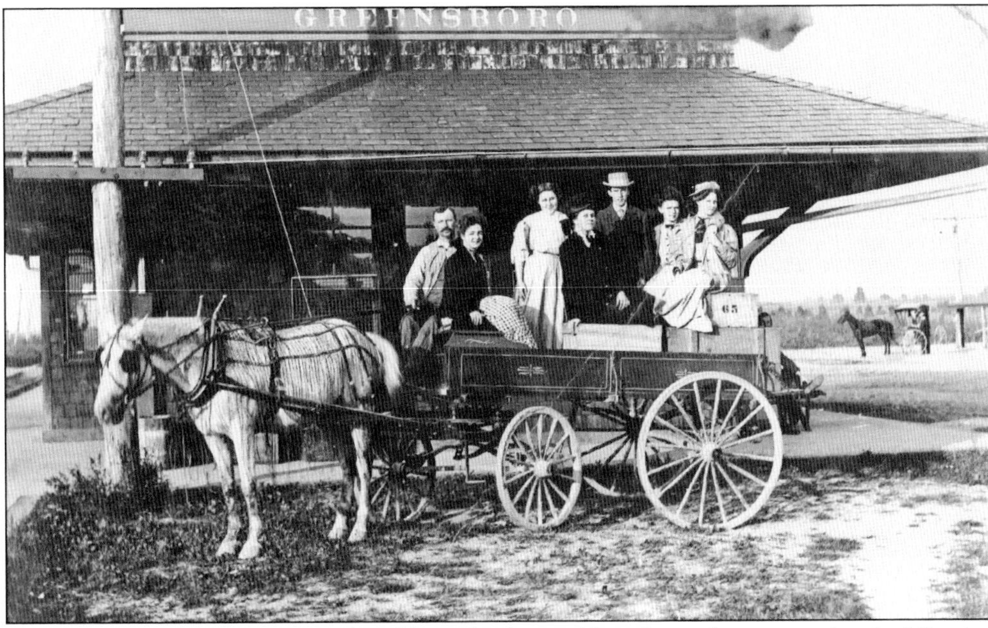

The Maryland and Delaware Railroad brought the world to Greensboro immediately following the Civil War. The stop at Greensboro provided a connection for Delaware's main rail line to Oxford, Maryland. Greensboro Train Station is pictured around 1910. Gail Grace stands in the middle of the wagon with Elsie Coursey seated at far left, according to Mable Riffle of Greensboro. (Courtesy Sara K. Edwards/Richard Smith.)

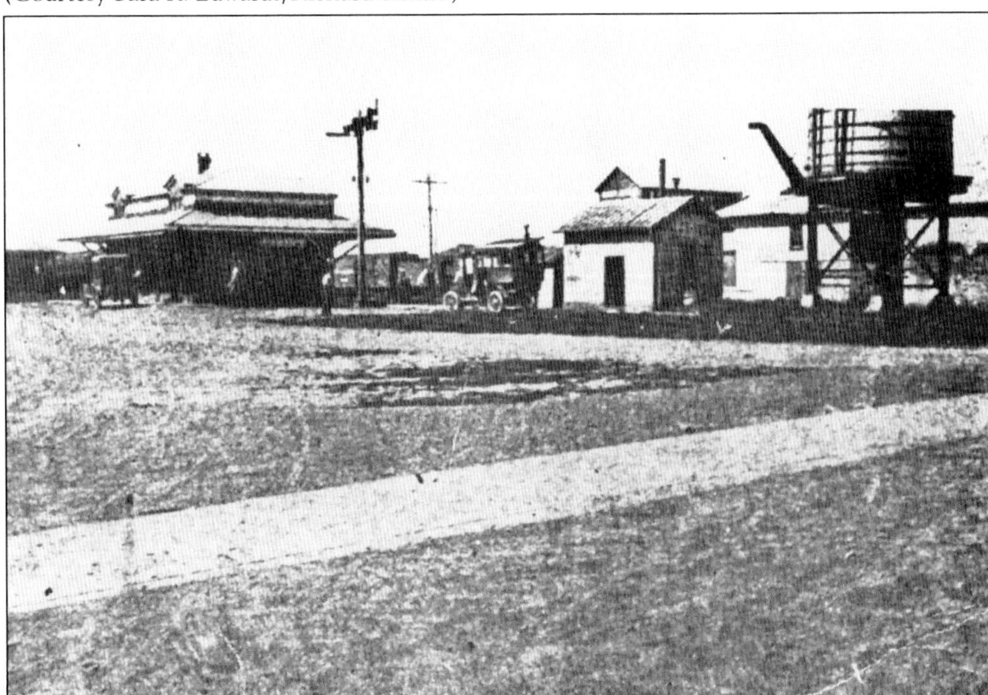

Greensboro saw railroad expansion after 1870, and by 1900, as many as six daily trains made their way through the town. (Courtesy Town of Greensboro.)

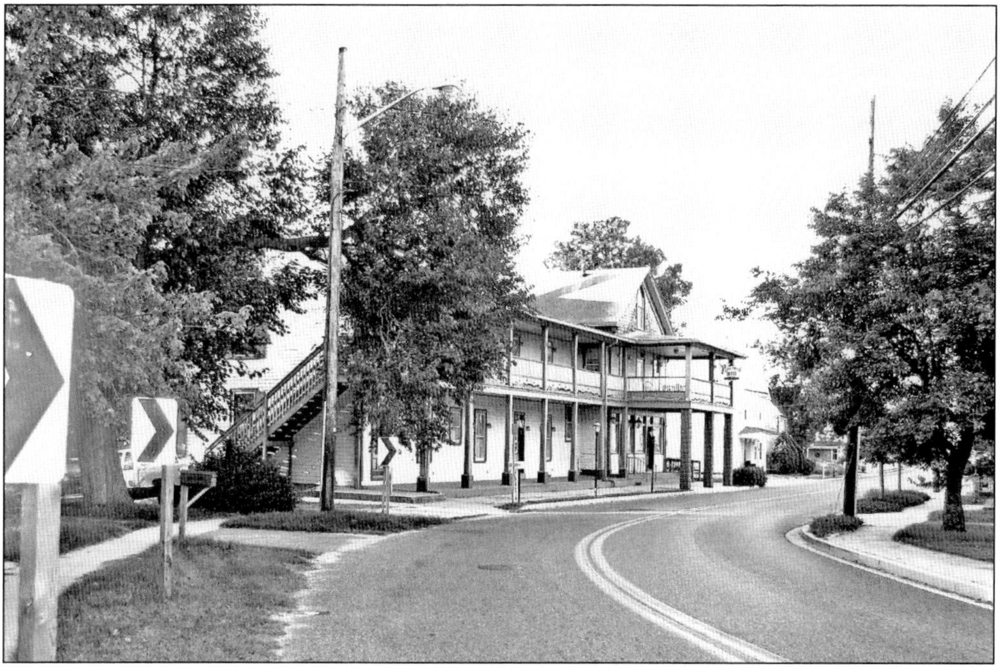

The Riverside Hotel (or Foster Hotel), originally constructed in 1912 by C. B. Jarman from the Roe Cannery, was first established to service visitors to the town and traveling salesmen. The hotel was state of the art with a telephone in every room. The first part of the 20th century saw growth in retail and manufacturing, and the hotel was frequently filled to capacity on weekends. (Courtesy J. C. Reveal.)

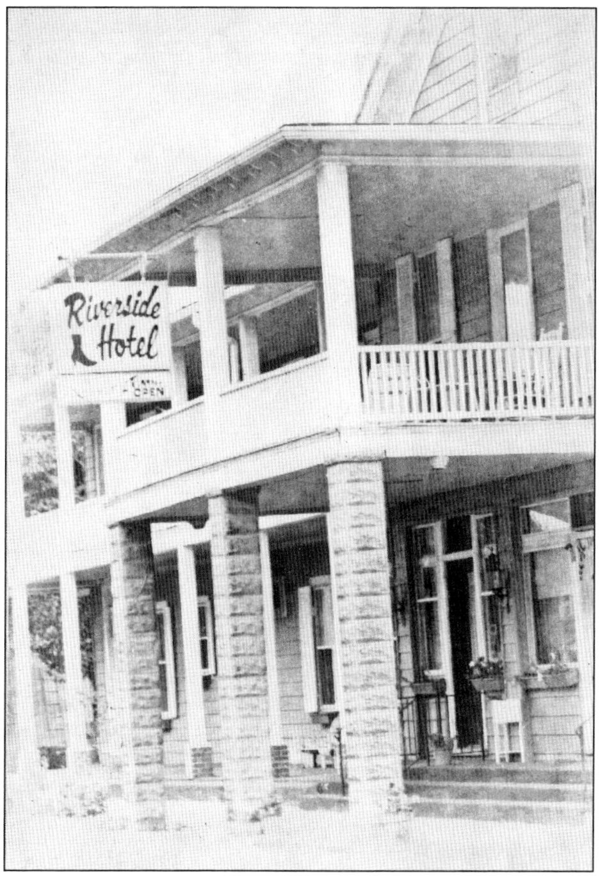

The hotel changed hands and names several times over the years. At one point, it operated as a restaurant and offered rooms for rent. (Courtesy *Times Record* newspaper.)

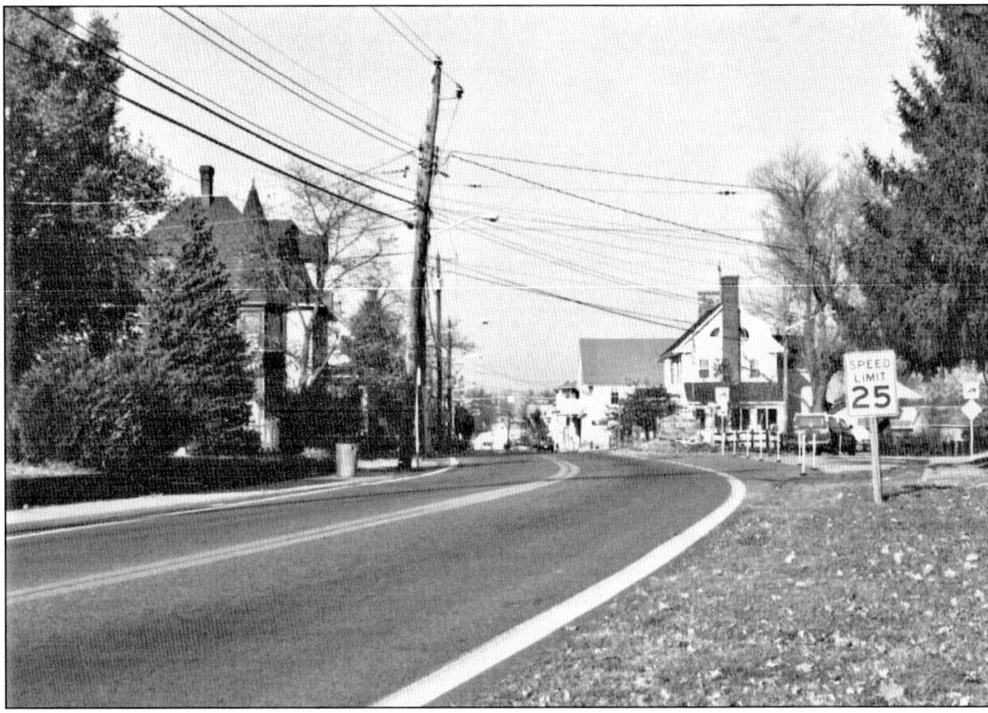

The entry to Greensboro on Main Street (Route 480) provides a welcoming view into the Greensboro Historic District. (Courtesy the Maryland Historical Trust.)

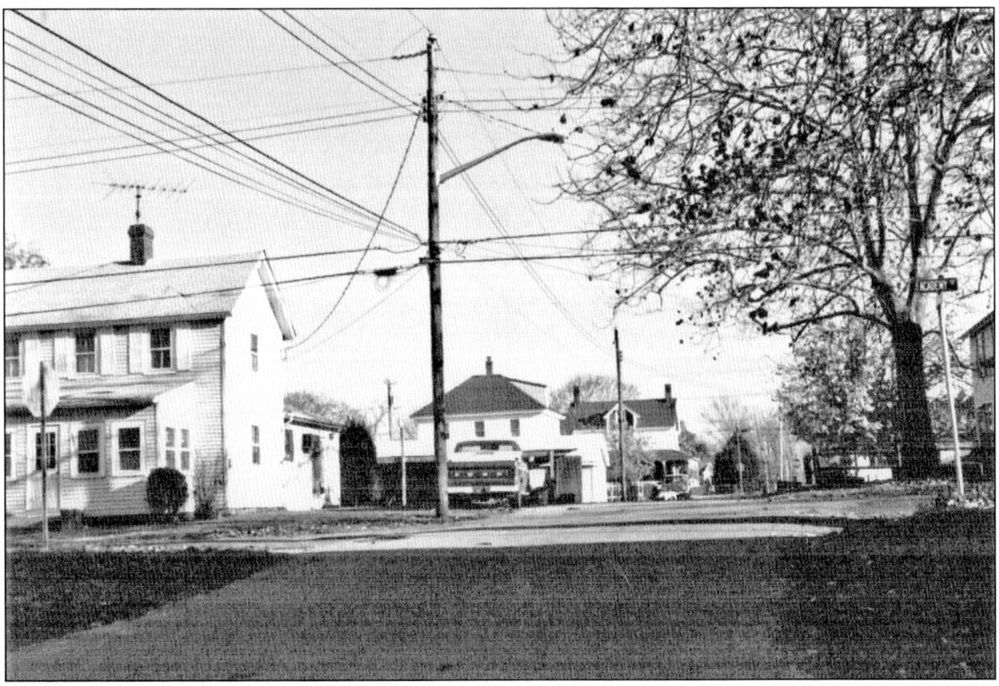

The quiet shade of Bernard Avenue and Academy Street provides a look into another aspect of Greensboro's historic district, with the Harrington House visible in the distance. (Courtesy the Maryland Historical Trust.)

Two

The Choptank River

The Choptank River and the town of Greensboro have maintained an intimate relationship since before 1732, when the Maryland General Assembly passed an act designed to found a town "at the bridge near the head of the Choptank River." It was determined early that the "S" curve, also known as the Great Bend, would be an ideal location for establishing a port of delivery and distribution to residents, primarily agricultural, who lived in the middle of the Delmarva Peninsula.

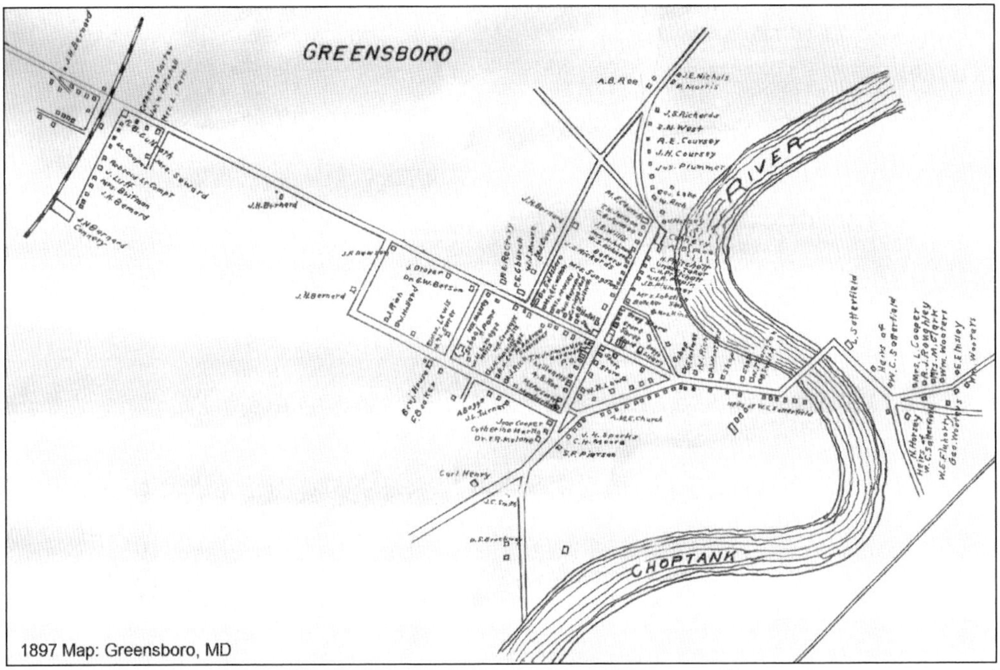

1897 Map: Greensboro, MD

This reproduction of the 1897 Caroline County map shows the town of Greensboro as it appeared that year, with the clear distinction of the "S" curve. (Courtesy Town of Denton.)

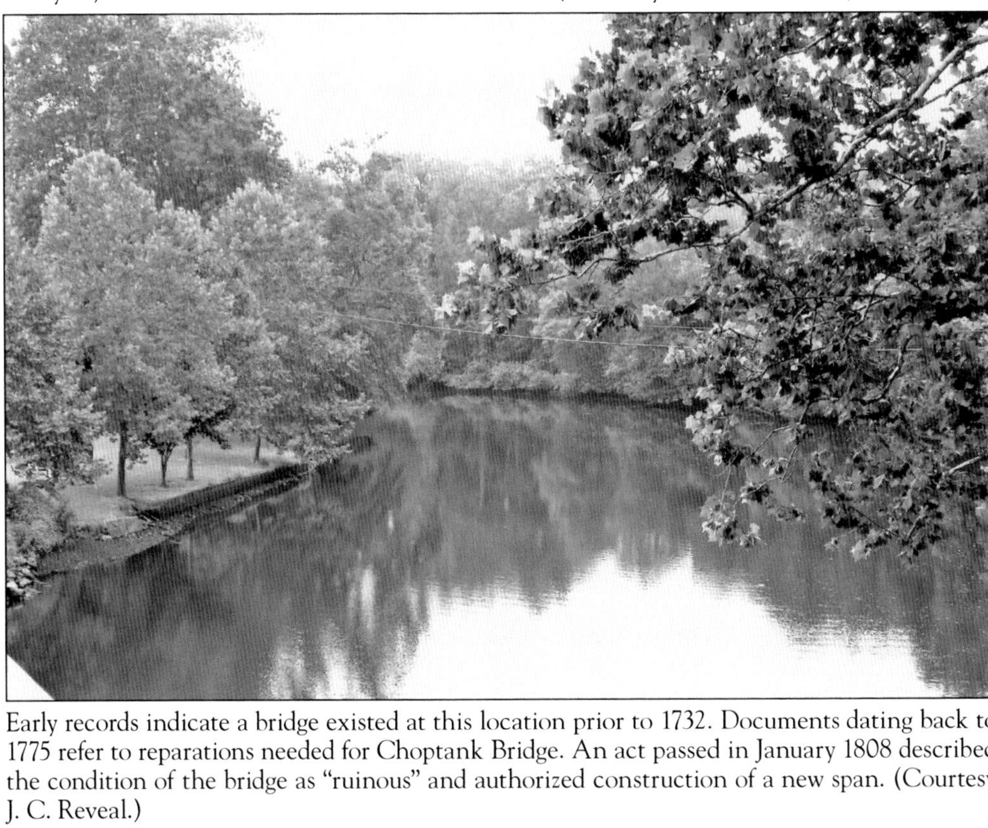

Early records indicate a bridge existed at this location prior to 1732. Documents dating back to 1775 refer to reparations needed for Choptank Bridge. An act passed in January 1808 described the condition of the bridge as "ruinous" and authorized construction of a new span. (Courtesy J. C. Reveal.)

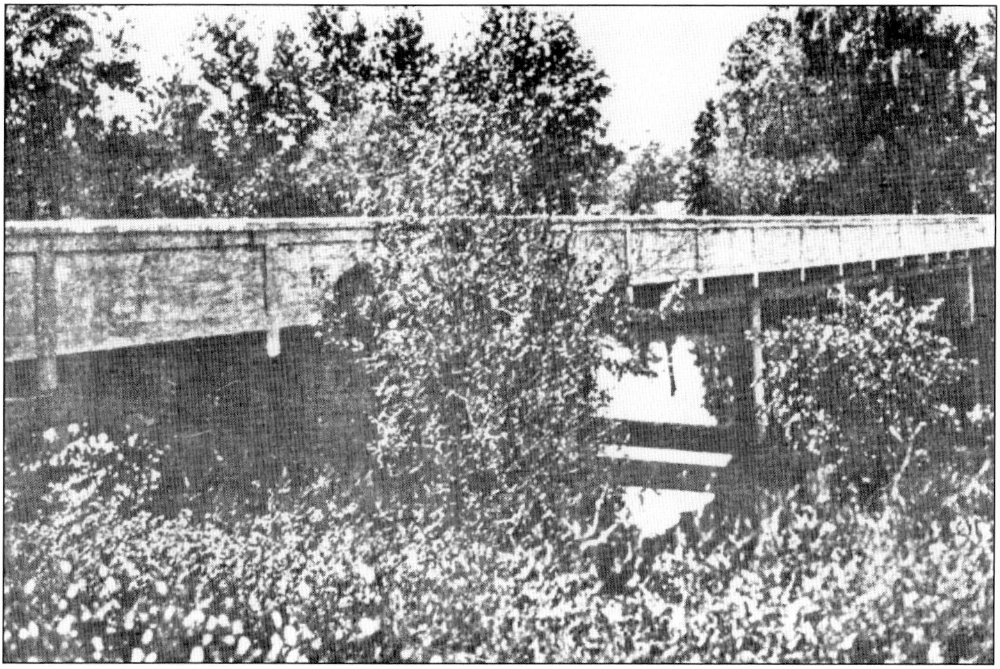

The Greensboro bridge, built in 1908, replaced the old timber bridge at this same point across the Choptank and provided improved access between Greensboro, on the west side of the river, and its growing neighborhoods on the east, as well as quick access to Delaware. (Courtesy Town of Greensboro.)

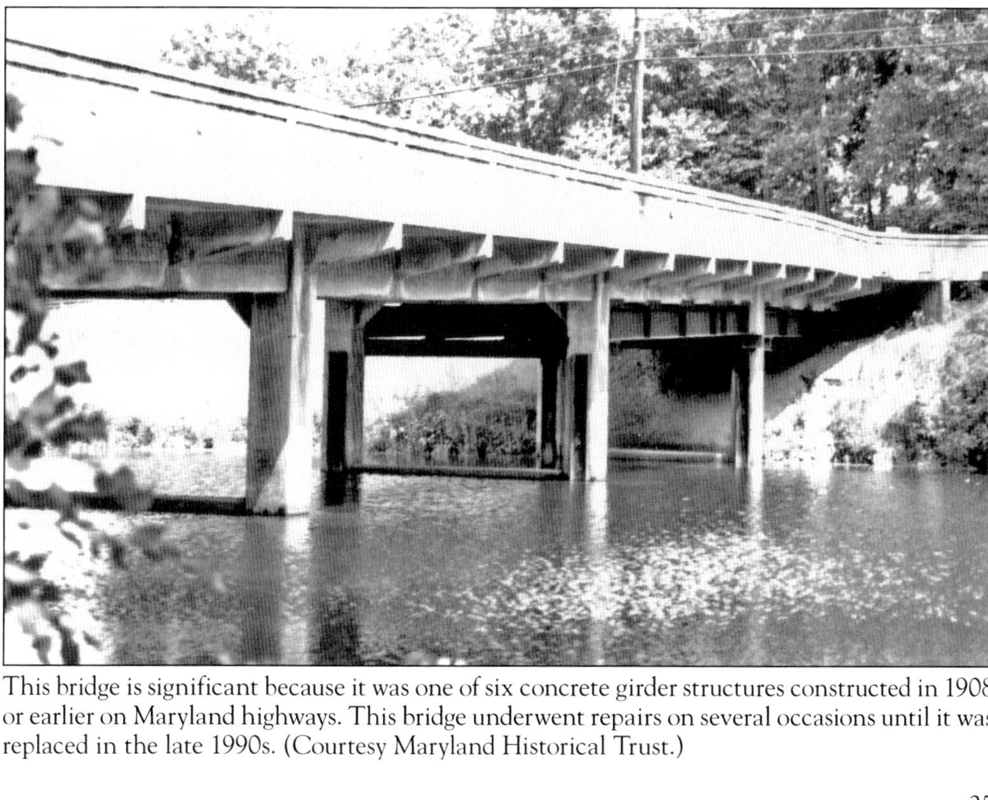

This bridge is significant because it was one of six concrete girder structures constructed in 1908 or earlier on Maryland highways. This bridge underwent repairs on several occasions until it was replaced in the late 1990s. (Courtesy Maryland Historical Trust.)

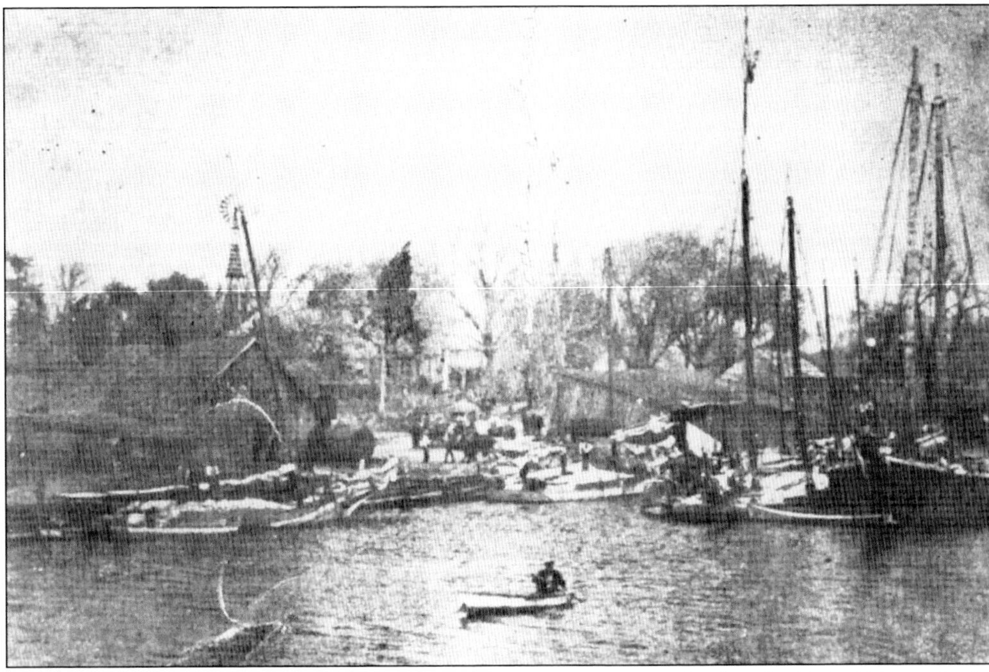

Brockway's Wharf around 1910 was home to many activities involved with shipbuilding. To the left is an oyster boat out of Baltimore, and the larger boat on the right is the *Walter P. Snow*. The loading and unloading of products, along with boat maintenance, are clearly portrayed here. (Courtesy Town of Greensboro.)

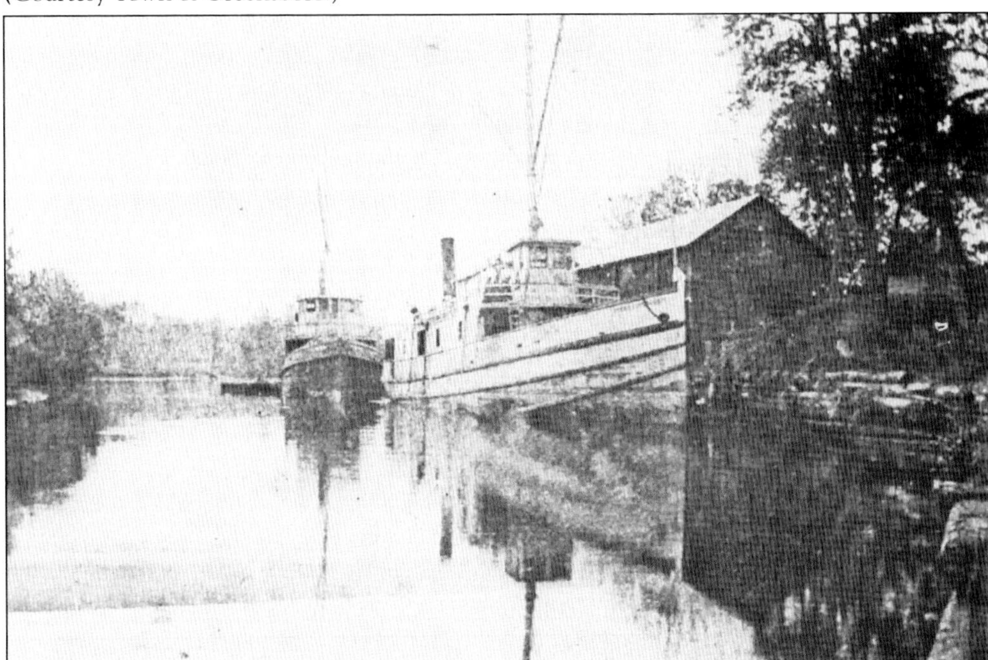

Although narrow, the Choptank River was deep enough to give shipbuilders the ability to construct boats such as the 1886 SS *Greensborough*. This boat served its purpose well until it was destroyed in a fire. (Courtesy Town of Greensboro.)

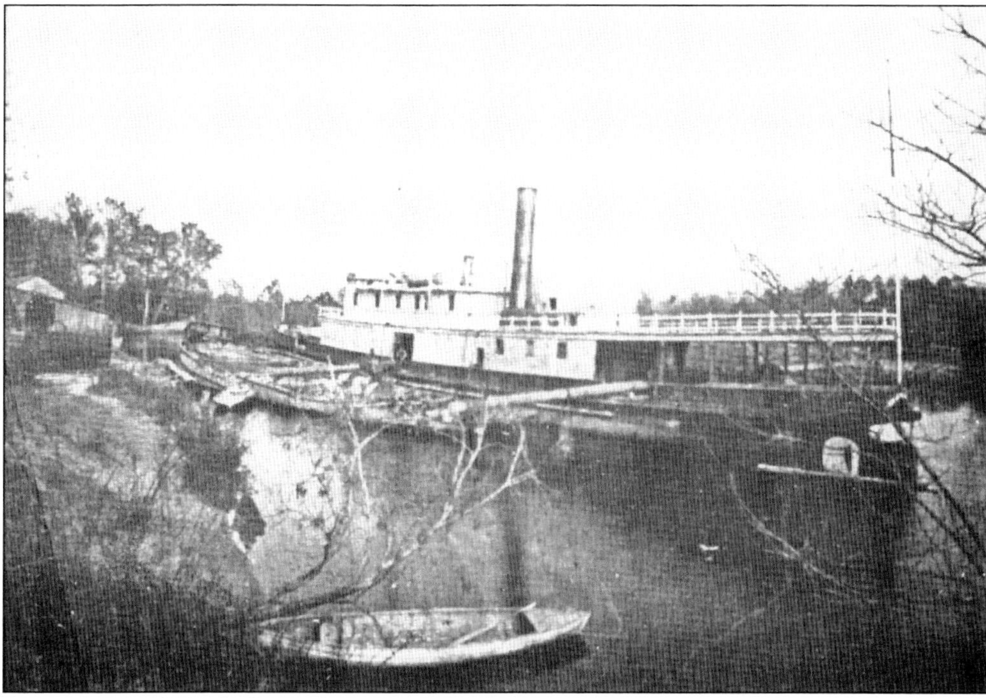

The remains of the hull can be seen as the SS *Greensborough* is being moved by the larger, unnamed ship on its starboard side. (Courtesy Town of Greensboro.)

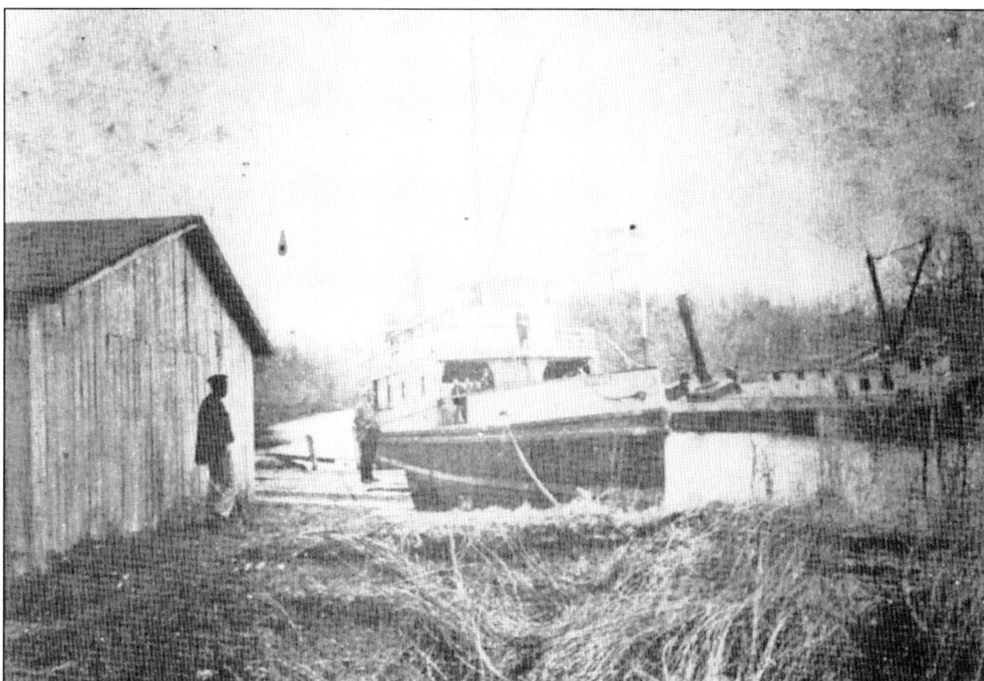

Shipbuilding in Greensboro was not without its crises and accidents, as evidenced by this *c.* 1910 image of the SS *Edenton* at Case's Wharf, with the wreck of the SS *Vesper* in the background. (Courtesy Town of Greensboro.)

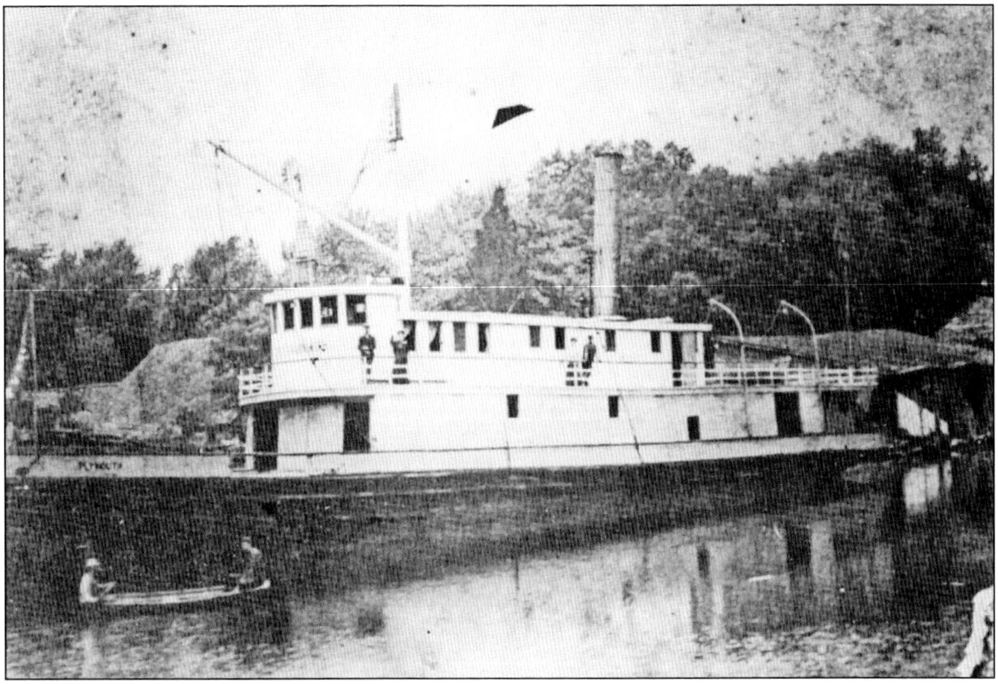

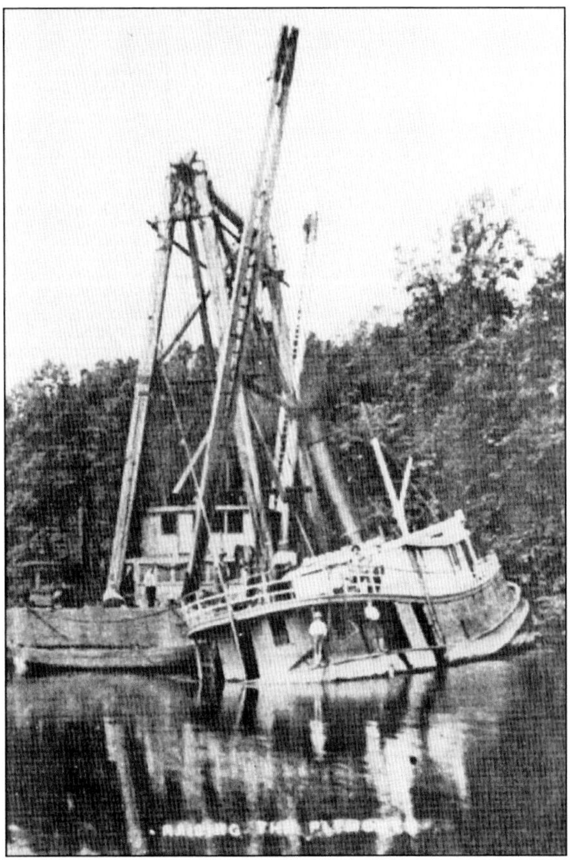

The picture above, of the SS *Plymouth* owned by Elias and Minnie Kenton (standing amidships), was taken in 1910. The SS *Plymouth* would soon meet with disaster, sinking into the Choptank. (Courtesy Town of Greensboro.)

Efforts were put forth to raise the SS *Plymouth* after it burned (left). (Courtesy Town of Greensboro.)

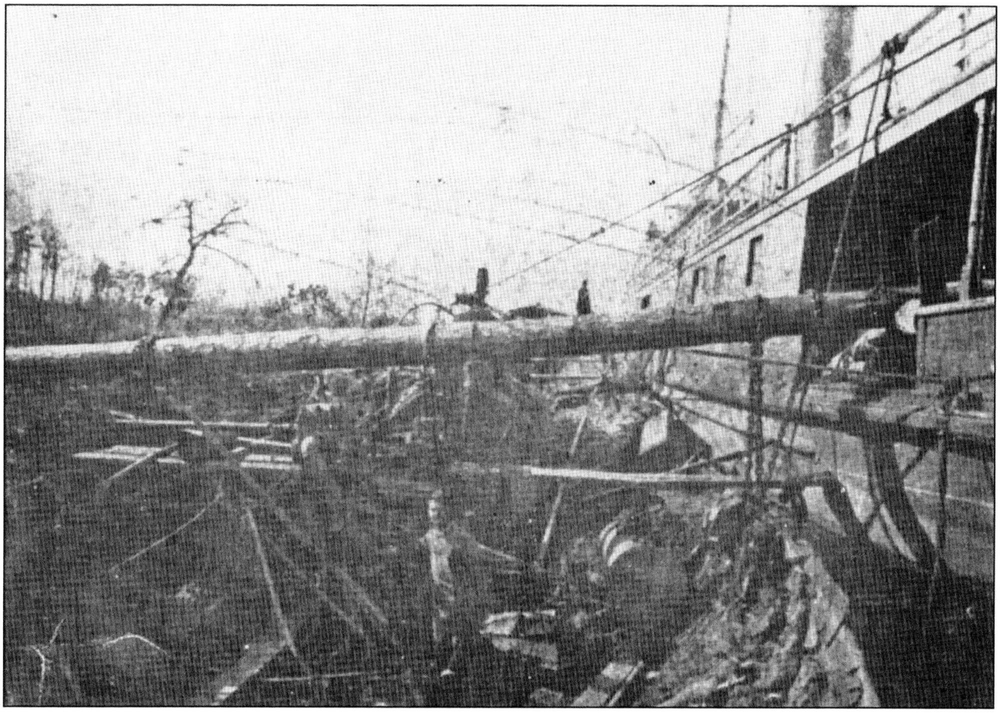

This is a close-up of the salvage of the SS *Vesper* around 1911. (Courtesy Town of Greensboro.)

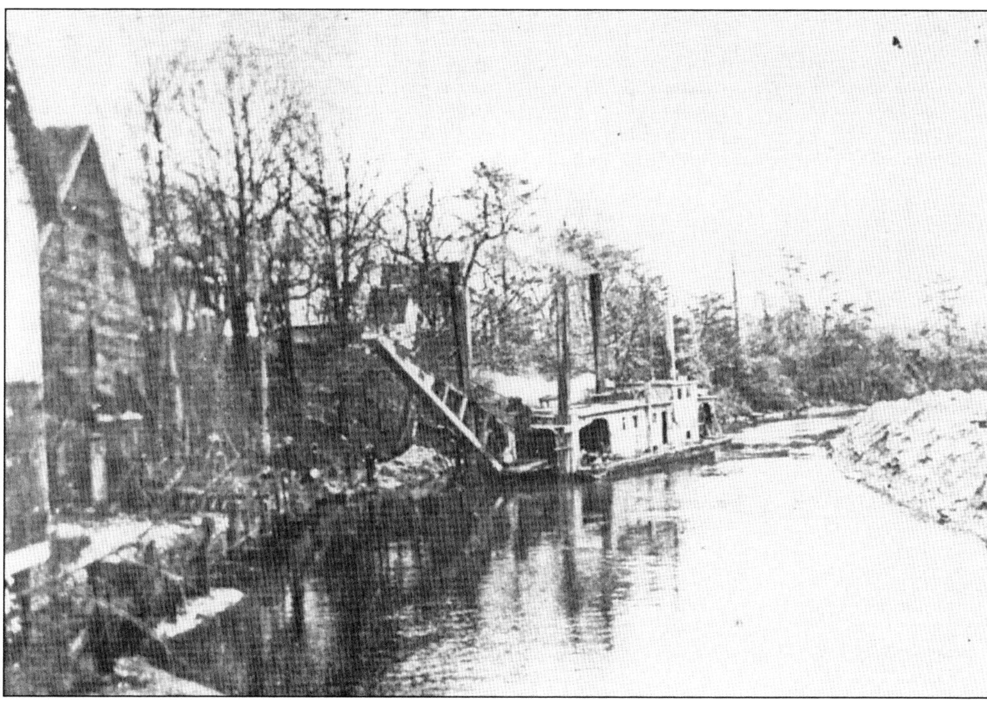

The waters were frequently dredged to ensure the necessary depth for shipbuilding. Here dredging occurs around 1878 near the bridge at Satterfield's warehouse, a business dependent upon the river. (Courtesy Town of Greensboro.)

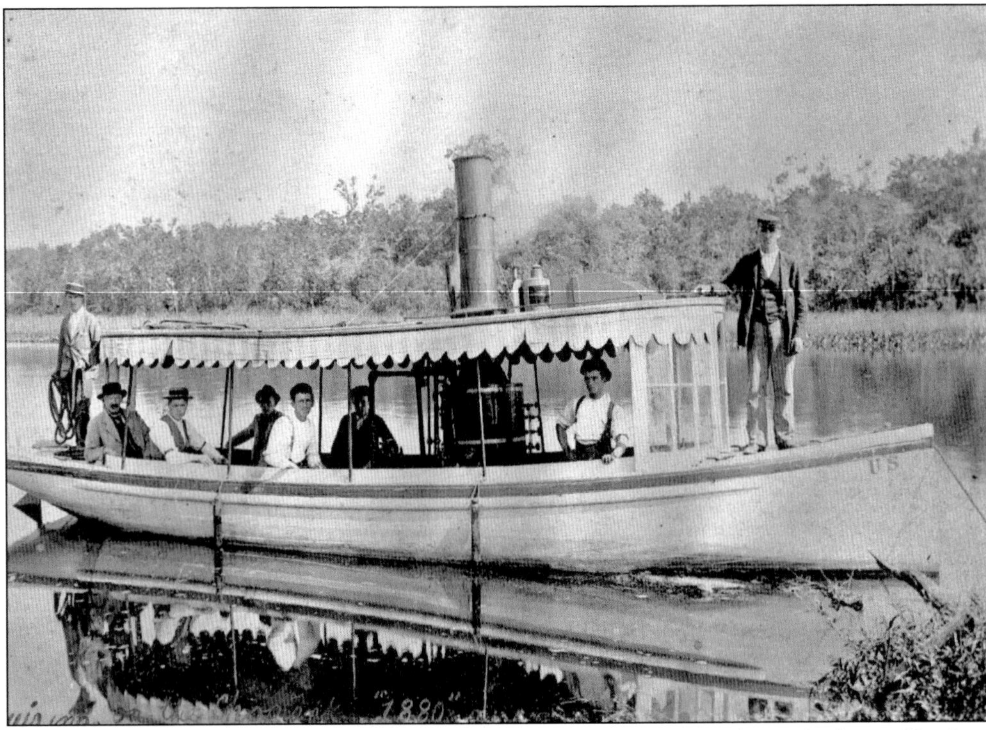

Capt. Benjamin House, one of Greensboro's prominent citizens, stands on the bow of his boat during a Sunday excursion around 1880. (Courtesy Town of Greensboro.)

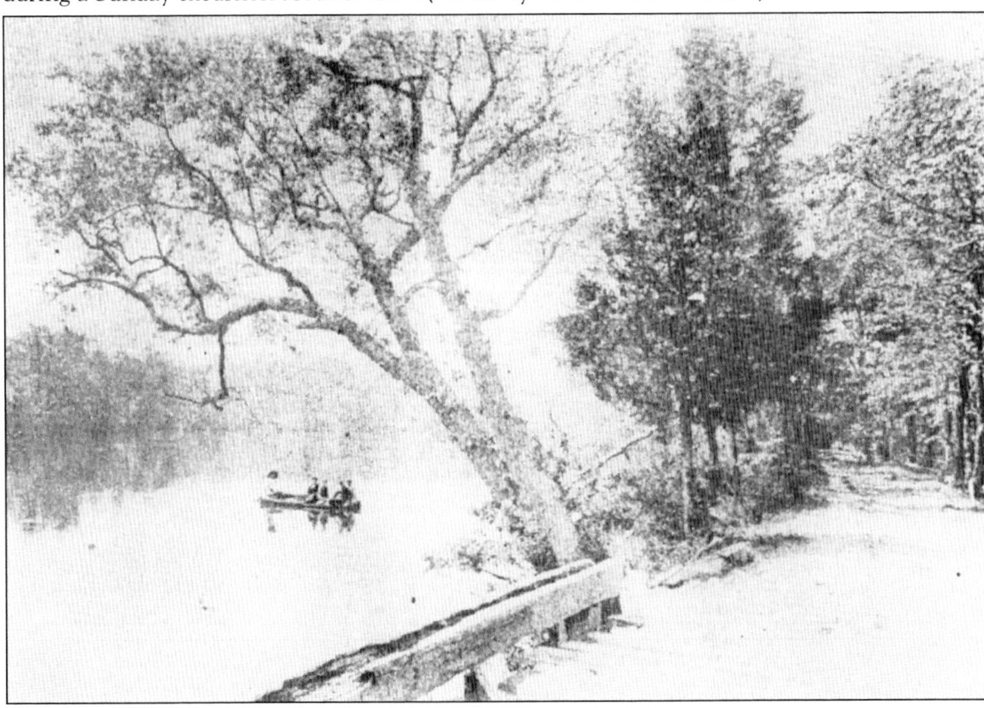

Fishing at Moore's Lake (later named Draper's Mill) near Red Bridges always remained a popular activity. (Courtesy Town of Greensboro.)

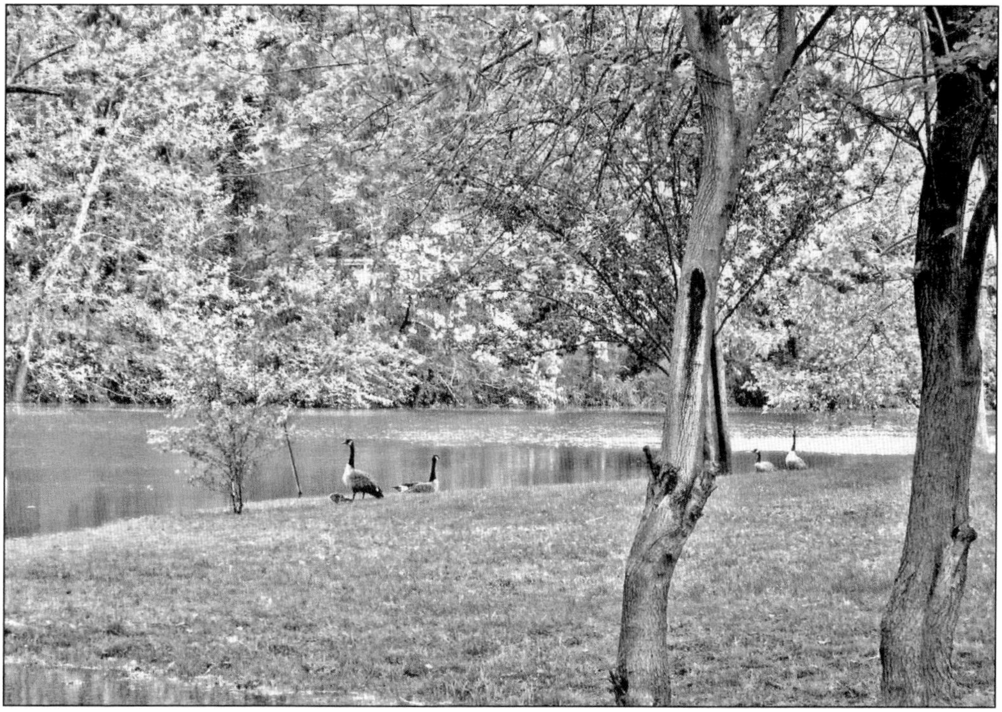

Whether a warm spring morning or a brisk autumn afternoon, the banks of the Choptank River bring out friends and family to enjoy a leisurely day. (Courtesy J. C. Reveal.)

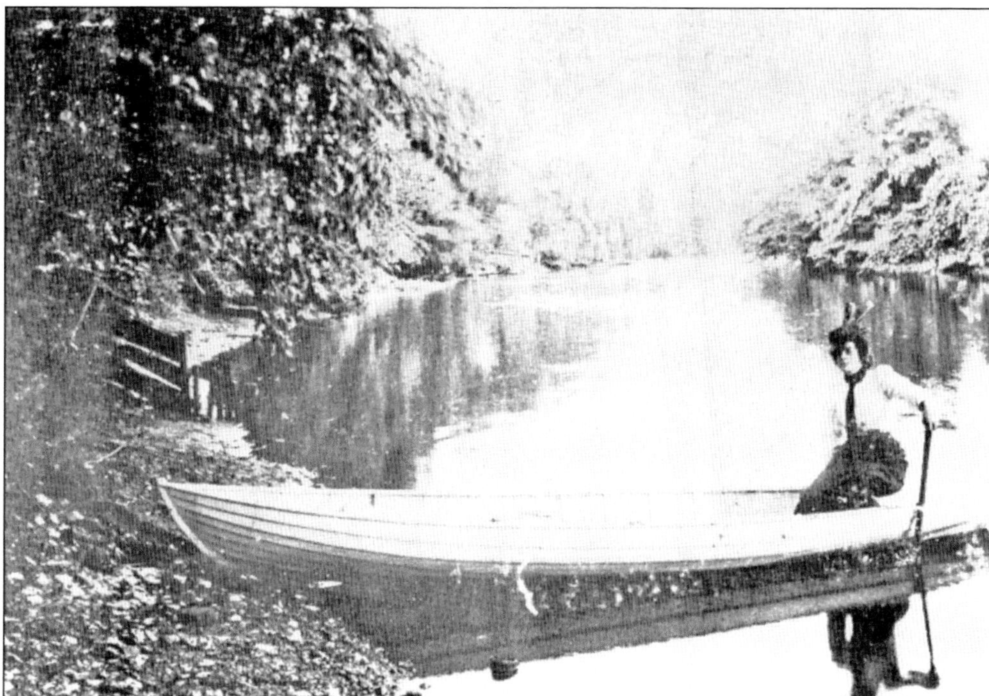

Regardless of how many people took advantage of a peaceful day, boating on the Choptank River was always a popular activity. (Courtesy Town of Greensboro.)

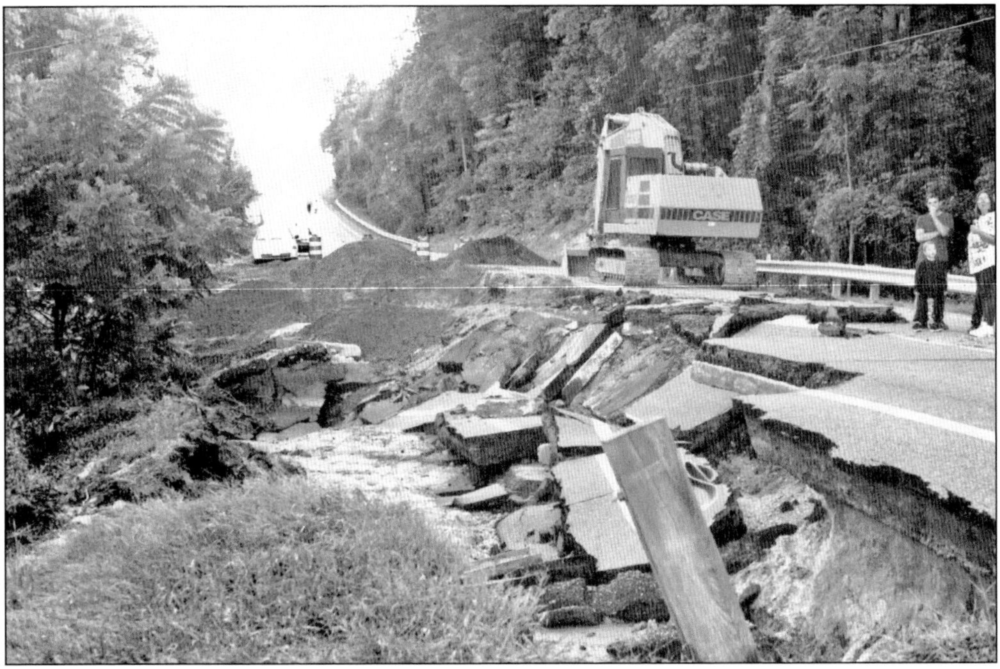

Small branches of the Choptank River were not immune to the effects of strong storms. The floodwaters at Forges Branch destroyed one section of Route 480 between Greensboro and Ridgely in 1999, making passage impossible. (Courtesy Cheryl Jones.)

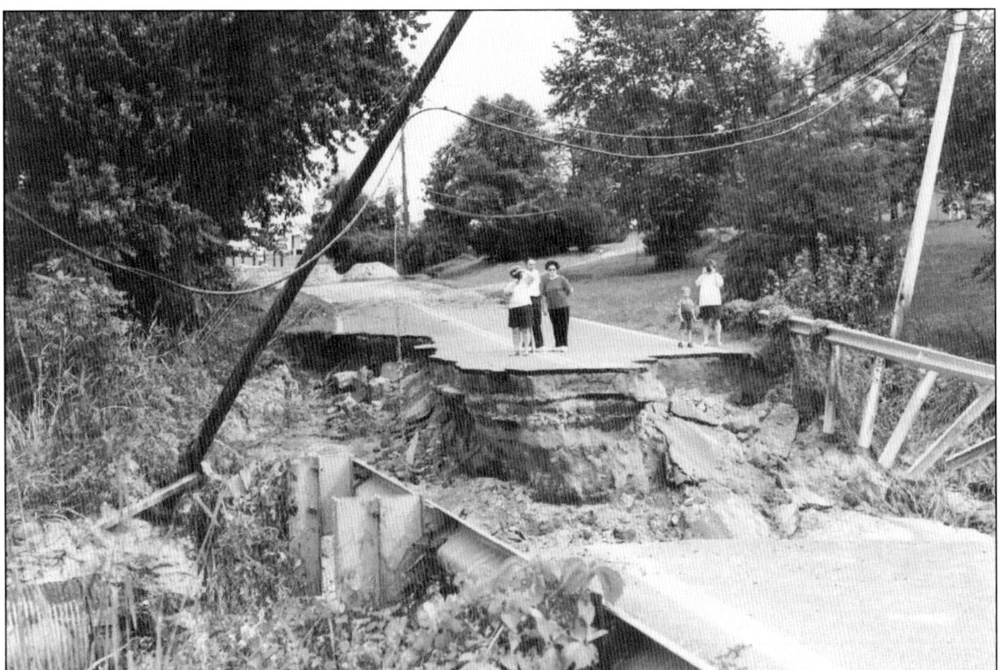

Damage from Hurricane Floyd in 1999 affected small roads and major highways alike. Residents Paul and Alice Dixon (center) with daughter, Mary Alice Dixon Cannon, inspect the damage done at Boyce Mill Road just outside of Greensboro. (Courtesy Cheryl Jones.)

Three

Religion

Much of Greensboro's history can be found in the small churches, and family and town cemeteries that dot the area. Greensboro has a strong religious community, with five churches in town and several more within a three-to-five-mile driving distance. One source states, "In Caroline County, as early as 1775, there was an appointment near Choptank Bridge. This appointment has become permanent in Greensborough. . . . This village has long been the head of a circuit, with its society and chapel. . . . In 1775 they had made appointments as low as Choptank Bridge, now Greensborough." This information, from Lednum's *A History of the Rise of Methodism in America*, shows that this arm of Christianity flourished in Caroline County. The society of Methodists had no formal location for its meetings until 1789, when Peter Harrington sold property to the Methodist Society for the building of a church. Among the guest ministers who preached there were Freeborn Garrettson and Francis Asbury. Frances Asbury, the Methodist bishop who promoted the circuit rider system, spoke at the church on several occasions. Garrettson, who freed his slaves upon converting to Methodism, was instrumental in organizing the Methodist Episcopal Church of the United States.

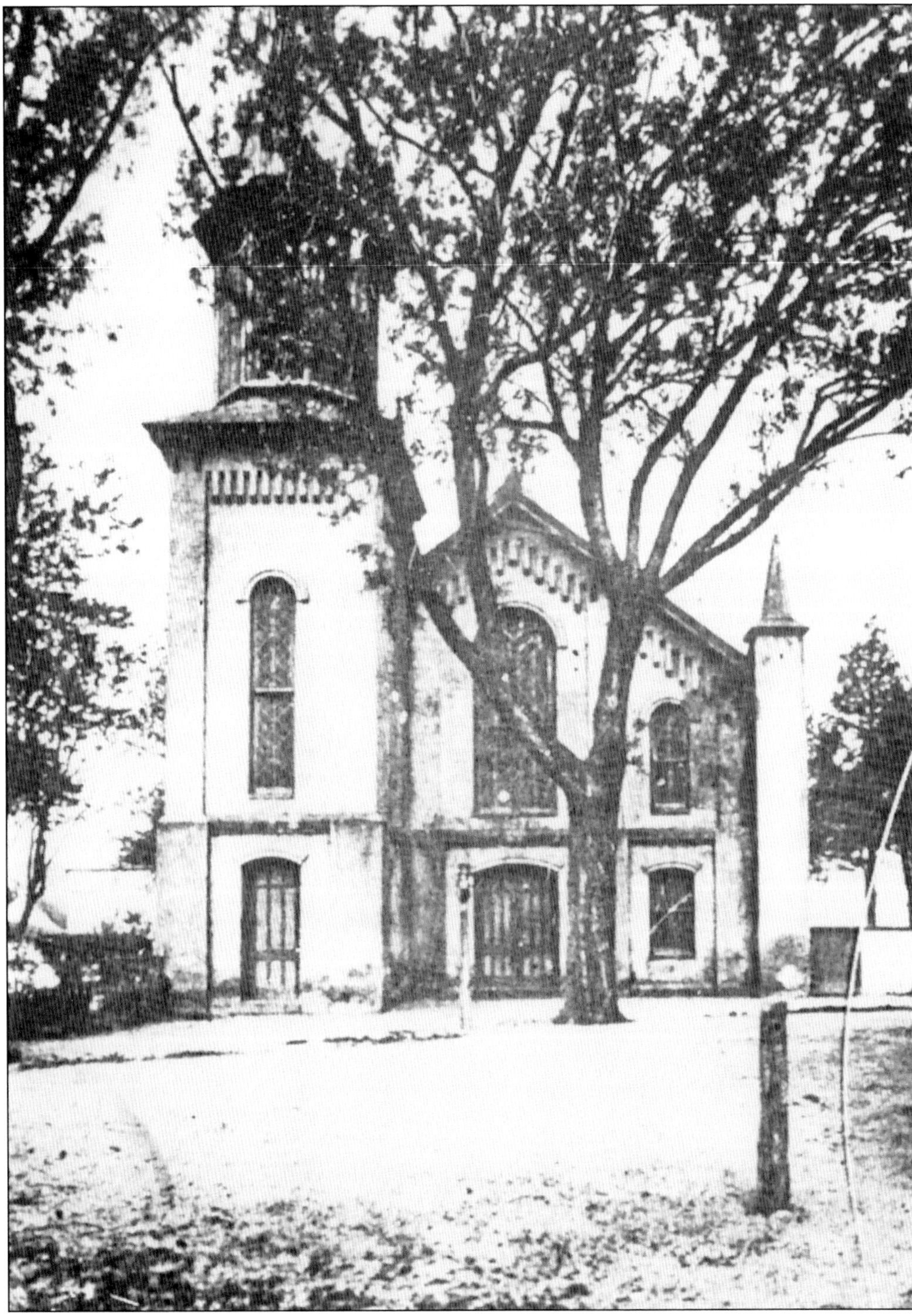

The first church to occupy this location was built on property owned by Peter Harrington and ceded to the Methodist Society in 1789; the second church, pictured here, was built in 1832 and remodeled in 1872. Other religious groups including the Protestant Church and the Holiness Church used this facility until it was razed around 1965. (Courtesy Town of Greensboro.)

One of the few pictures taken inside the second Methodist church of Greensboro shows Paul V. Fryer and Rachel Bilbrough on their wedding day. (Courtesy Joan Cesarini.)

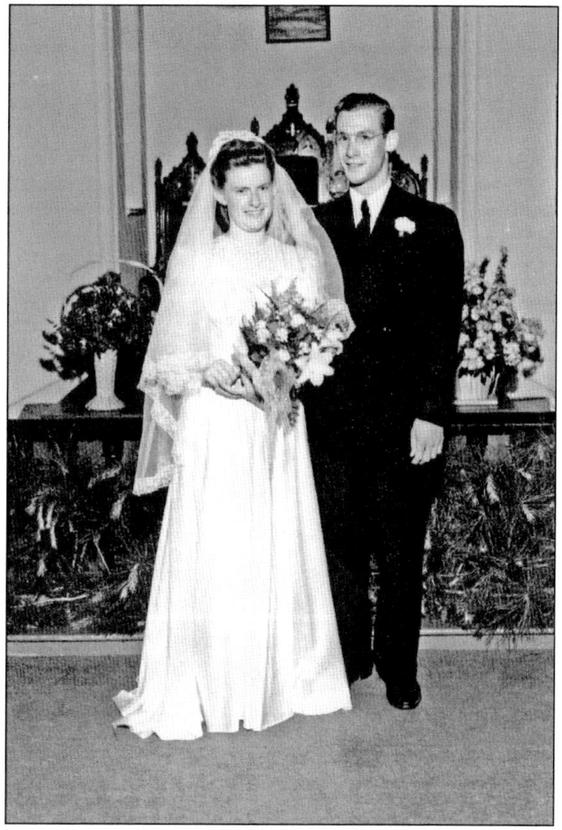

This bell was retrieved from the second Methodist church and placed at the site of the original Methodist cemetery. (Courtesy J. C. Reveal.)

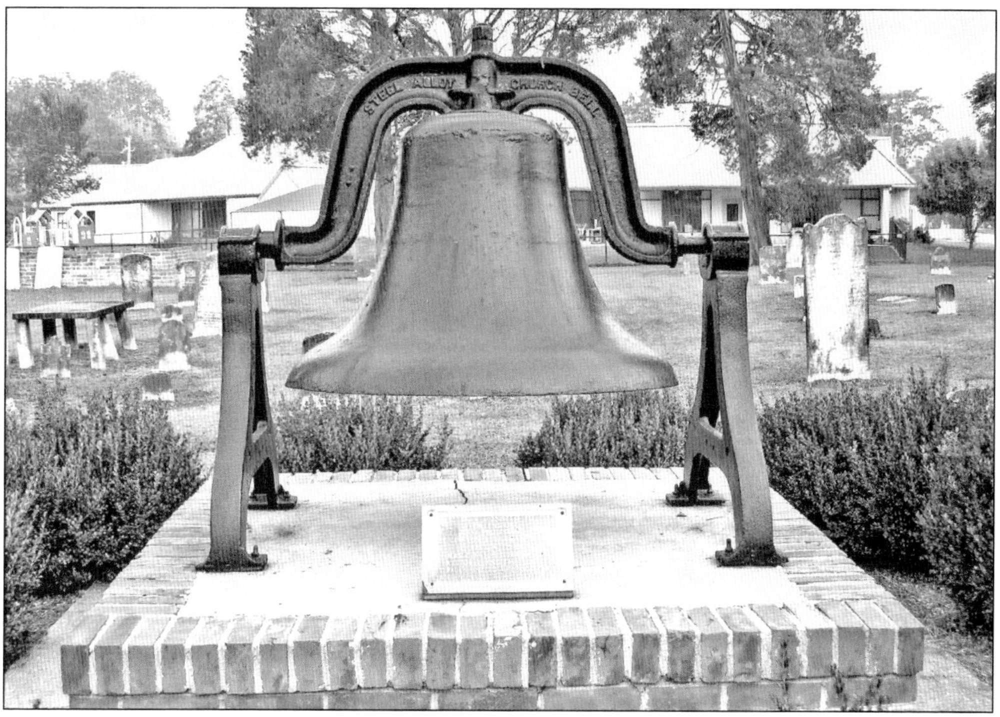

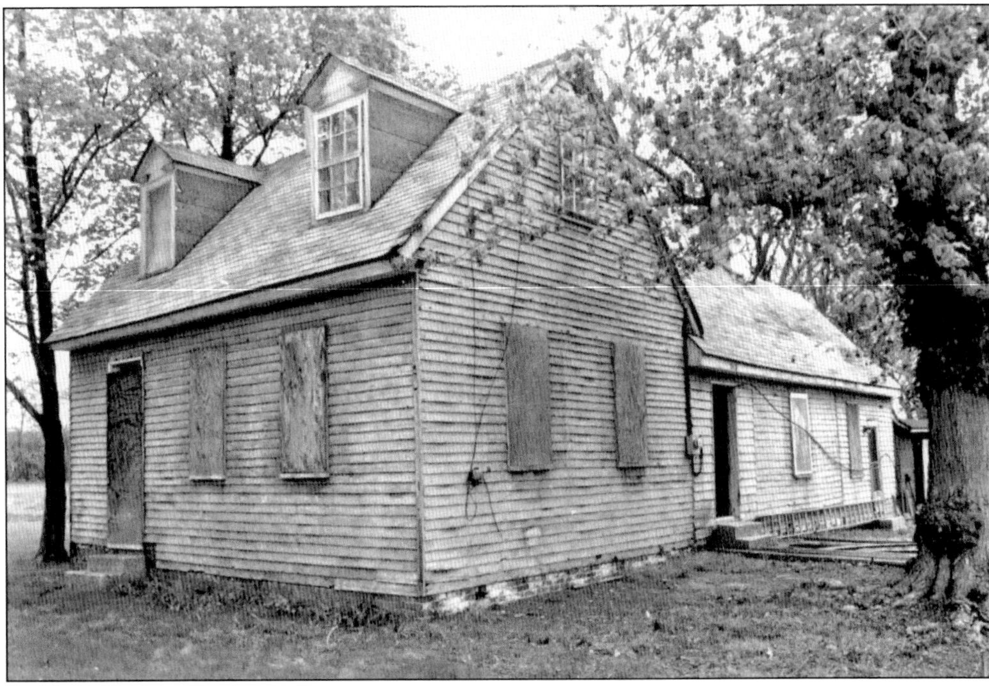

The Old Parsonage, built around 1813, was used by the old Methodist Church until the new church was built in 1904. It fell into a state of disrepair after 1900. (Courtesy the Maryland Historical Trust.)

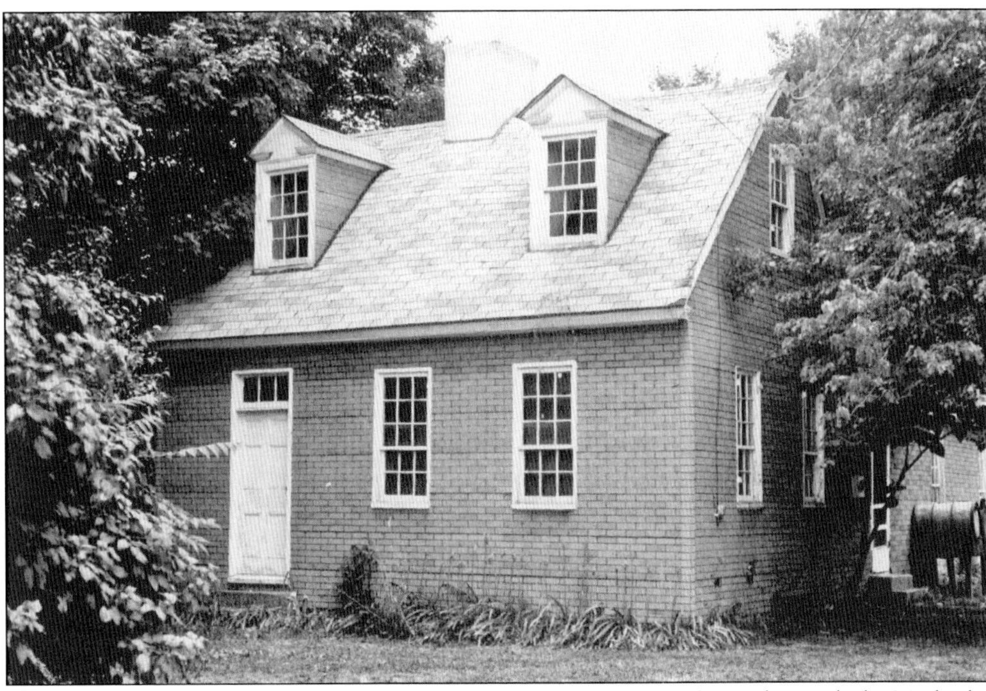

The Old Parsonage, also known as the Leonard house because of its relationship with the Methodist Church, is historically significant to both the town and the religious community. (Courtesy the Maryland Historical Trust.)

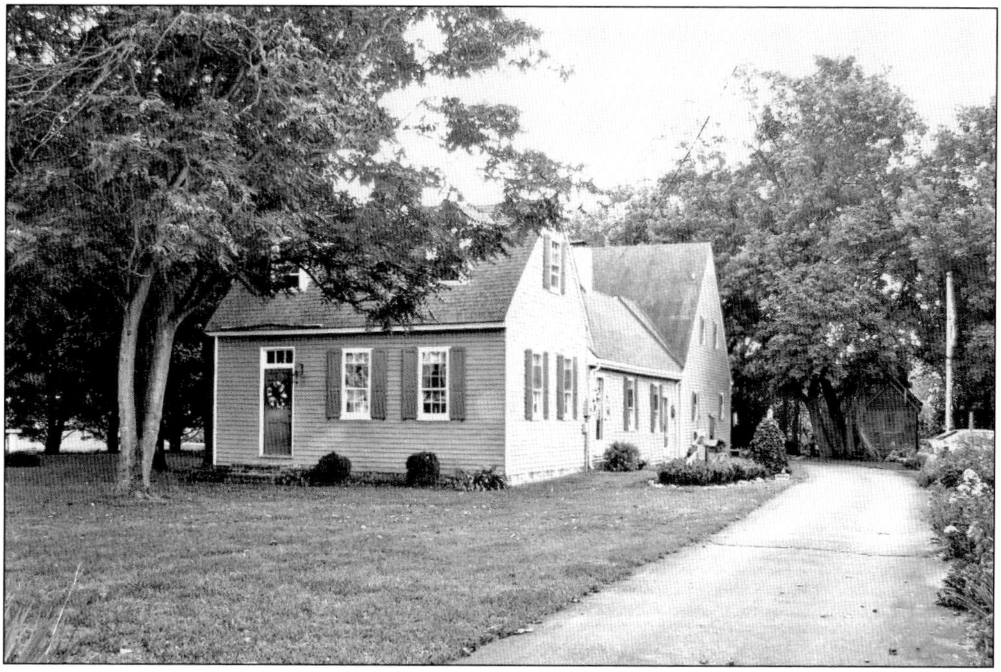

The current owners, Clyde and Elsie Embert, faithfully restored the old part of the inside of the parsonage to its original appearance while renovating the outside as well. In 1986, the Old Parsonage was listed on the National Register of Historic Places, and it remains the only building in Greensboro to be so recognized. (Courtesy J. C. Reveal.)

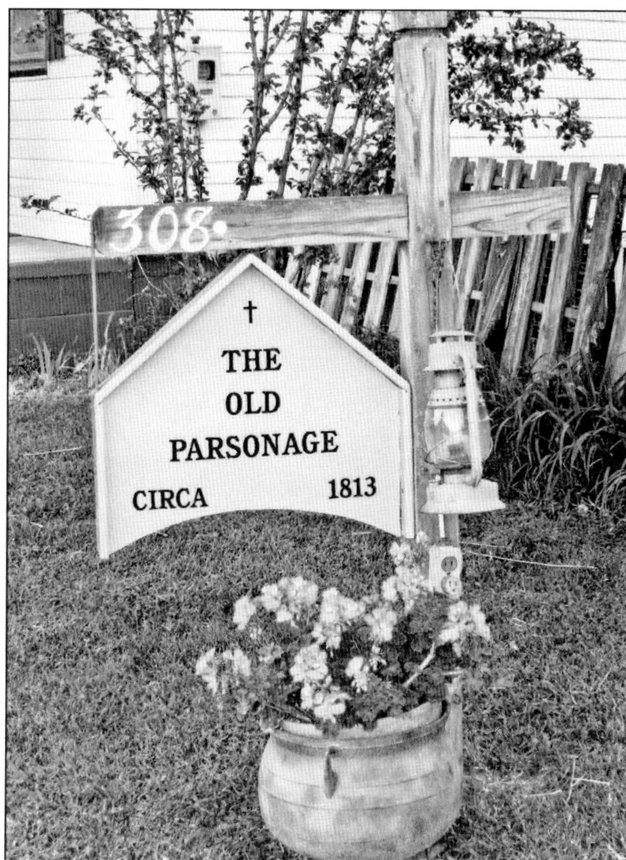

The sign welcoming visitors and friends to the home of Clyde and Elsie Embert stands on Main Street just at the north end of town. (Courtesy J. C. Reveal.)

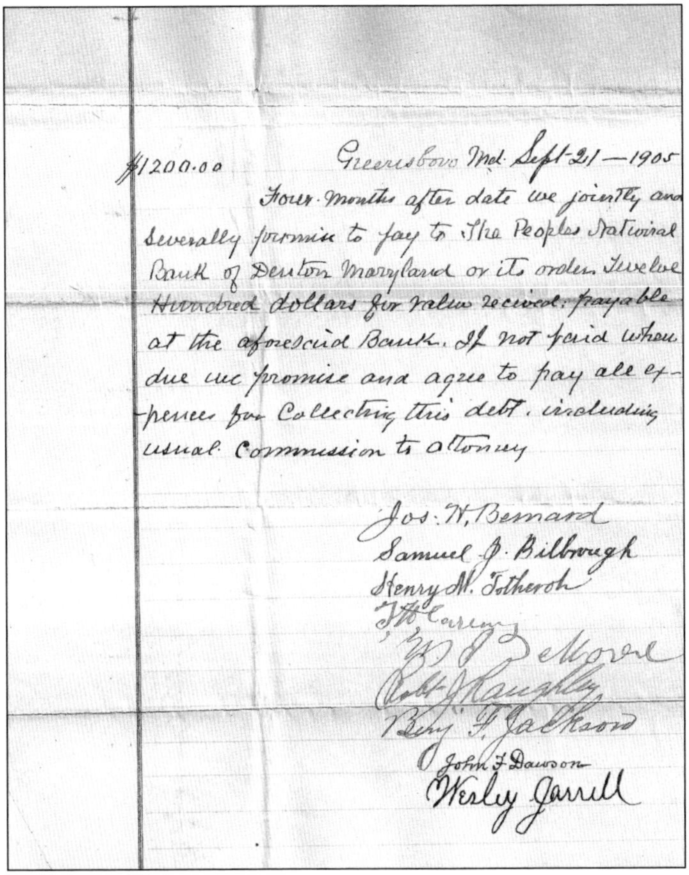

$1200.00 Greensboro Md. Sept-21—1905

Four months after date we jointly and severally promise to pay to The Peoples National Bank of Denton Maryland or its order Twelve Hundred dollars for value received: payable at the aforesaid Bank. If not paid when due we promise and agree to pay all expenses for Collecting this debt. including usual Commission to attorney

Jos. W. Bernard
Samuel J. Bilbrough
Henry M. Totheroh
T. W. Carey
W. J. DeMoore
Robt J. Haughley
Benj. F. Jackson
John F. Dawson
Wesley Jarrell

On September 21, 1905, the board of St. Paul's Methodist Episcopal Church borrowed $1,200. This promissory note reflects the signatures of many of Greensboro's most important citizens and businessmen—names that remain important to the town's history. (Courtesy St. Paul's Methodist Church.)

In 1905, growth of the Methodist congregation necessitated the building of a new church, St. Paul's Methodist Episcopal Church. The members obtained property two blocks west of downtown Greensboro and constructed the new, larger accommodations. (Courtesy J. C. Reveal.)

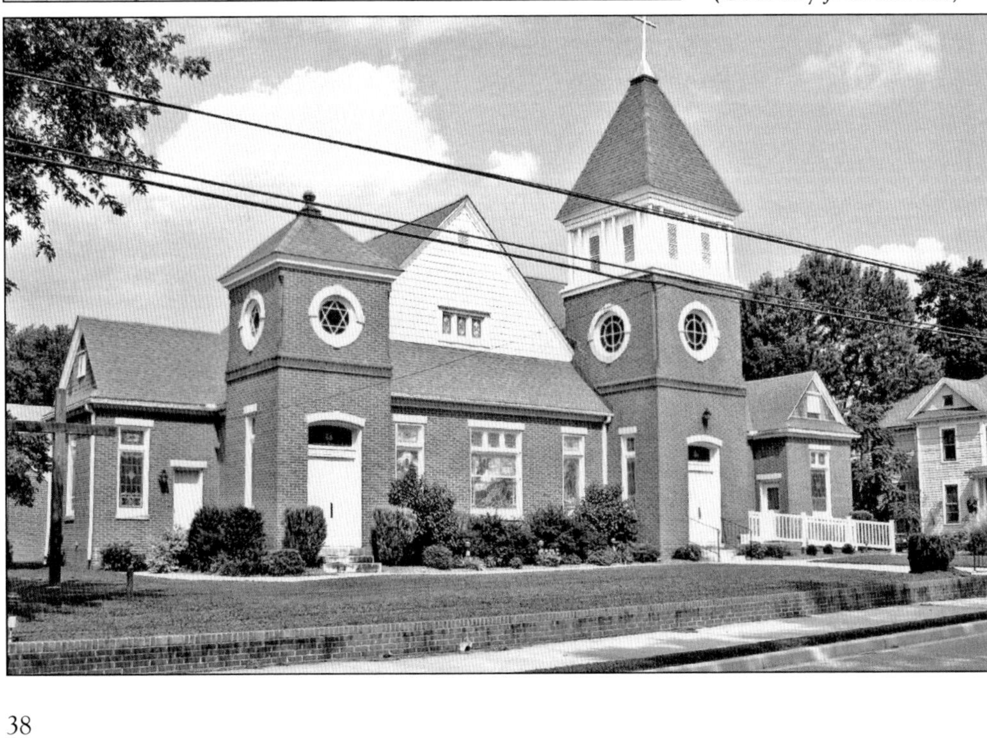

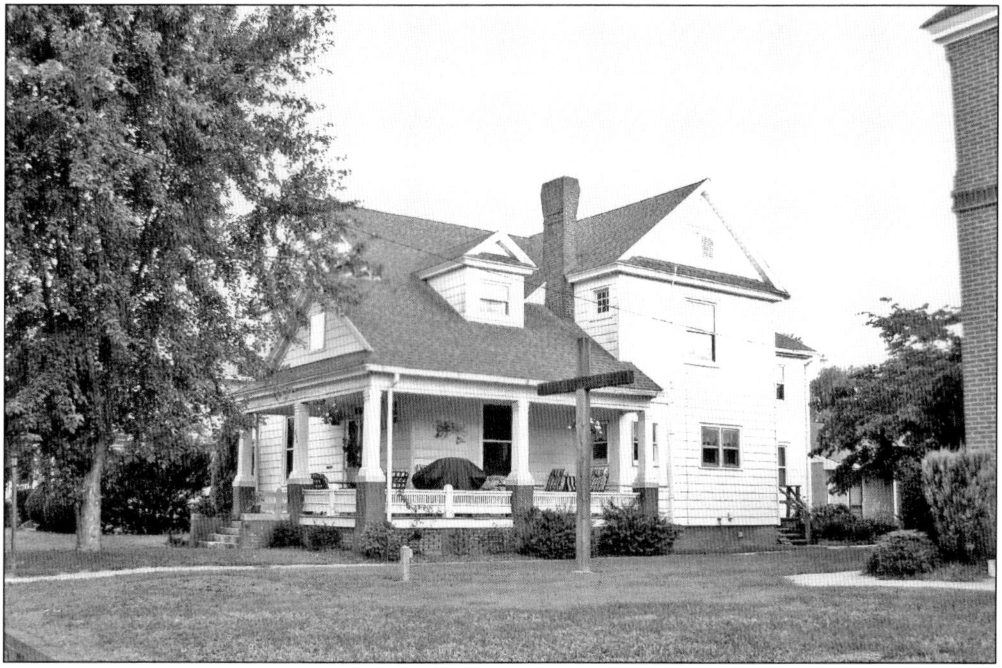

The St. Paul's Methodist Episcopal Church parsonage is one of the lovely historic homes in Greensboro. It was erected about the same time as the church, approximately 1905. (Courtesy J. C. Reveal.)

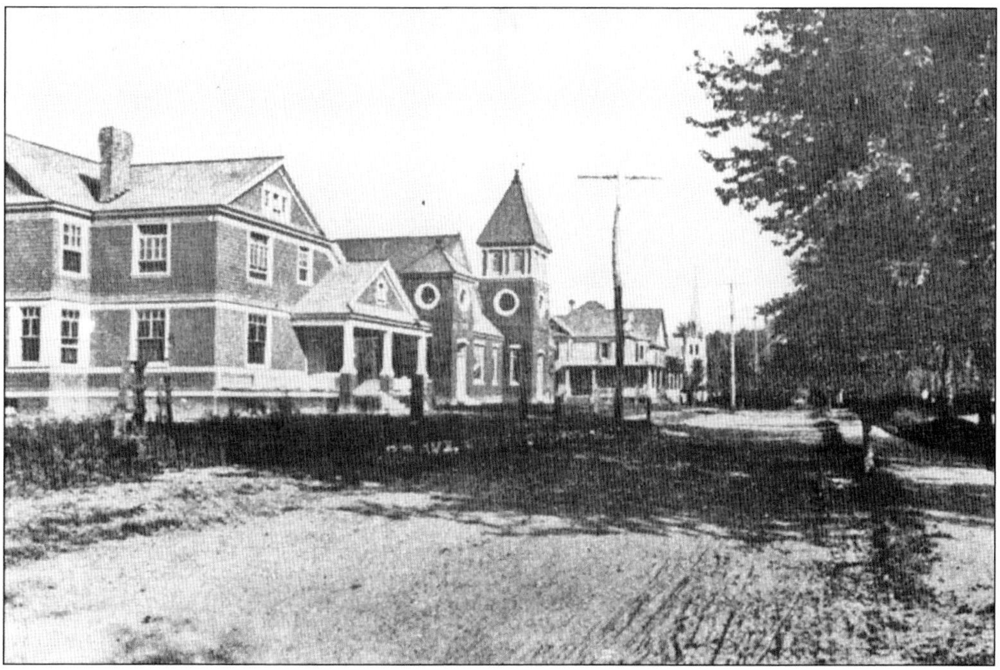

This view of Sunset Avenue looking east shows the original building next to St. Paul's Methodist Episcopal Church, which is currently the parsonage. Originally a brick building, it underwent renovations that included more modern siding and restructuring of the front porch. (Courtesy Town of Greensboro.)

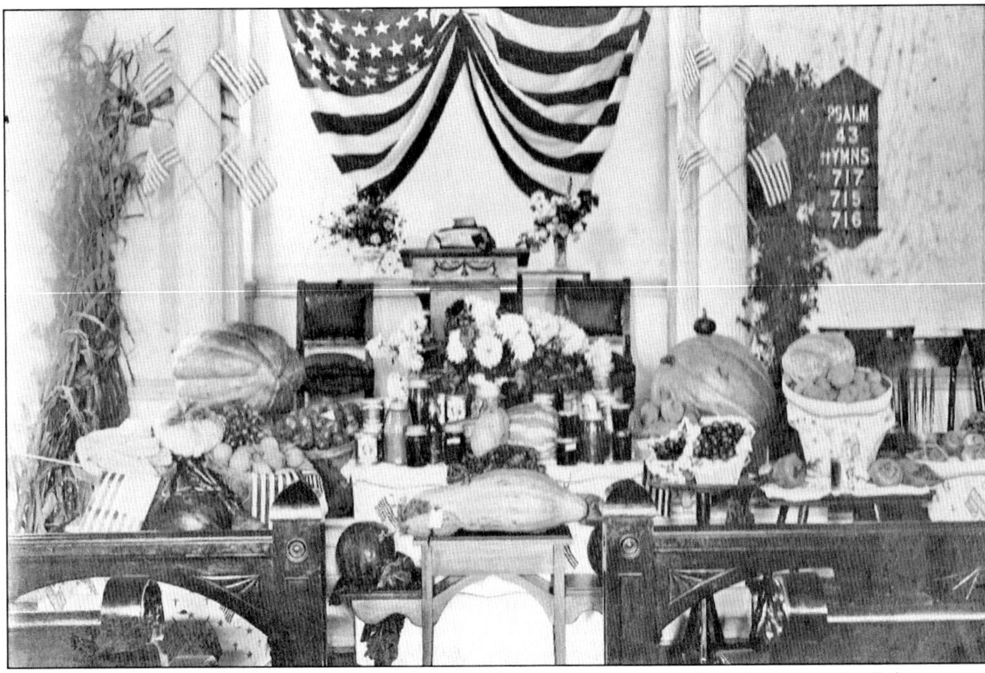

Agriculture is recognized for its importance to the area, as seen in this photograph of the annual Harvest Home celebration at St. Paul's Methodist church. This picture is significant to the town's history as it was taken by Henry Cohee, one of the primary photographers of the area. (Courtesy St. Paul's Methodist Church.)

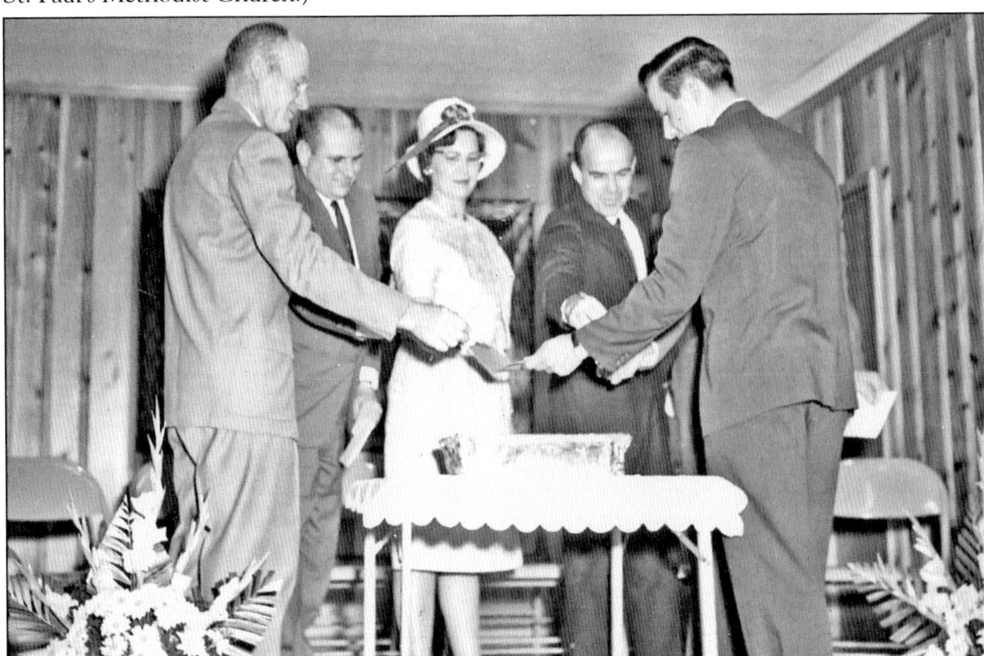
St. Paul's Church members—from left to right, Richard Porter, Ray Breeding, Joyce Ober, Goldsborough Stafford, and Reverend William Hankins—happily burn the St. Paul's mortgage papers in 1965. (Courtesy St. Paul's Methodist Church.)

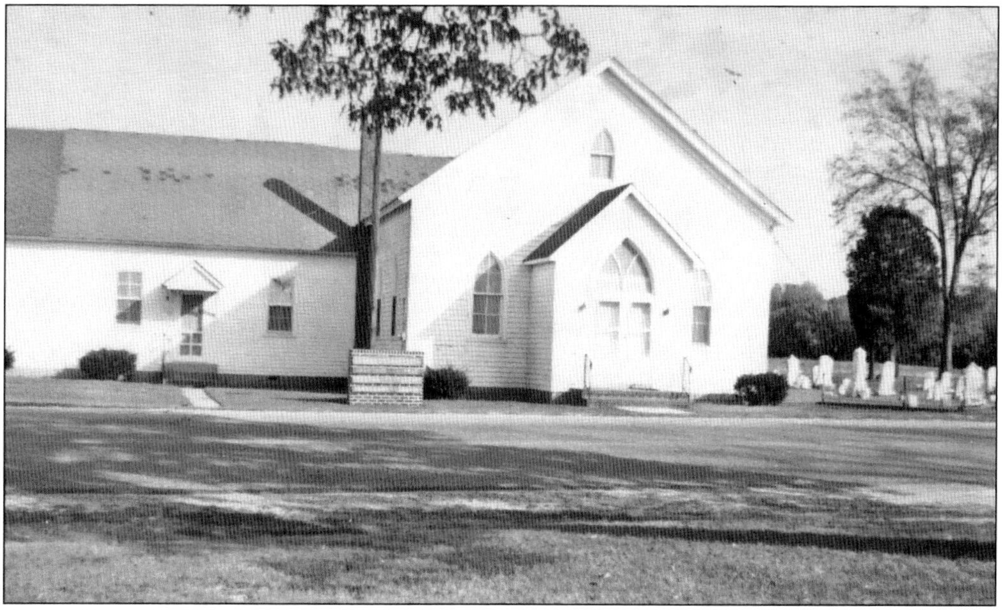

Burrsville Methodist church, sister to St. Paul's United Methodist Episcopal church, is located in a pastoral setting, a short drive from Greensboro on Knifebox Road in Burrsville, Maryland. (Courtesy Joan Cesarini.)

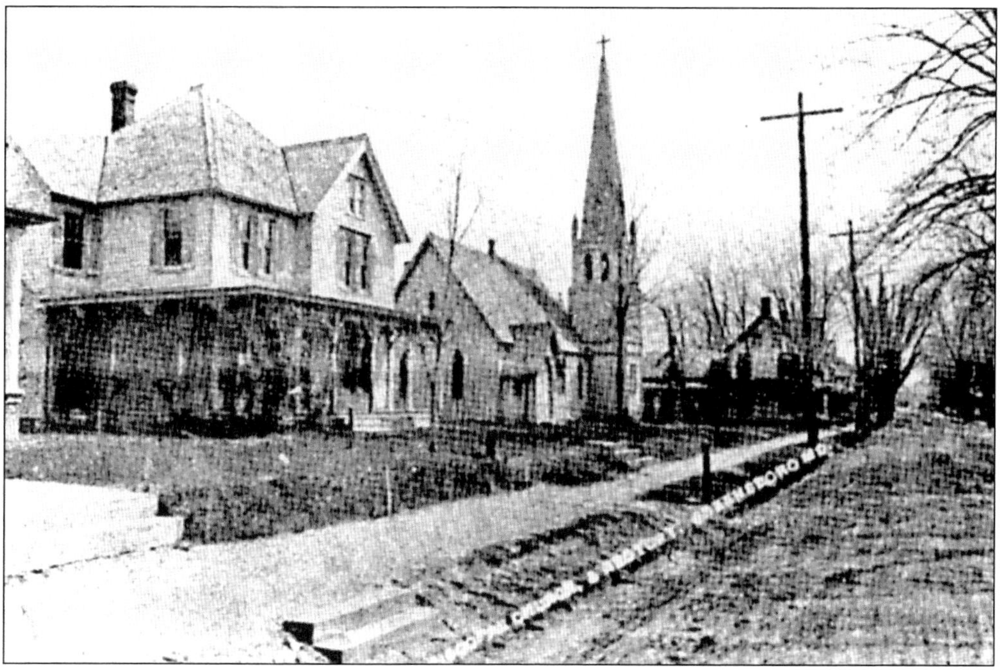

The Church of the Holy Trinity was the result of efforts by Angeline Goldsborough and Ella Betts and was based on their knowledge of local children who had no church or religious education. Goldsborough and Betts organized a Sunday school, and a Mr. Ernst presented the idea of a new church to a convention at Easton in 1870. A new parish was formed. The church building was completed and dedicated on April 13, 1875. The congregation diminished to a point where the church was no longer used, and the building was razed in the 1960s. (Courtesy Town of Greensboro.)

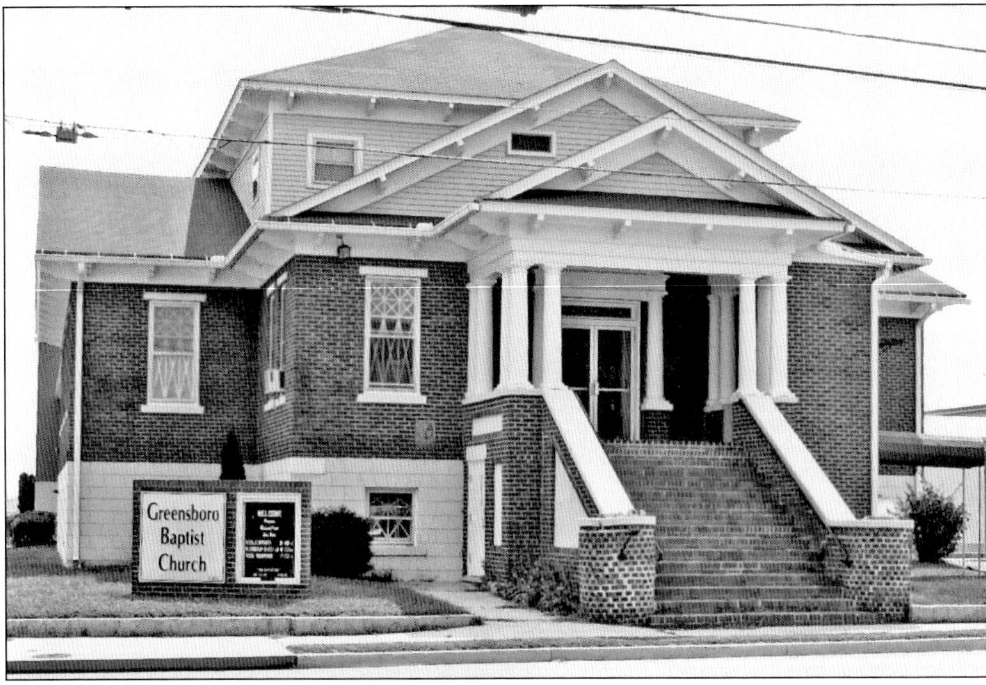

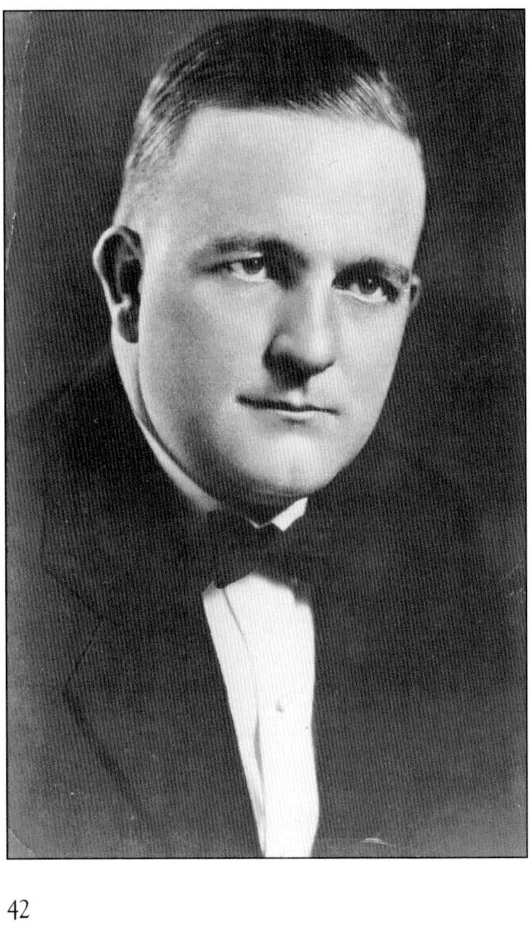

The Greensboro Baptist Church was established in June 1920, and the first service was held on July 3, 1920, in a tabernacle that occupied this site. Eight hundred people attended. On July 5, 1920, a second service was held with attendance at 1,200. (Courtesy J. C. Reveal.)

The church was officially organized on November 1, 1920, with Rev. Melvin G. Morris as pastor and 24 charter members. (Courtesy Greensboro Baptist Church.)

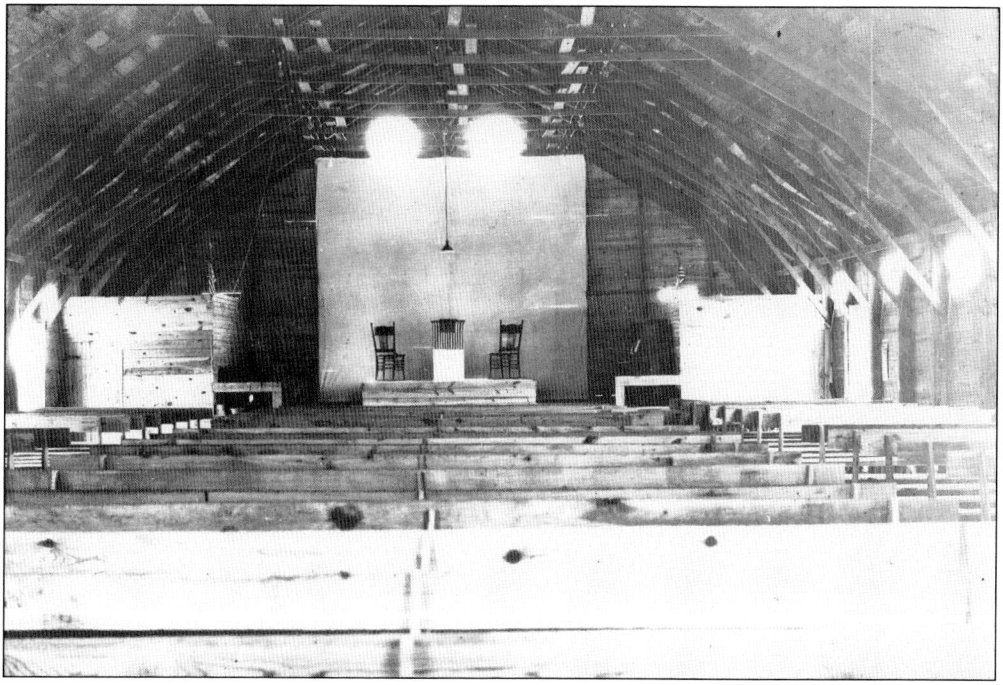

Prior to the building of the Greensboro Baptist church, the congregation met at a Baptist tabernacle. On March 8, 1921, the congregation voted to build a permanent church. (Courtesy Greensboro Baptist Church.)

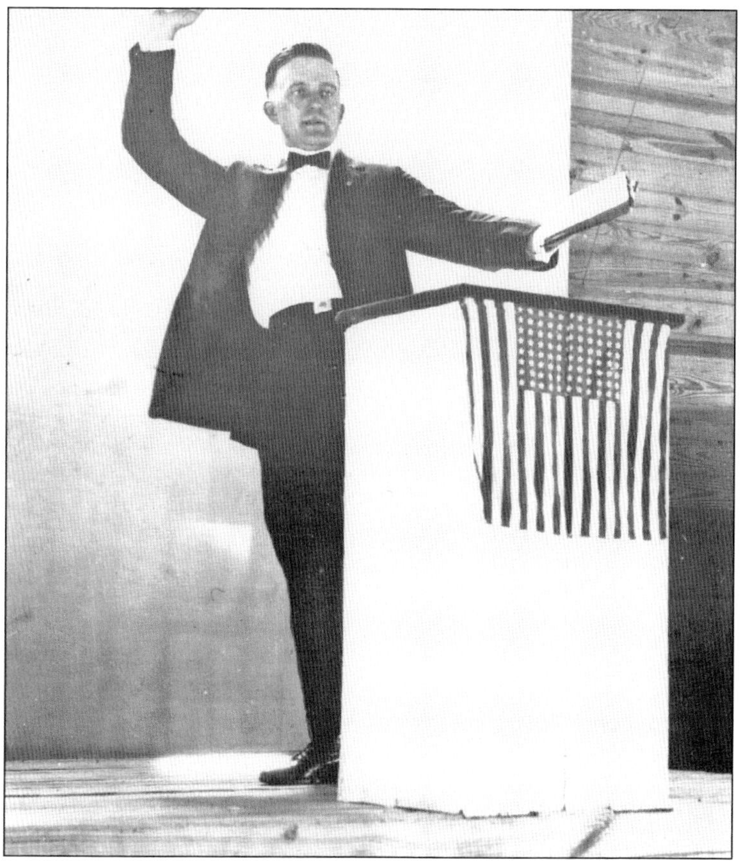

The charismatic Rev. Melvin Morris preaches in the tabernacle before the church building is constructed. (Courtesy Greensboro Baptist Church.)

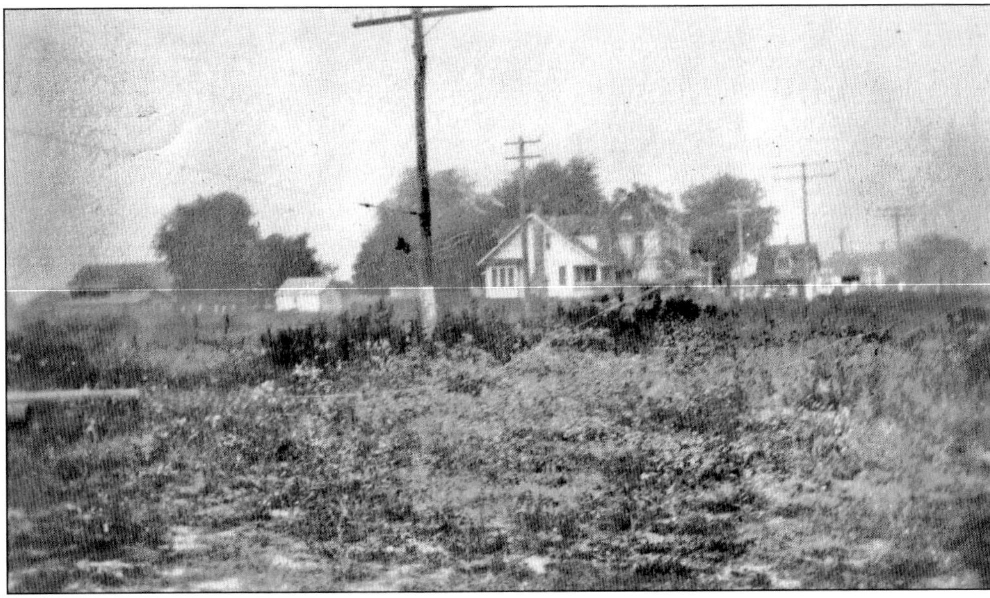

By June 1921, the tabernacle had been removed and the lot readied for construction. (Courtesy Greensboro Baptist Church.)

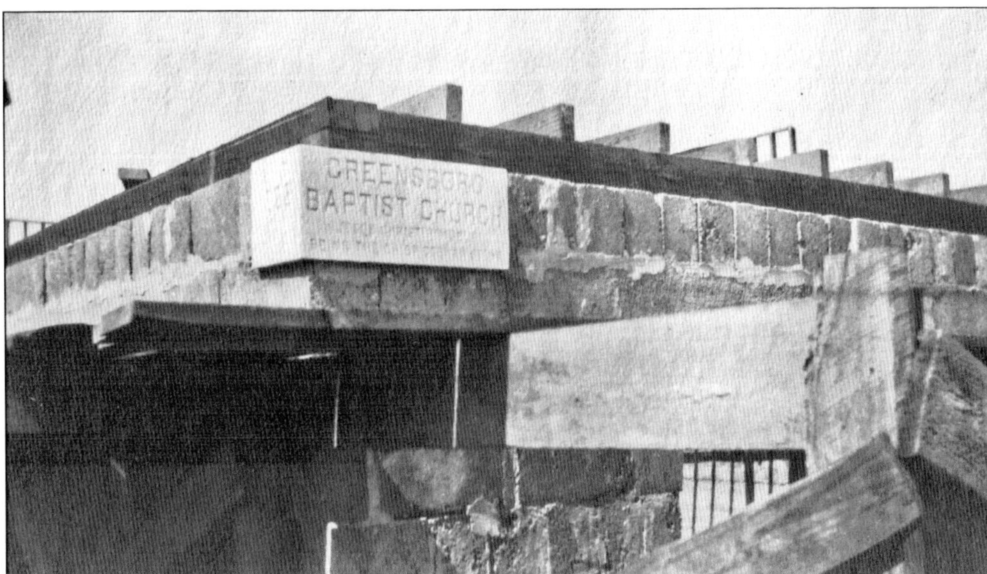

One of the first actions in the construction of the church building was to lay the cornerstone. (Courtesy Greensboro Baptist Church.)

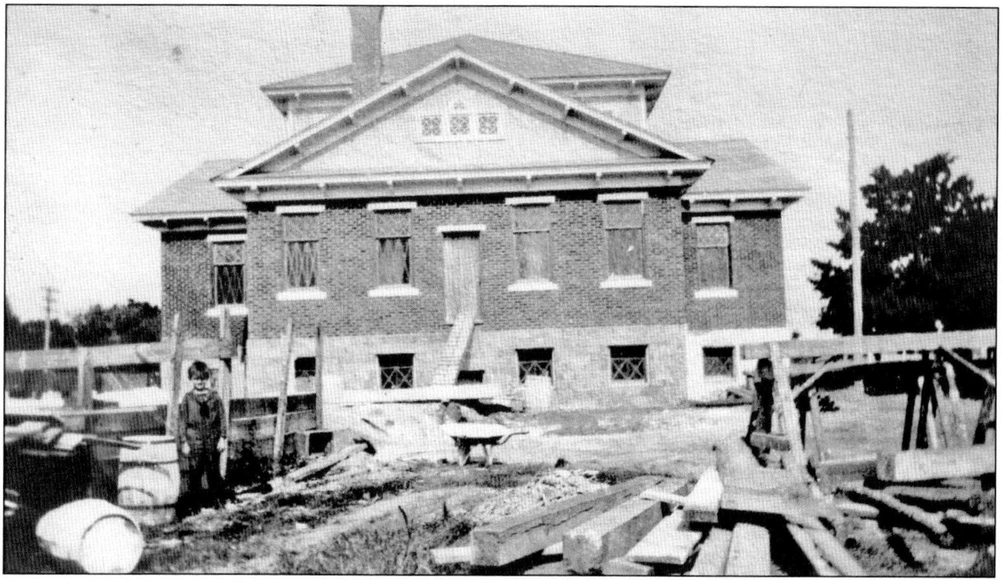

As seen in this view of the back of the church, it was a building that was substantial in size from its very beginning, designed to hold its large and growing congregation. (Courtesy Greensboro Baptist Church.)

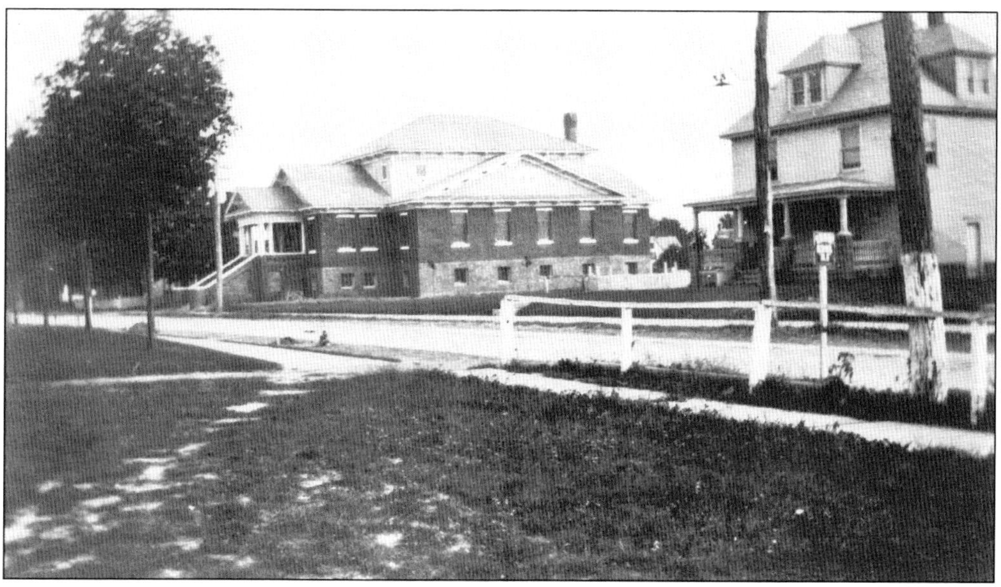

The house seen in the right of this picture was eventually bought and served as the parsonage. (Courtesy Greensboro Baptist Church.)

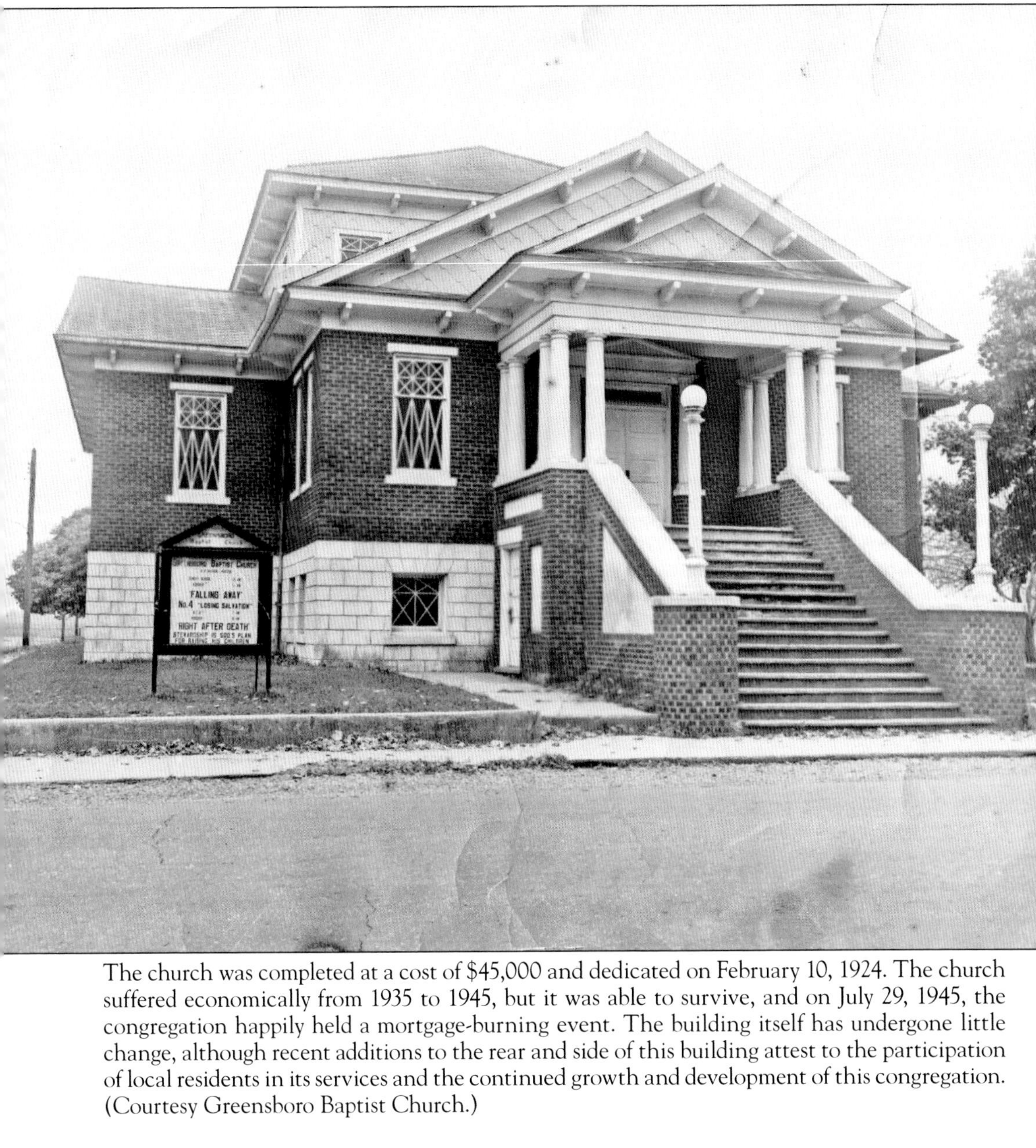

The church was completed at a cost of $45,000 and dedicated on February 10, 1924. The church suffered economically from 1935 to 1945, but it was able to survive, and on July 29, 1945, the congregation happily held a mortgage-burning event. The building itself has undergone little change, although recent additions to the rear and side of this building attest to the participation of local residents in its services and the continued growth and development of this congregation. (Courtesy Greensboro Baptist Church.)

Mount Pleasant Methodist Church has served the local African American community since 1864, when Rev. John A. Dennis built the first church and named it Dennis Temple. Rev. P. M. Shelton constructed the present building in 1905. On May 28, 1905, it was dedicated as Mount Pleasant church in a ceremony that began with the congregation singing "We're Marching to Zion" while parading through town. (Courtesy J. C. Reveal.)

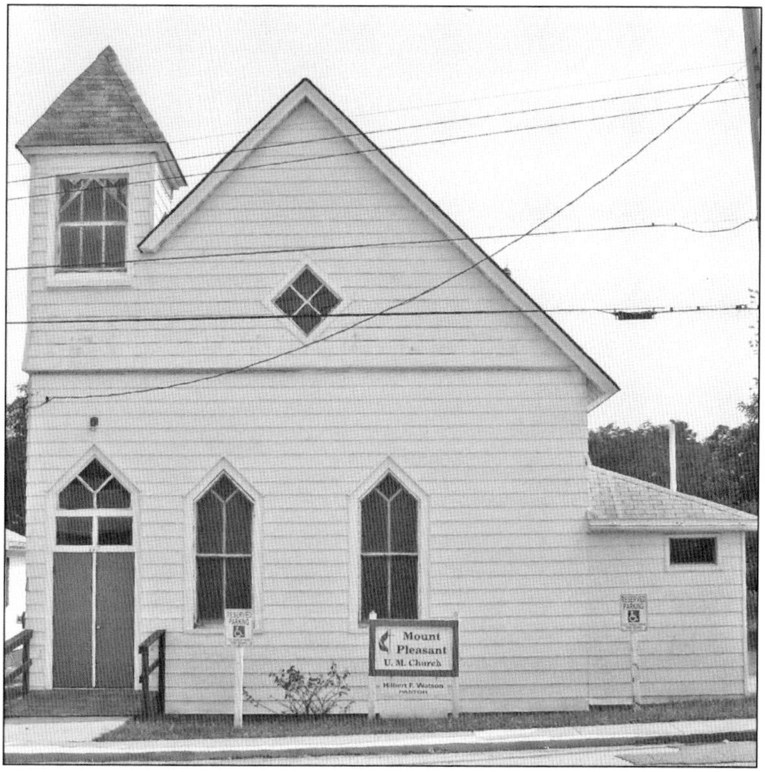

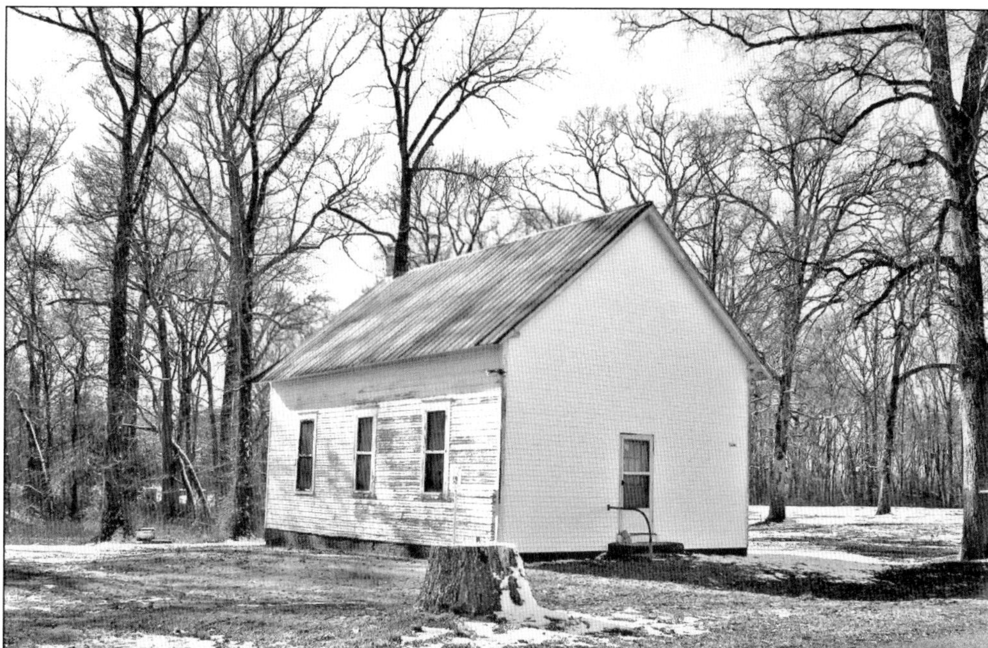

Irwin's Chapel, a second African Methodist Episcopal (AME) church is located a short drive northwest of the town on Union Road. It is nestled in a small wooded area and surrounded by an old, historic cemetery. (Courtesy J. C. Reveal.)

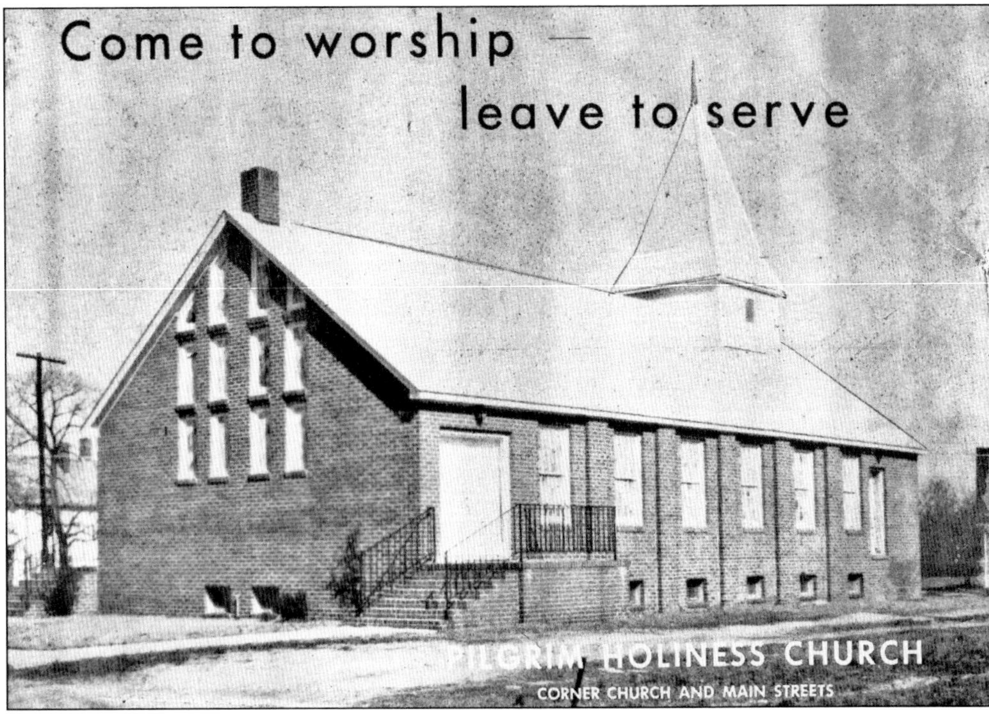

Originally named the Pilgrim Holiness Church, this later became the Wesleyan Church of Greensboro. The church was founded by Rev. Alford Clark in 1935. (Courtesy Joan Cesarini.)

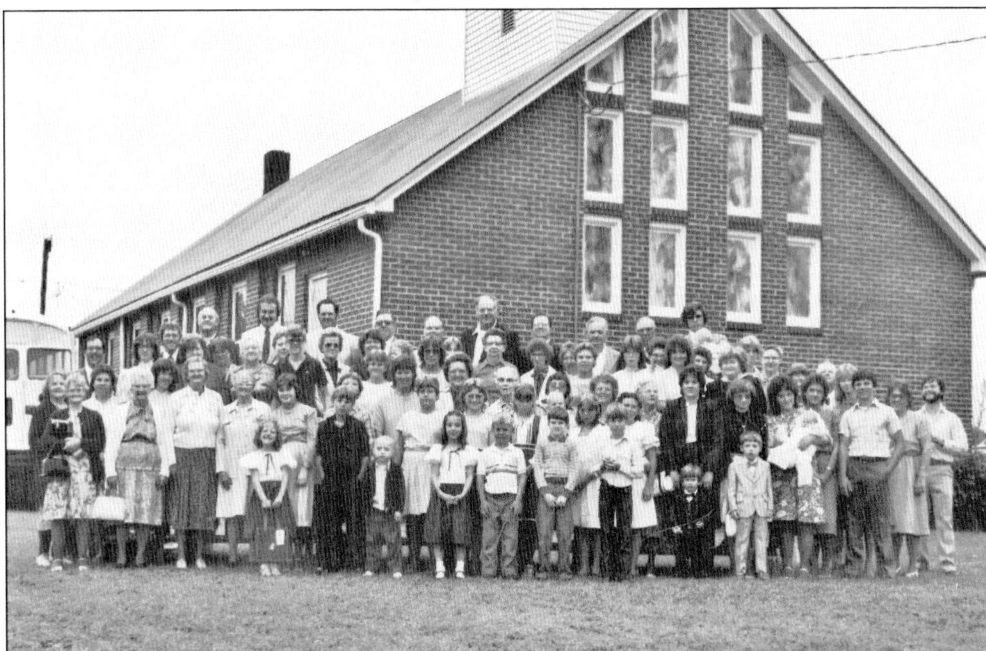

The congregation of the Wesleyan Church of Greensboro is pictured here in the 1970s, prior to moving the church to its new location, approximately one quarter of a mile north just outside of the Greensboro town border. (Courtesy Joan Cesarini.)

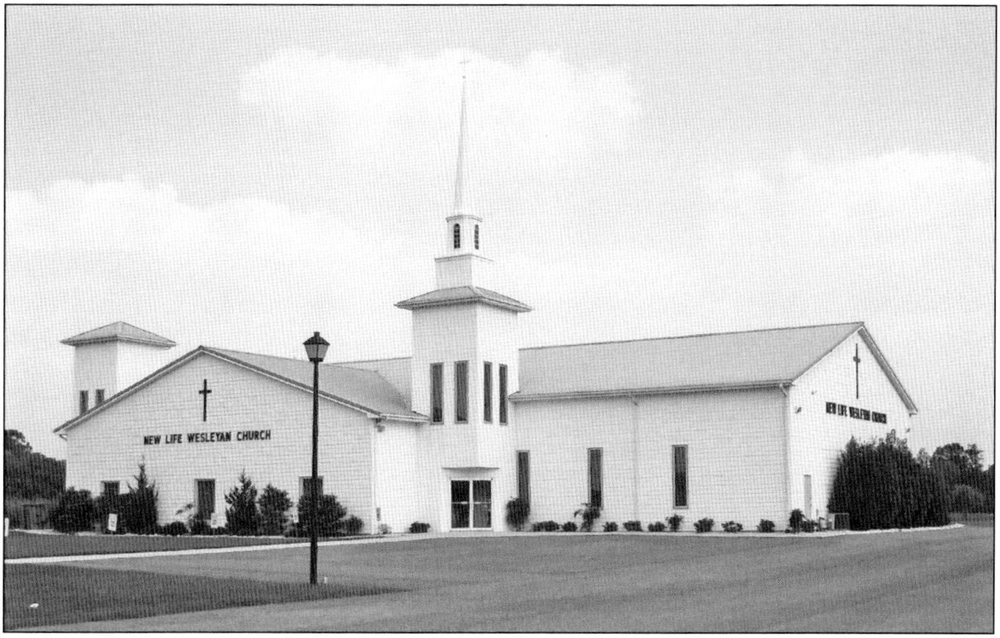

In 2004, the New Life Wesleyan Church opened the doors of its new building, situated just outside the town limits. This active congregation had outgrown its previous location, and this building was completed to accommodate its growing flock. (Courtesy J. C. Reveal.)

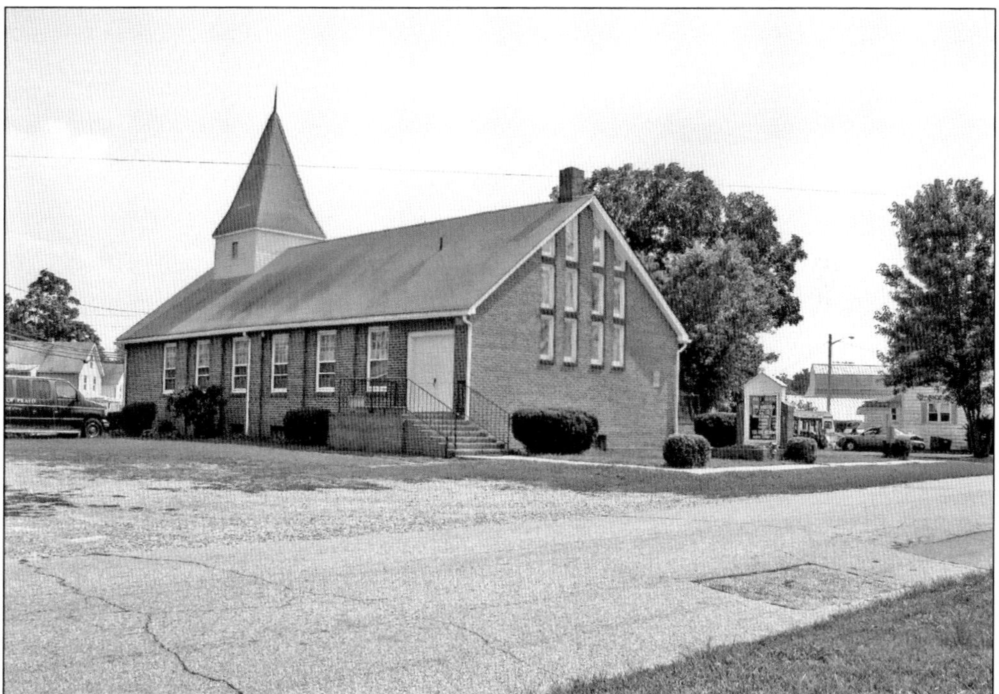

The New Council of God Ministries Church, an apostolic congregation, was established in Greensboro in 2004. Although not comparable in size to the Methodist, Baptist, or Wesleyan churches, it enjoys a dedicated following. (Courtesy J. C. Reveal.)

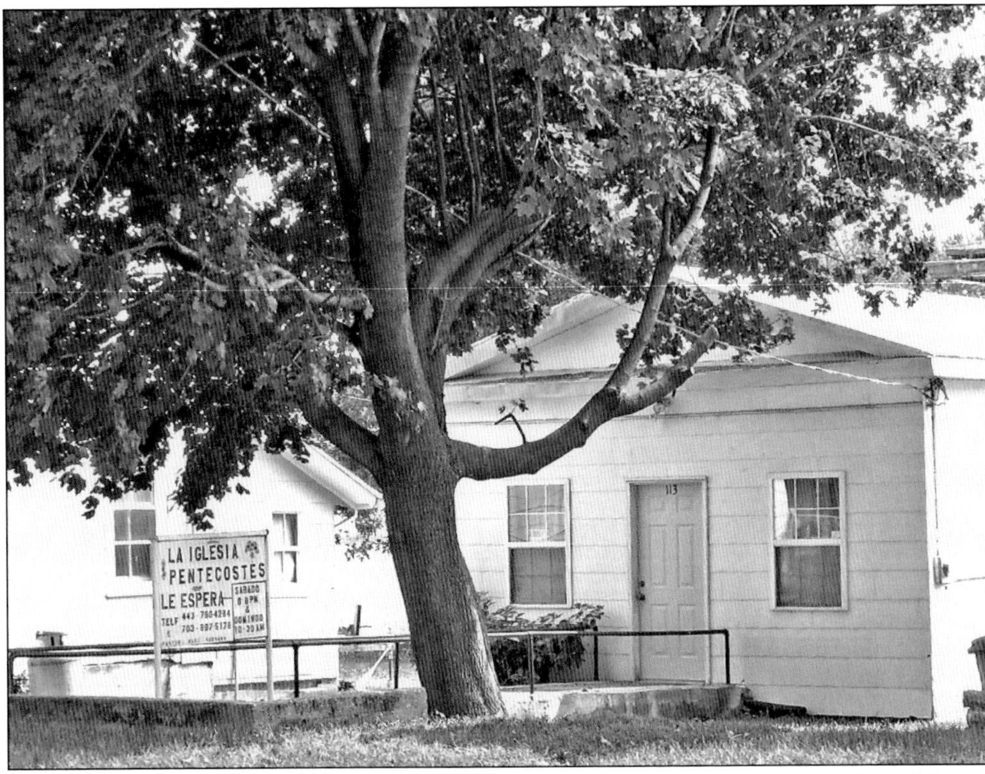

In recent years, Greensboro has welcomed into its community a growing number of Latino residents, who have brought with them their deep religious convictions. This small building in the heart of Greensboro provides this group with a place to practice their religious beliefs. (Courtesy J. C. Reveal.)

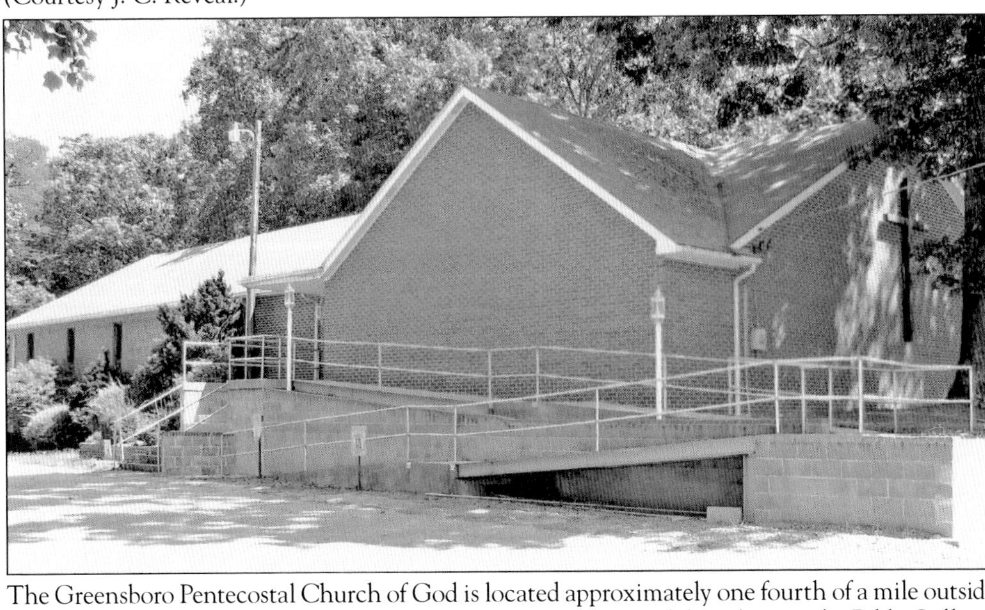

The Greensboro Pentecostal Church of God is located approximately one fourth of a mile outside of the town limits in a quiet, wooded area. It is also the home of the Chesapeake Bible College. (Courtesy J. C. Reveal.)

Social functions thrived in the religious community. Reverend E. Linwood Horseman of the Greensboro Pilgrim Holiness Church and his wife, Ethel, prepare for a Sunday school outing around 1952. (Courtesy Joan Cesarini.)

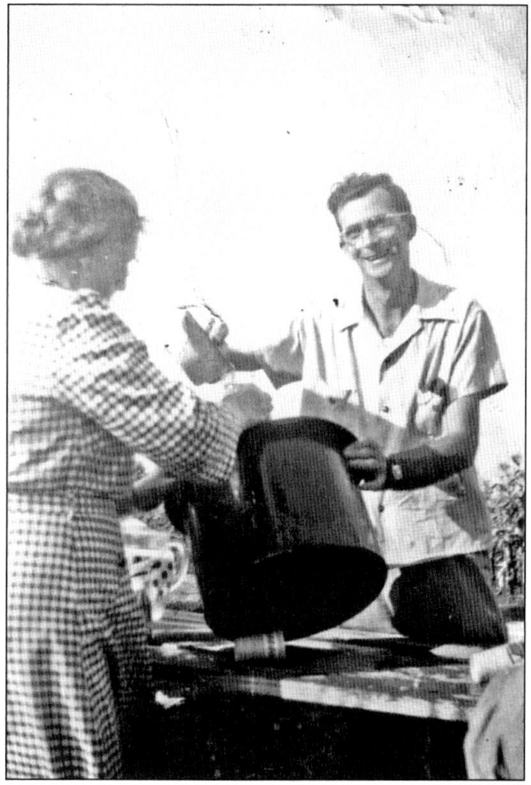

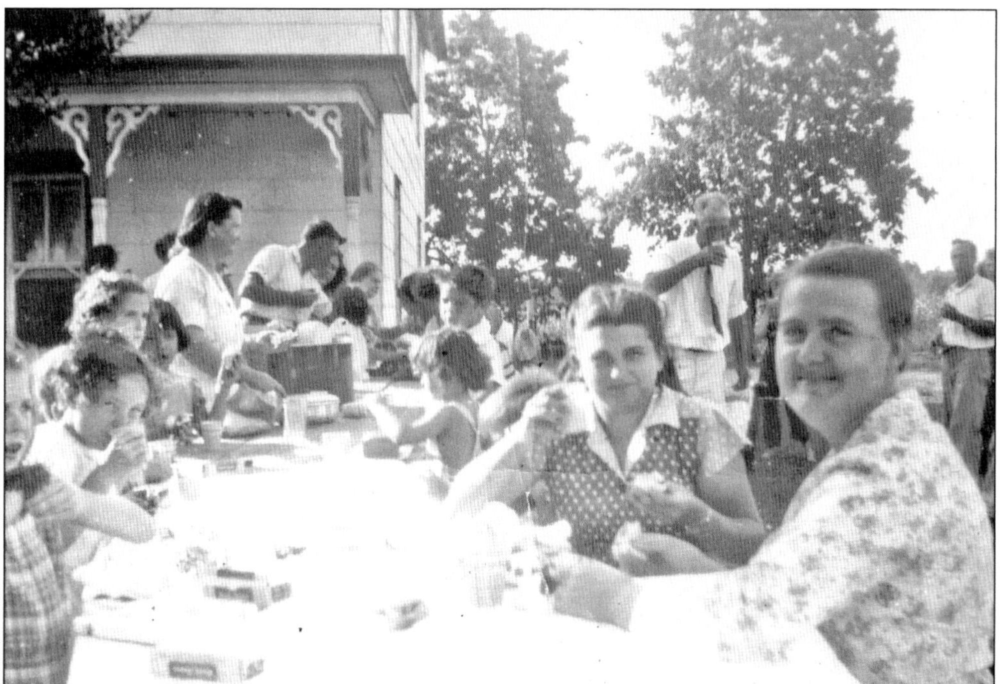

Members of the Pilgrim Holiness Church of Greensboro Sunday school enjoy an outing at Butler Farm in the 1940s. (Courtesy Joan Cesarini.)

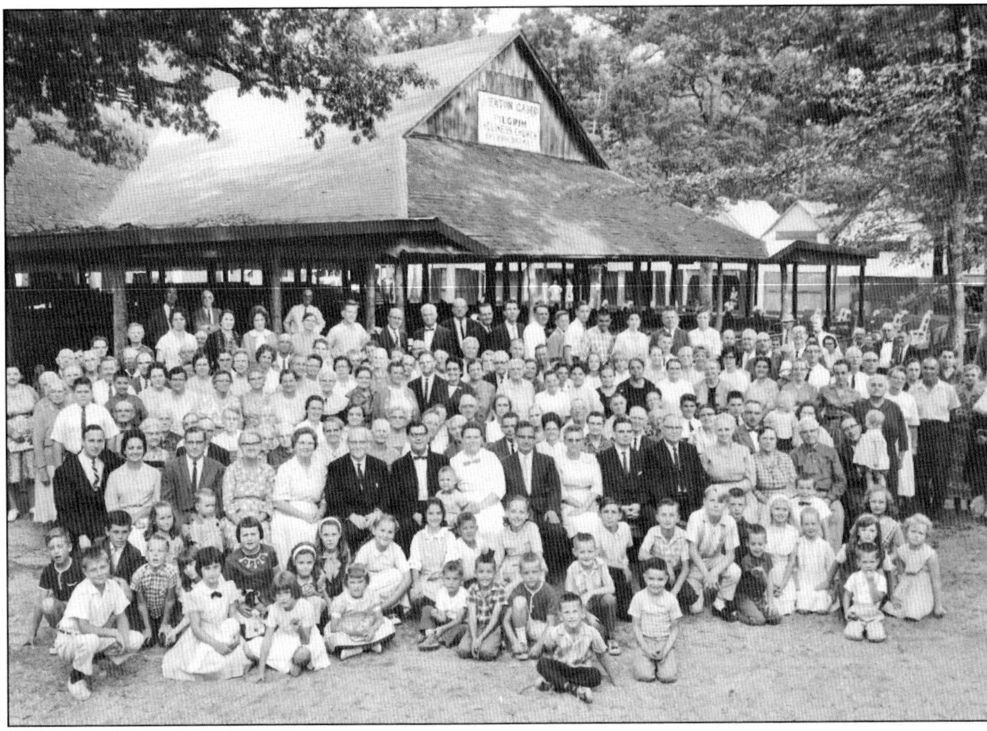

Denton Camp of Pilgrim Holiness Church, previously Pentecostal Camp, enjoyed a large attendance around 1968. (Courtesy Joan Cesarini.)

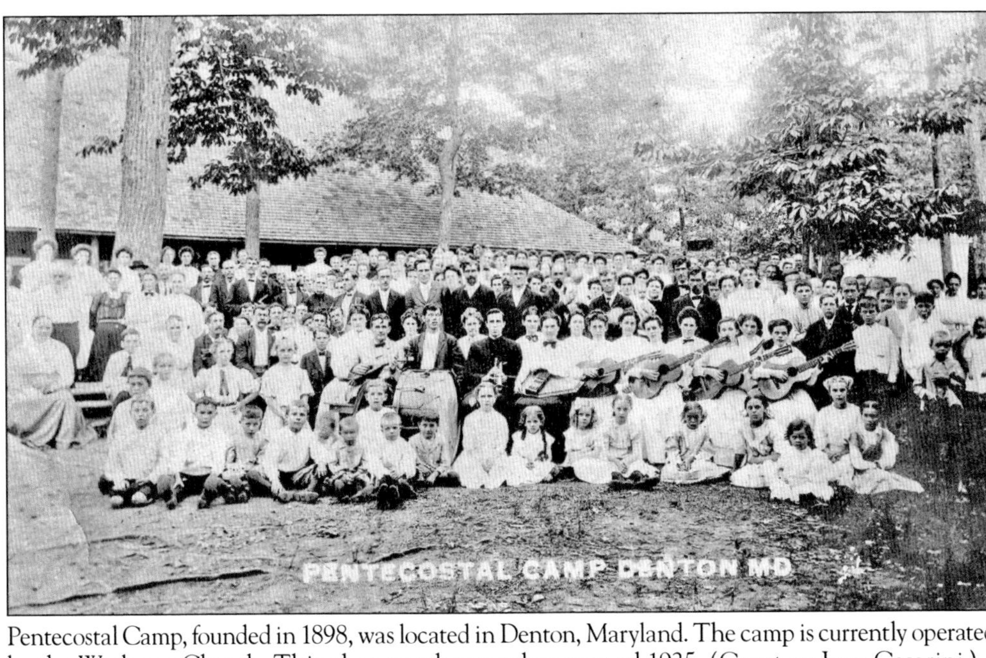

Pentecostal Camp, founded in 1898, was located in Denton, Maryland. The camp is currently operated by the Wesleyan Church. This photograph was taken around 1925. (Courtesy Joan Cesarini.)

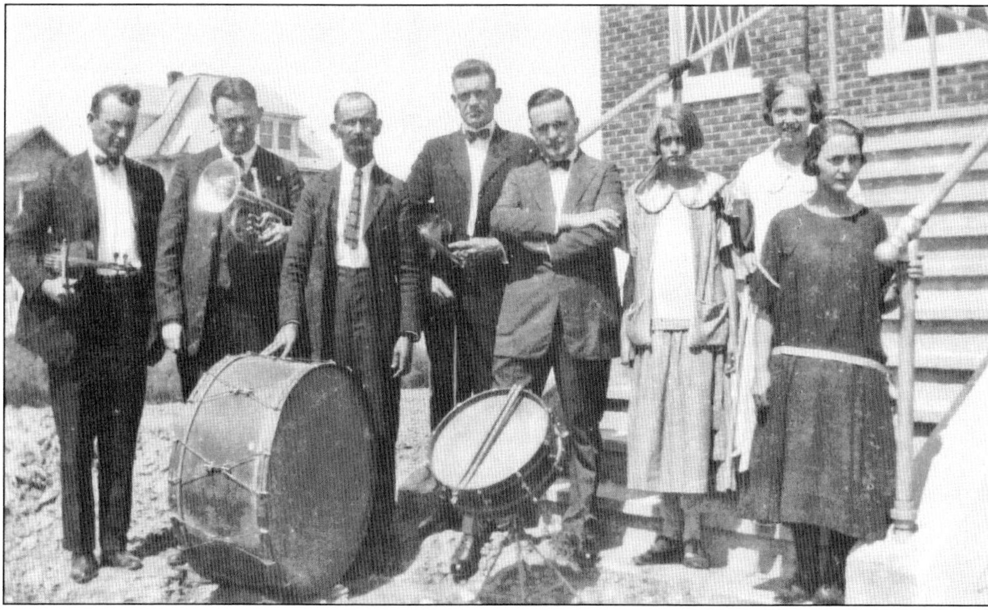

The marching band of the Baptist Church, pictured around 1925, included, from left to right, Harry Draper, Thomas Thornton, Harry Karcher, J. Edgar Shockley, Rev. Melvin Morris (the pastor), Daisy Pickett, Elizabeth Snediker, and Edith Edward Hughes. (Courtesy Greensboro Baptist Church.)

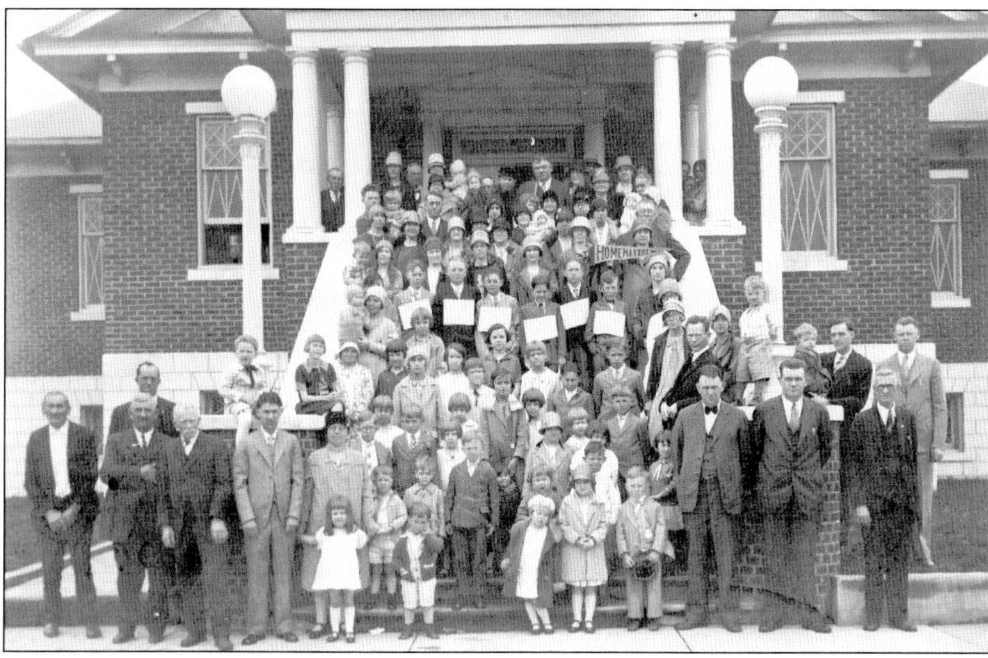

The Baptist Church congregation, shortly after the completion of the new Greensboro Baptist church, poses for the camera around 1925. (Courtesy Greensboro Baptist Church.)

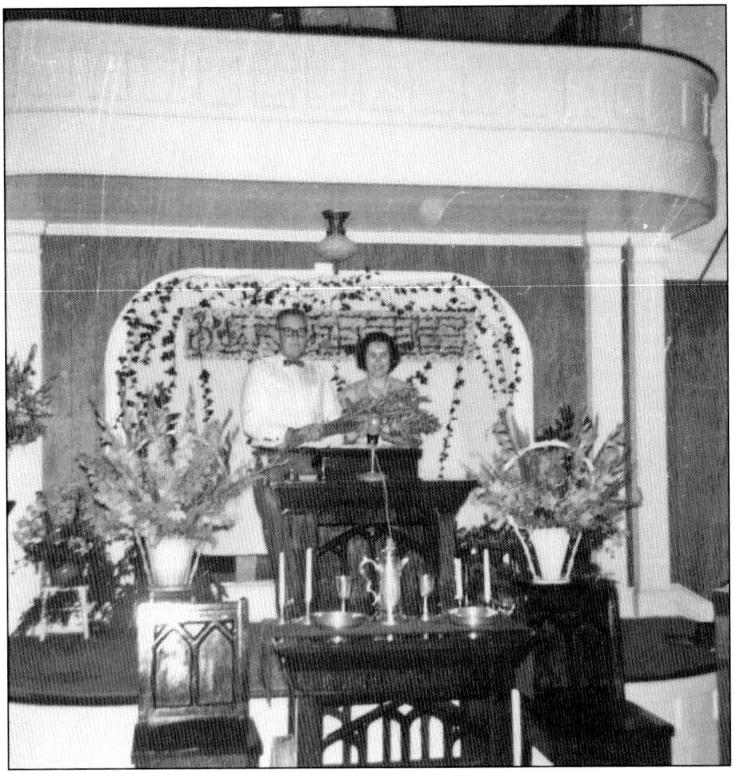

Baptist Church members Maurice Howard and Ida Mae Shields participate at one of the Youth Sunday events. (Courtesy Greensboro Baptist Church.)

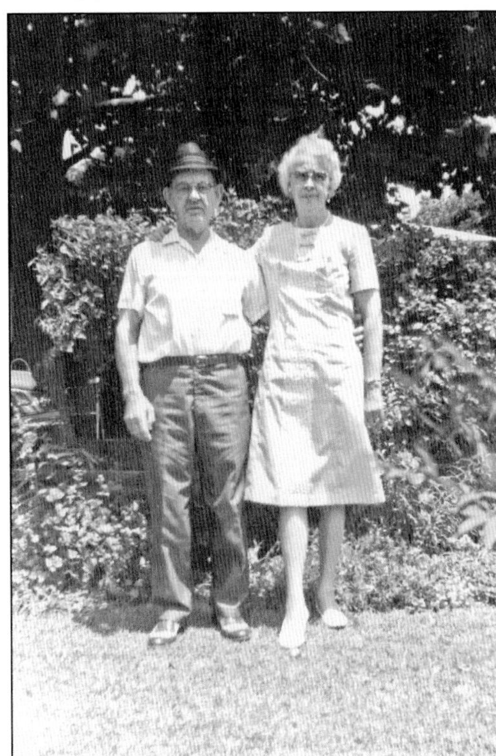

Nolan and Helen Edwards are remembered as being among the most active members of the Greensboro Baptist Church. (Courtesy Greensboro Baptist Church.)

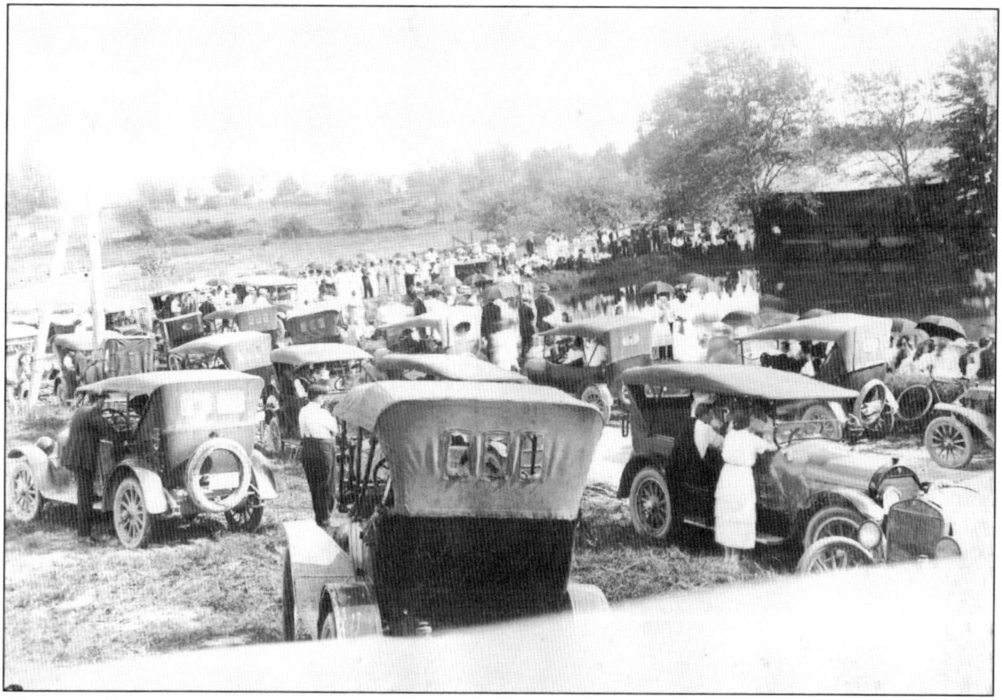

The act of baptism is core to the tenets of the Baptist Church. This *c.* 1920 photograph reflects the gathering for a baptism at Pippin's Pond. (Courtesy Greensboro Baptist Church.)

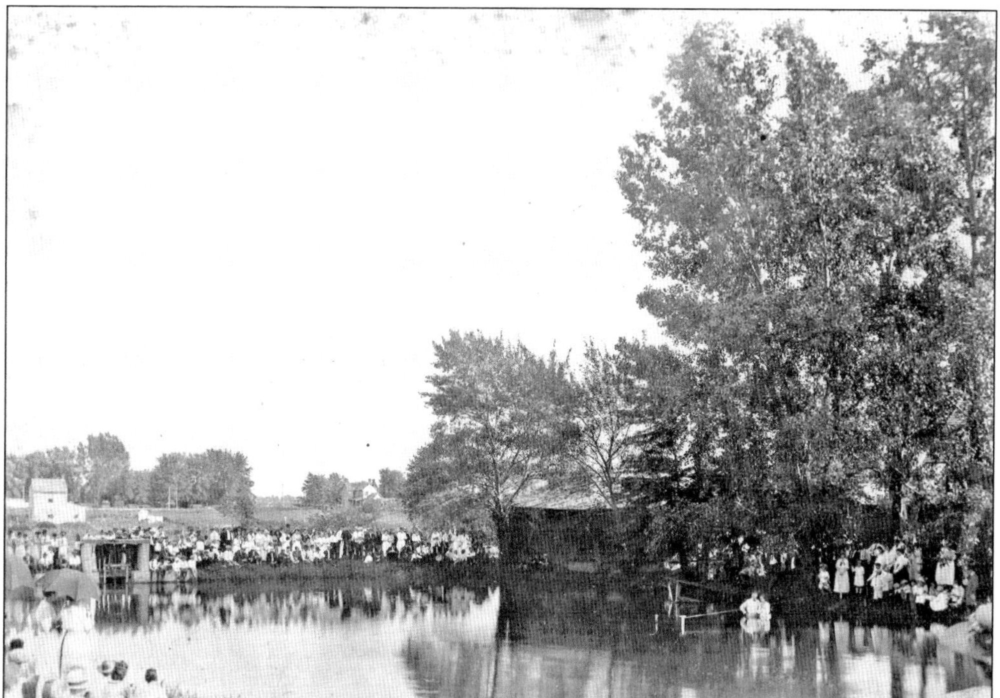

The Baptist Church held a baptism at Pippin's Pond in 1920. The event was attended by most of its thriving congregation. (Courtesy Greensboro Baptist Church.)

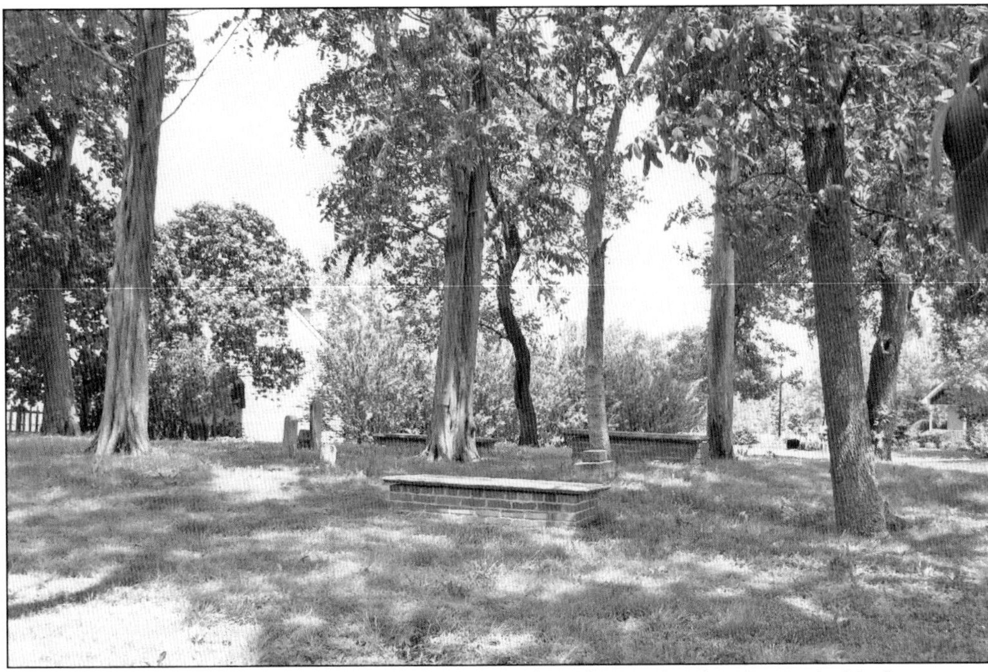

One of the oldest cemeteries in Greensboro, situated on the north side of town, holds the remains of the Hughlett and Comegys families. Several of the tombs are built above ground, and their tombstones have lengthy remembrances. (Courtesy J. C. Reveal.)

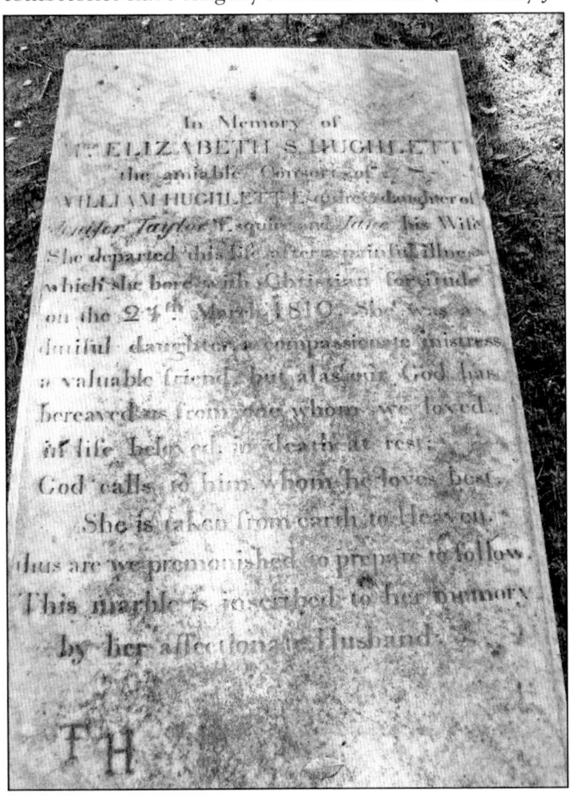

The grave site of Elizabeth Hughlett reflects the following: "In memory of Mrs Elizabeth Hughlett the amicable consort of William Hughlett Esquire and daughter of Junifer Taylor Esquire and Jane his wife. She departed this life after a painful illness which she bore with Christian fortitude on the 27th March 1810. She was a dutiful daughter, a compassionate mistress, a valuable friend, but alas our God has bereaved us from one whom we loved in life beloved in death at rest. God calls to him whom he loves best. She is taken from earth to Heaven thus we are premonished to prepare to follow. This marble is inscribed to her memory by her affectionate husband." (Courtesy J. C. Reveal.)

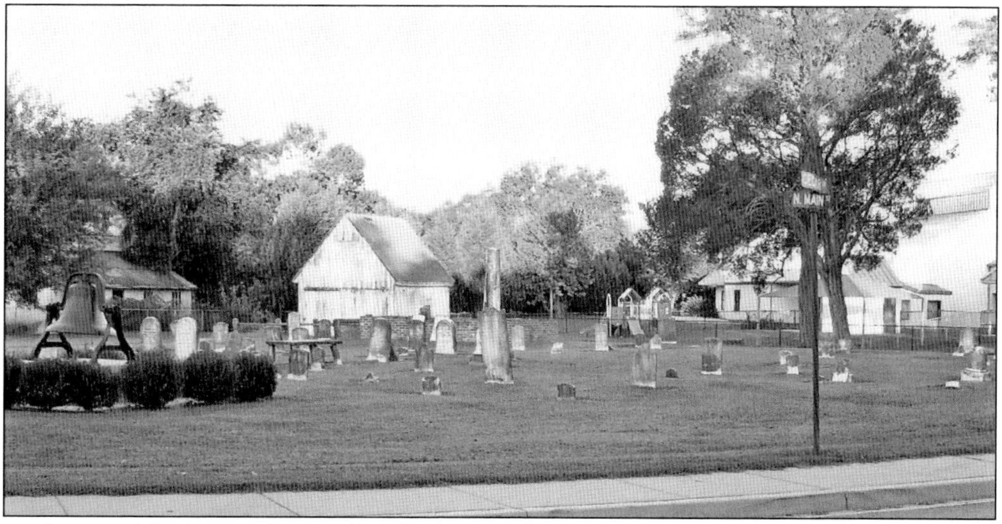

At the site of the first Methodist church in Greensboro, this cemetery holds the remains of many founding families. (Courtesy J. C. Reveal.)

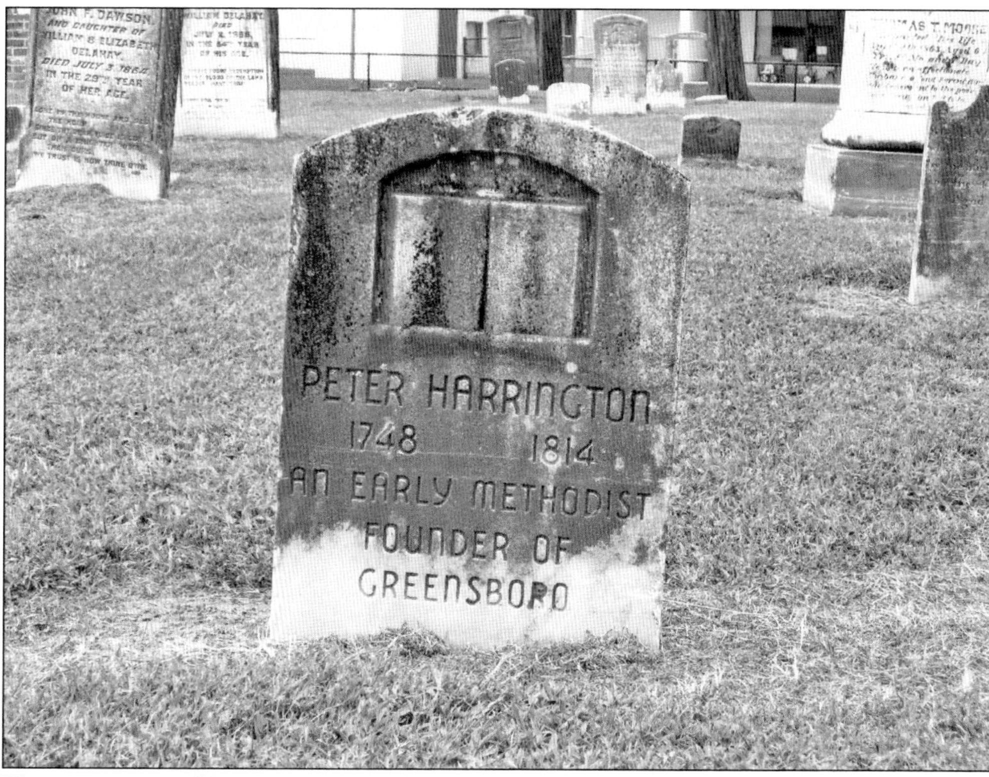

This gravestone of Peter Harrington (1748–1812), an early Methodist founder of Greensboro, is in the old cemetery behind the original location of the first Methodist church located in Greensboro. (Courtesy J. C. Reveal.)

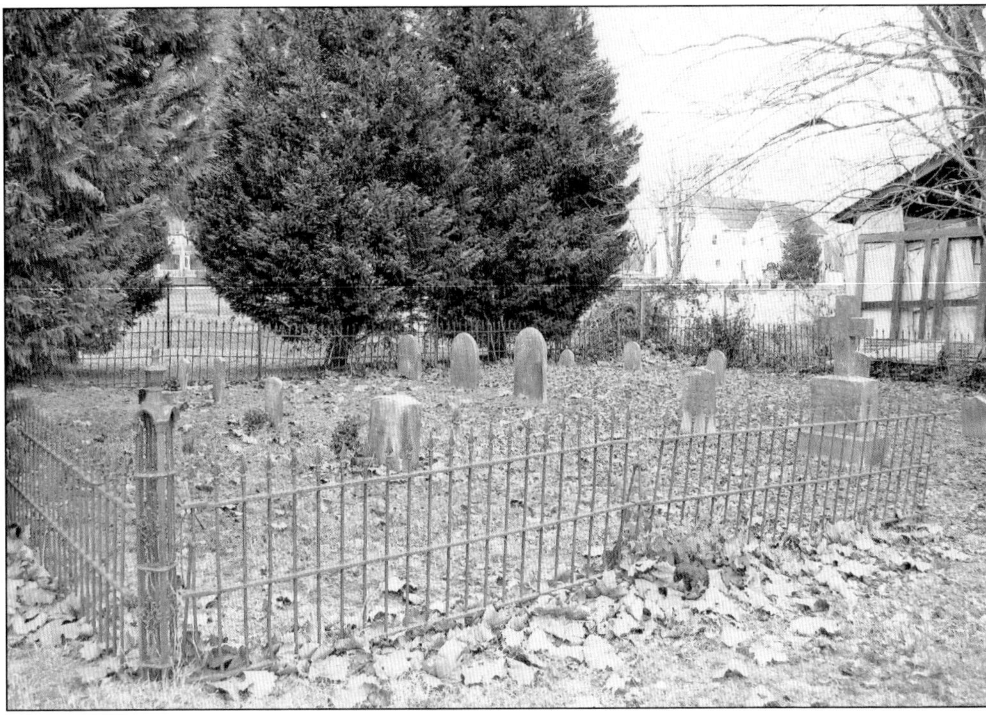

This small family cemetery holds the remains of the Turner family of Greensboro. Although descendants have moved on, the cemetery is lovingly maintained by volunteers and new owners of the property. (Courtesy J. C. Reveal.)

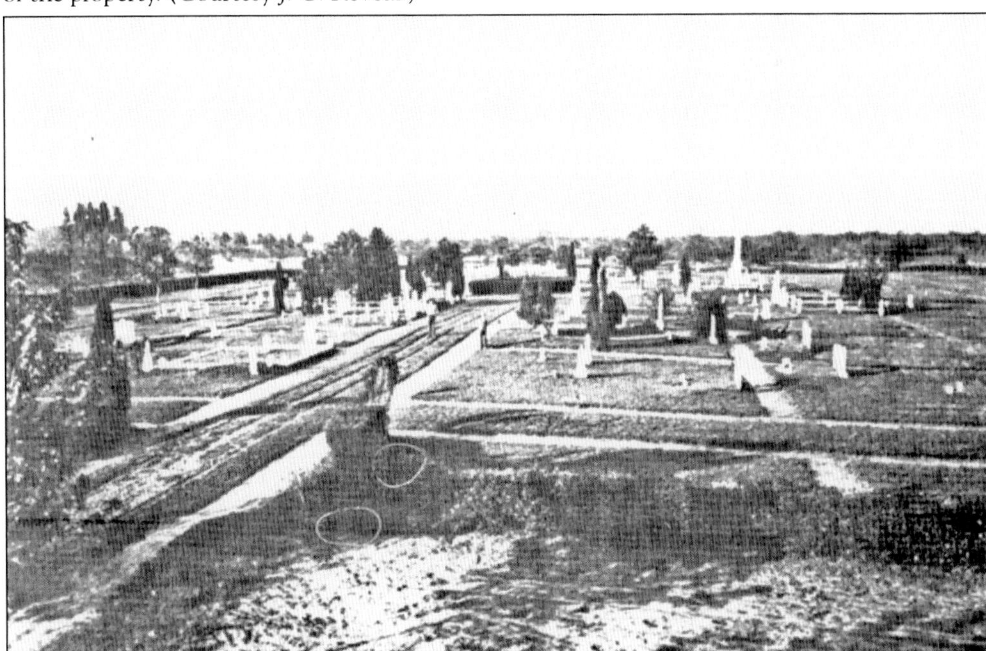

The Greensboro Cemetery, pictured in the 1890s, was established in 1873. (Courtesy Town of Greensboro.)

Four

EDUCATION

Prior to the 1816 law establishing the Public Free Schools of Maryland, public education was all but unknown. The precise date that Greensboro saw its first public school established is lost to history, but it is assumed to be around 1816. In the mid-1800s, a two-story building was erected to provide an education for Greensboro's youth. The Odd Fellows Hall occupied the second floor, which was later used by a private school. The building was renovated in 1845 and continued as a school building until 1873, by which time the number of students had significantly increased, requiring a larger building. That year, W. C. Satterfield worked with the Caroline County Board of Education to construct a new school near the Choptank Bridge. Classes were conducted at this location until 1876, when the building succumbed to a mysterious fire. Local folklore holds that the school was built on cemetery ground and that anything built on the land would be destroyed by fire. The Greensboro Academy was erected in 1876 and served the town's children through their high school years until construction of the Greensboro School in 1920.

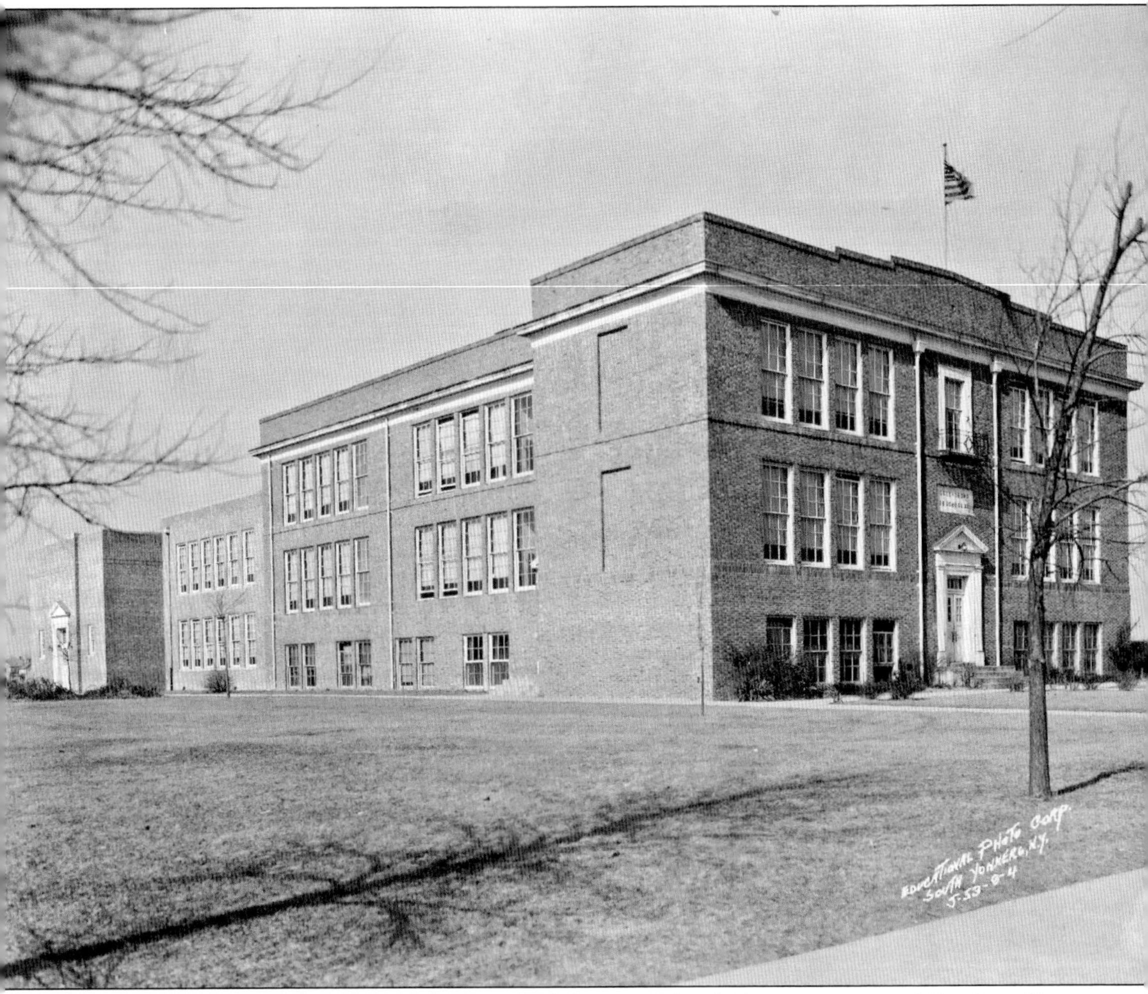

In 1906, "an act to authorize the Board of County School Commissioners of Caroline County to organize a High School to be located in the town of Greensboro" was passed. It was not, however, until 1920 that a new school was actually built in Greensboro. During its lifetime, the Greensboro School housed the first through the 12th grades. (Courtesy Caroline County Board of Education.)

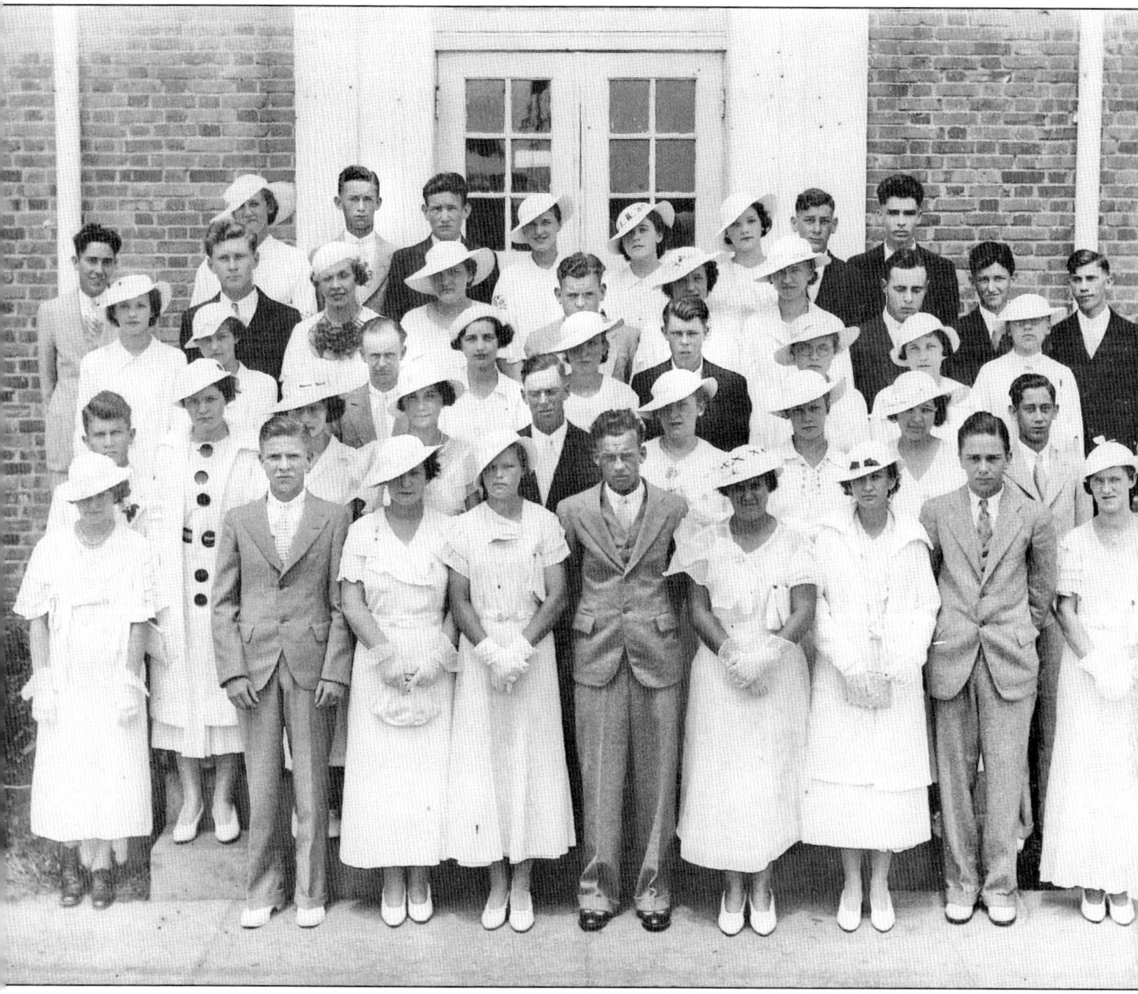

The 1934 graduating class from the Greensboro High School prepares to march into its future. (Courtesy Joan Cesarini.)

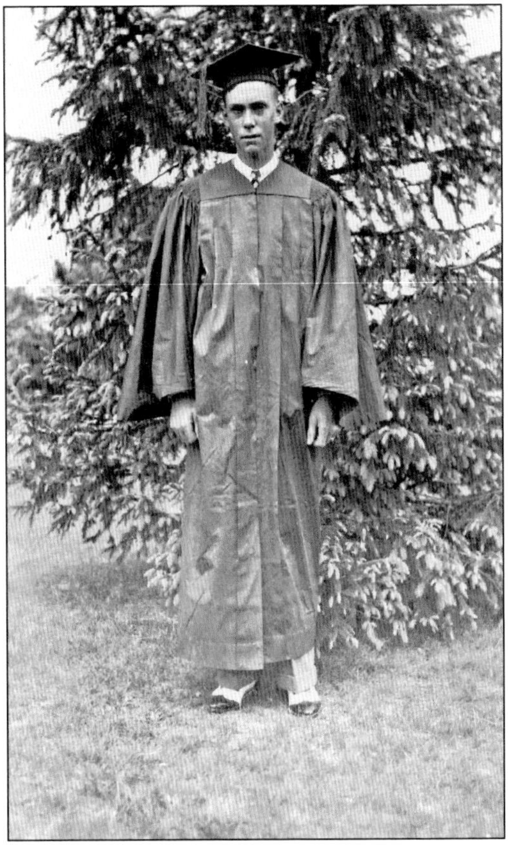

Local resident Ralph Dukes is pictured on his graduation from high school in 1934. (Courtesy Joan Cesarini.)

The R. B. Culbreth home, located on West Sunset Avenue, served as a boardinghouse for teachers at the local school during the late-19th and early-20th centuries. (Courtesy Town of Greensboro.)

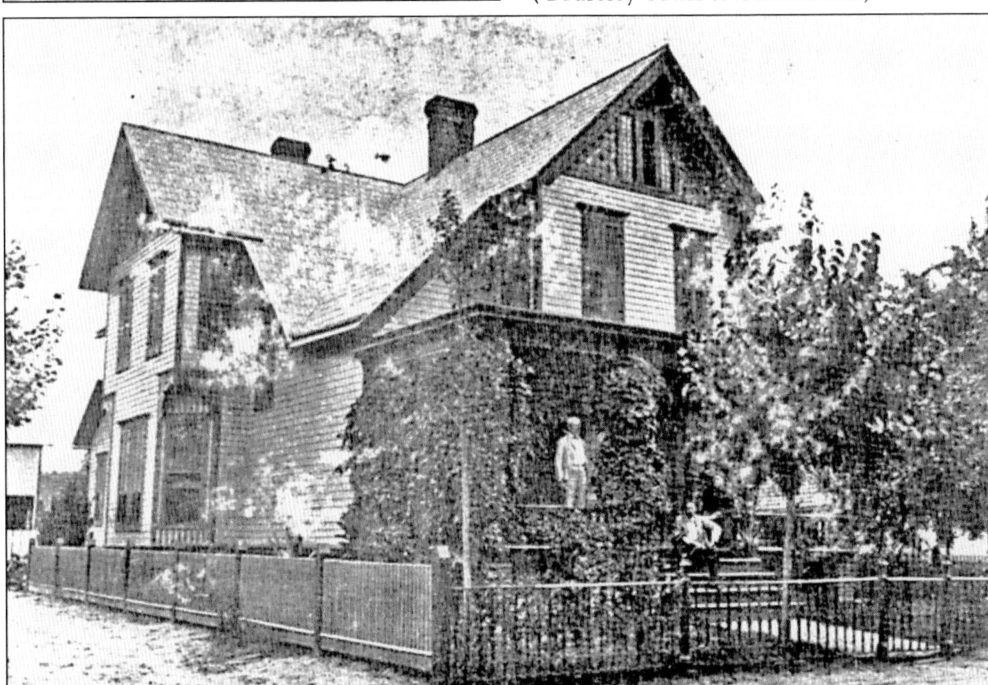

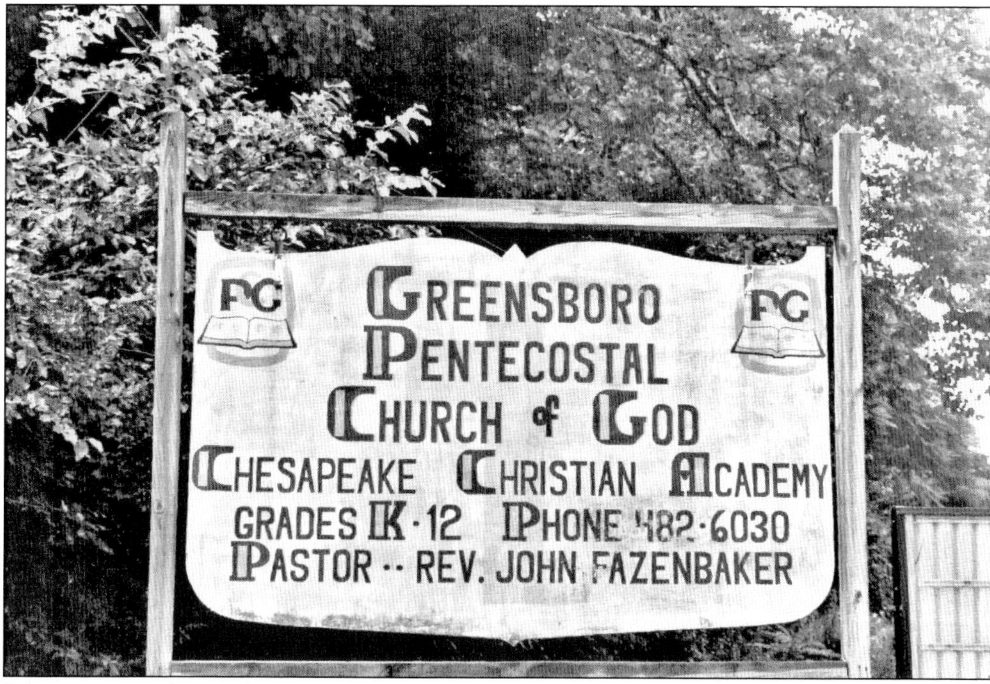

Education in and around Greensboro comes in a variety of sizes, shapes, and needs. The Chesapeake Bible College maintains a distance learning center at the Greensboro Pentecostal church, providing religious education for its students. (Courtesy *Times Record* newspaper.)

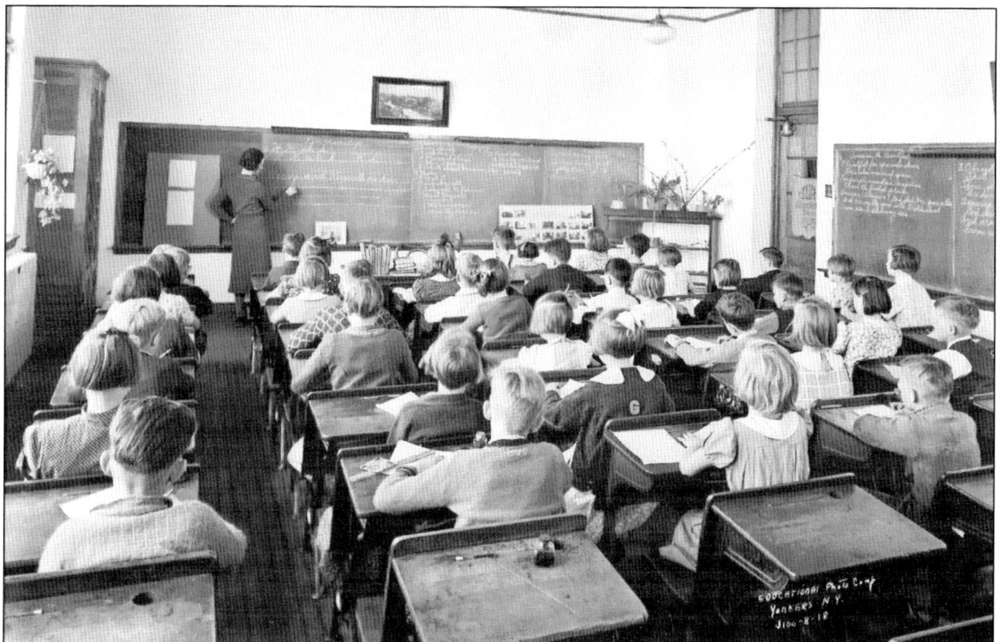

The *c.* 1938 fourth-grade class at Greensboro School prepares for the day's studies. During its lifetime, the school housed classes from first through 12th grade. (Courtesy Caroline County Board of Education.)

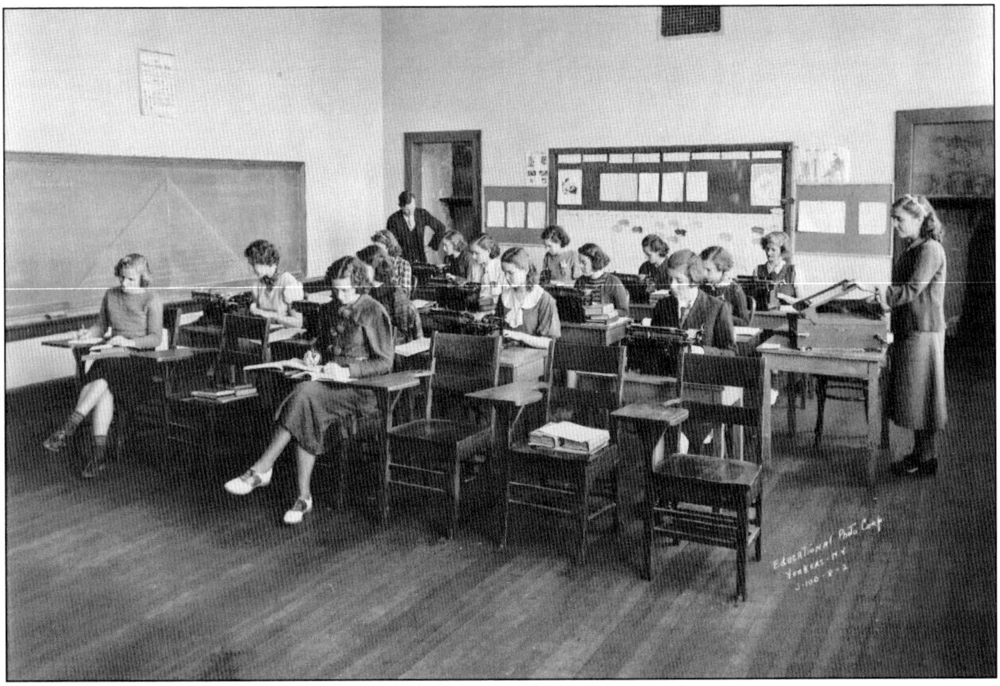

This Greensboro typing class, pictured about 1940, was taught by G. B. Hastings and offered primarily to young women. Hastings later became the principal of the Greensboro School. (Courtesy Caroline County Board of Education.)

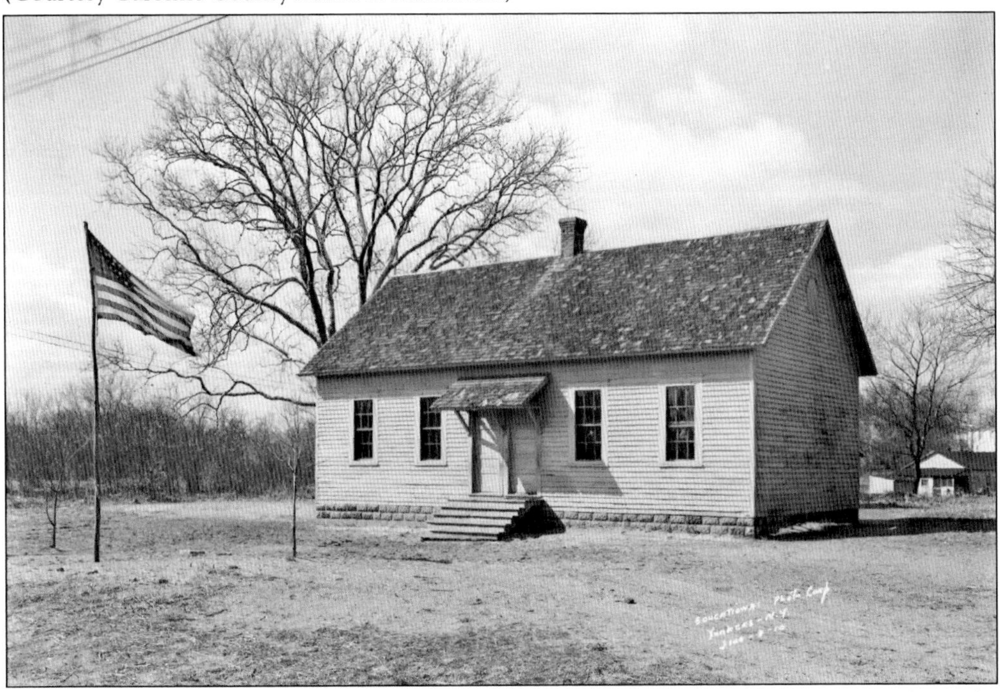

Although segregated, education was extended to all children. This 1930s pictures show the Greensboro Colored School, located within the town boundaries. The building has been converted to a residence with some modifications. (Courtesy Caroline County Board of Education.)

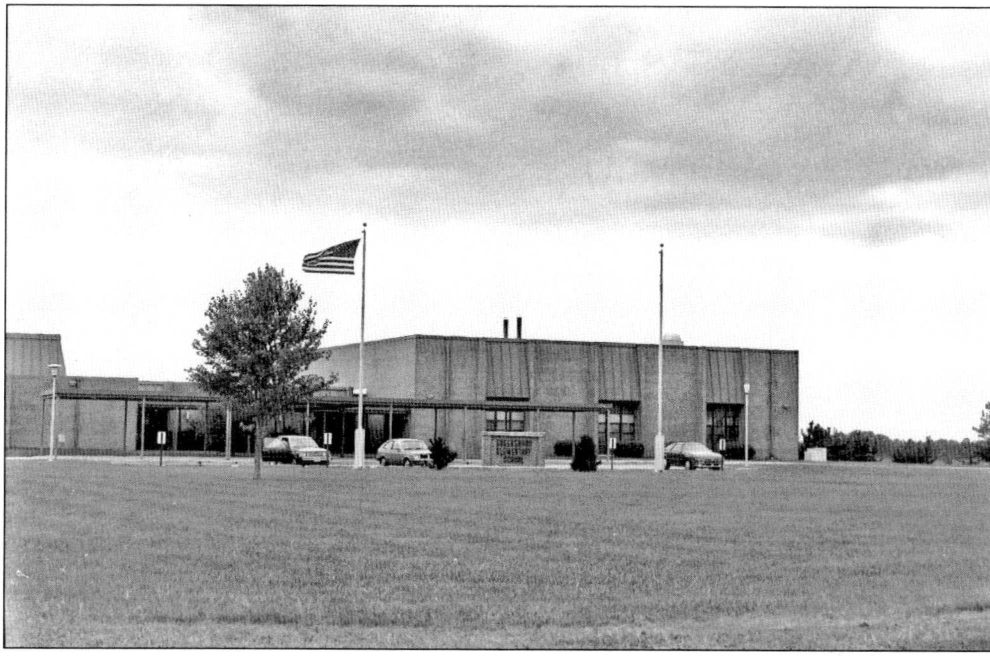

As the population continued to grow throughout the region, it became apparent that additional school space was needed to accommodate families with young children. The Greensboro Elementary School opened its doors in 1974 and extended just beyond town boundaries to incorporate the surrounding rural areas and small towns. (Courtesy *Times Record* newspaper.)

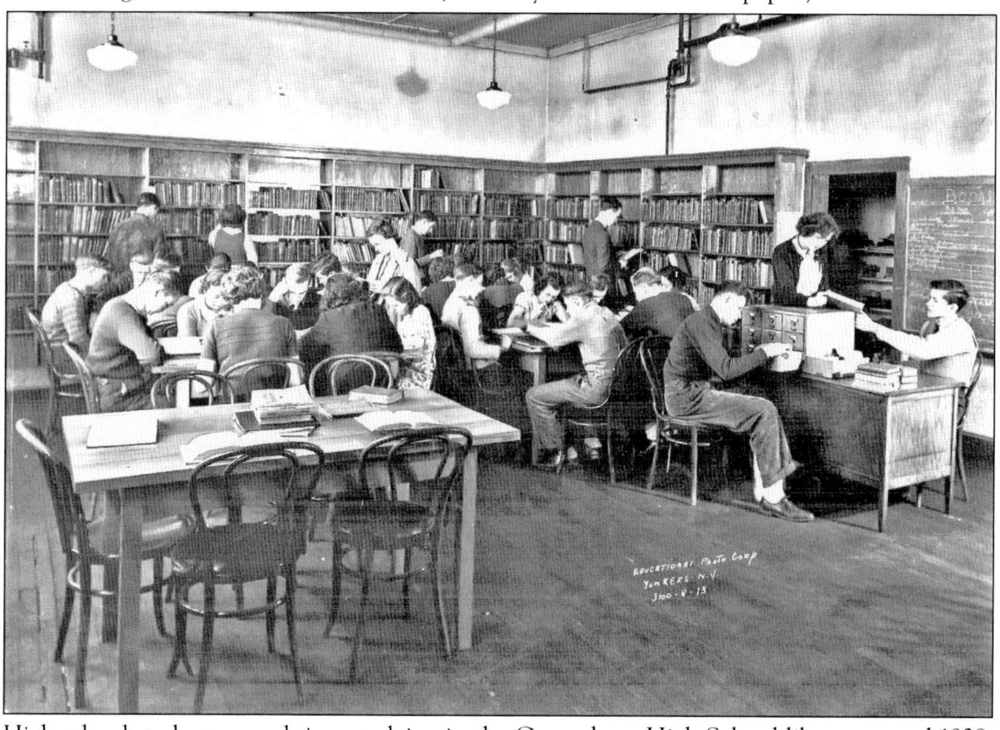

High school students spend time studying in the Greensboro High School library around 1938. (Courtesy Caroline County Board of Education.)

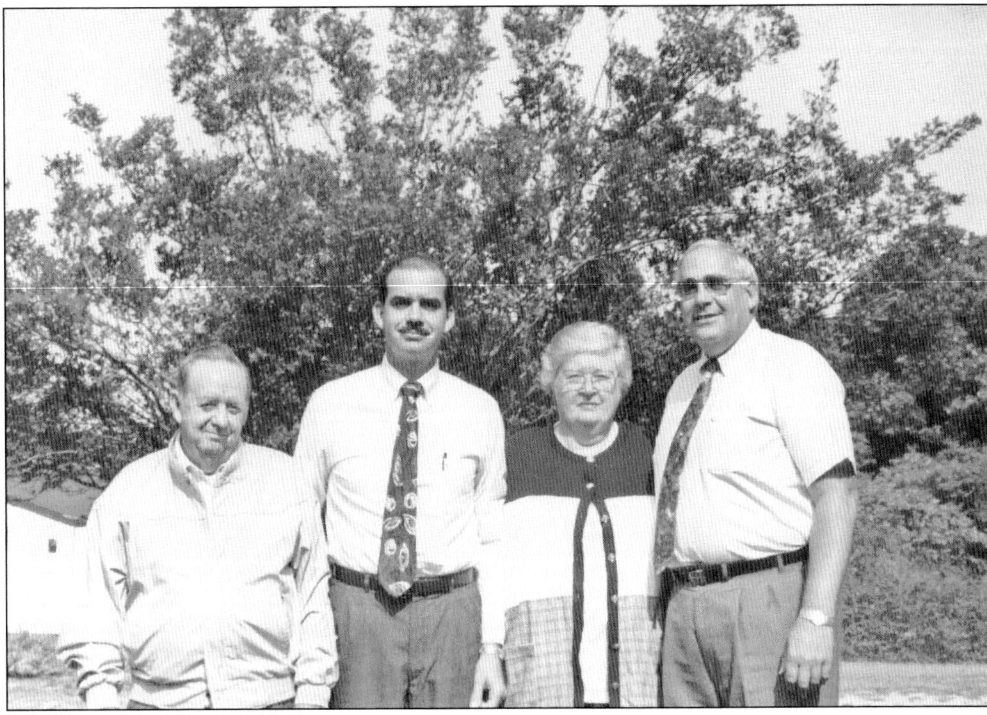

With growth came an infrastructure of vital importance to the town. In the mid-1990s, the Friends of the Caroline County Library recognized the need for a north county branch and began to raise money for such a project. Friends members preparing for the new library in Greensboro are Mayor Ed Weaver, Dr. Joe McCarthy, Carol Russell (president of the Greensboro Business and Civic Association), and Richard Harfeld (a member of the GBCA). (Courtesy *Times Record* newspaper.)

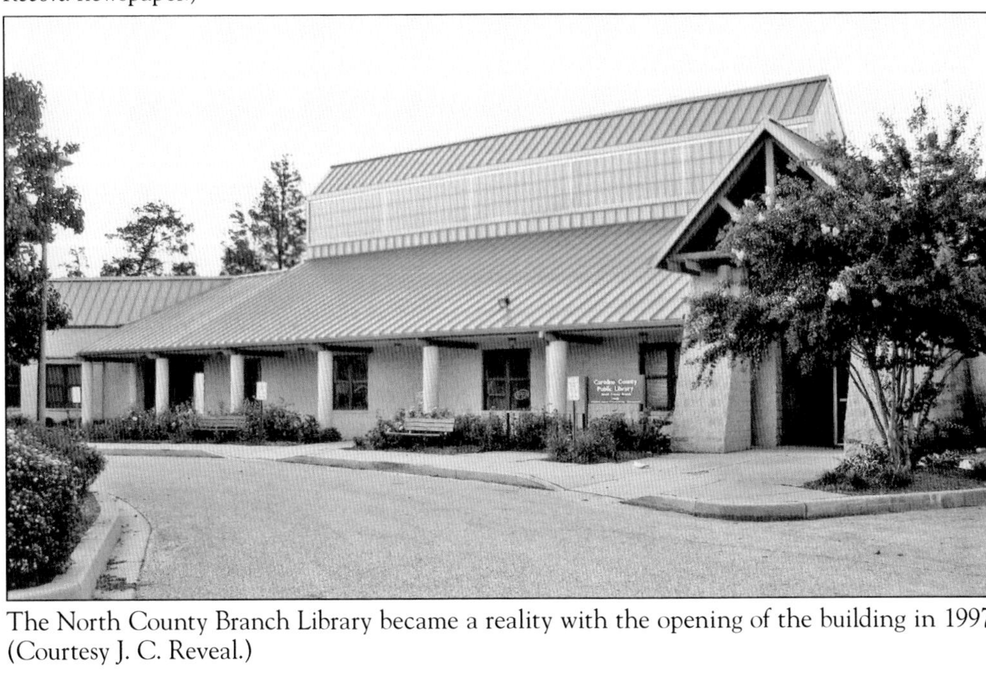

The North County Branch Library became a reality with the opening of the building in 1997. (Courtesy J. C. Reveal.)

Five

Historic Homes

Many of Greensboro's houses have stood the test of time and have their own stories to tell. Styles range from Federal to Colonial to Victorian, from Italiante to American Farmhouse, and most reflect the size of families that occupied them. Many residences have undergone renovations and survived with only moderate changes to their appearance. The flavor of Greensboro survives in these houses, which speak of a bygone time that continues to live in the town even as it grows. The Maryland Historical Trust historians have documented the history of many of the homes and buildings that have survived through the years.

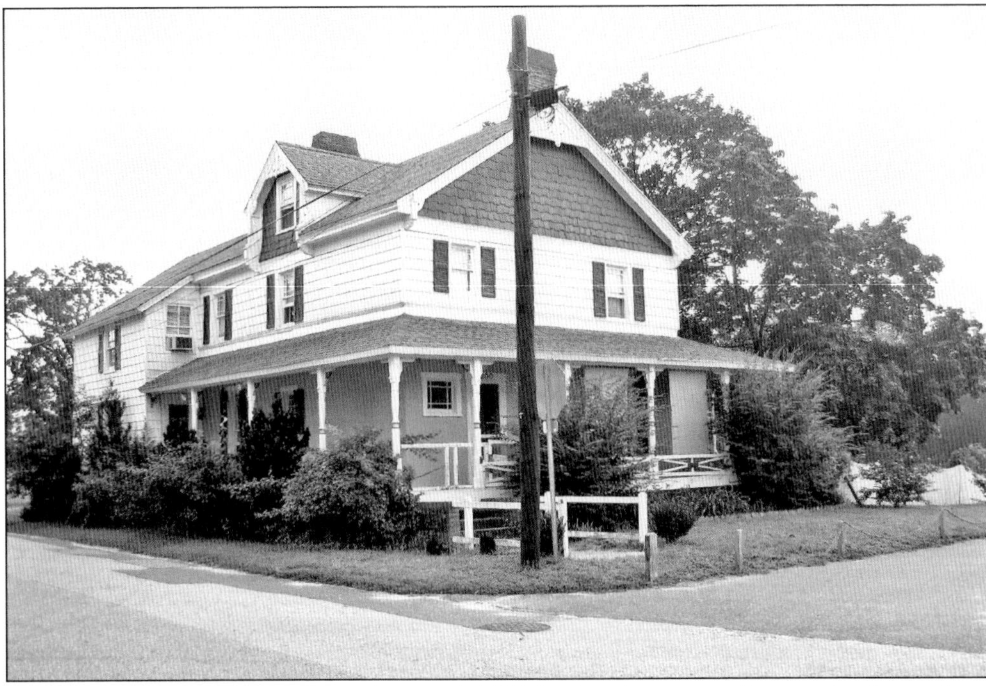

The Peter Harrington House was built around 1787. This building originally served as the residence of Peter Harrington, who is credited with founding Greensboro, along with his grandfather, Peter Rich. (Courtesy J. C. Reveal.)

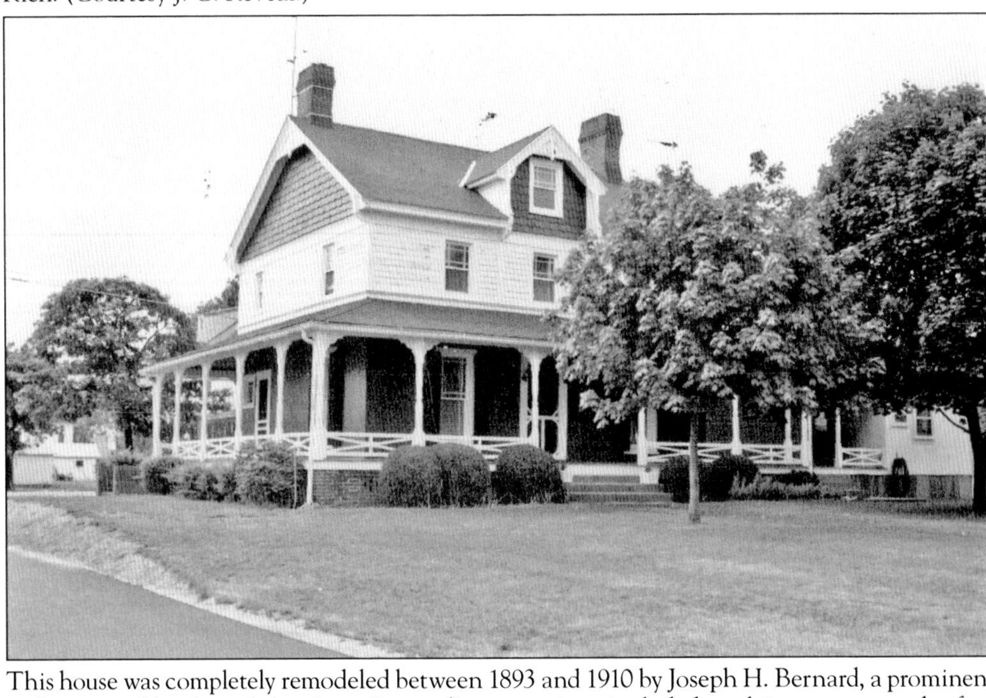

This house was completely remodeled between 1893 and 1910 by Joseph H. Bernard, a prominent architect and banker of the time. Bernard's renovations included applying stucco to the first story, covering the original brick, and some of the original character has been lost. (Courtesy the Maryland Historical Trust.)

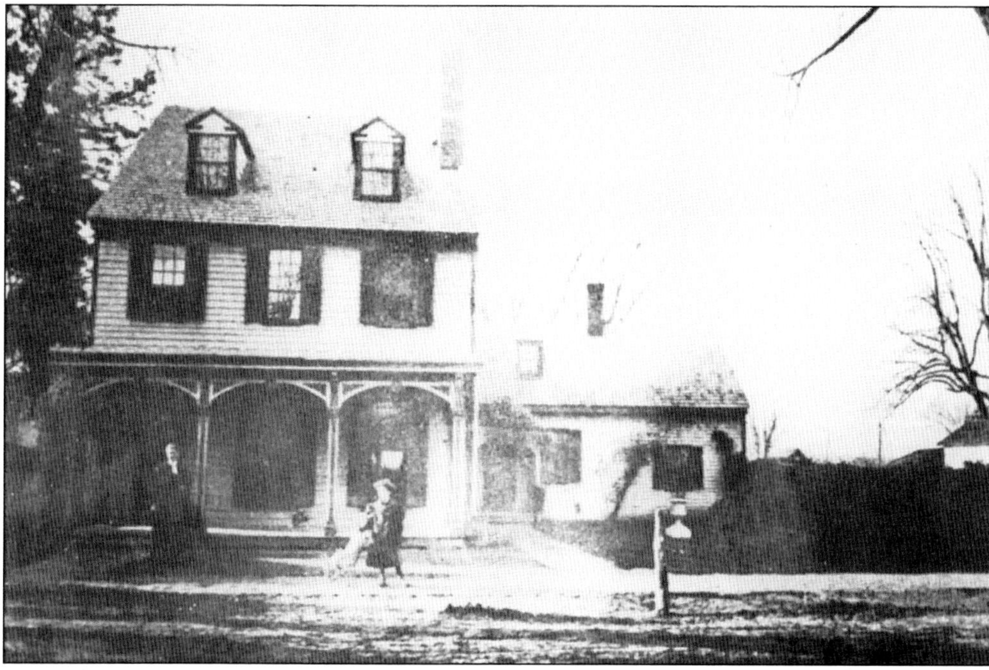

Massey/Boulais house is the only surviving townhouse in the town of Greensboro. The two-story wing to the north side (right) is the original 1790 house. (Courtesy Town of Greensboro.)

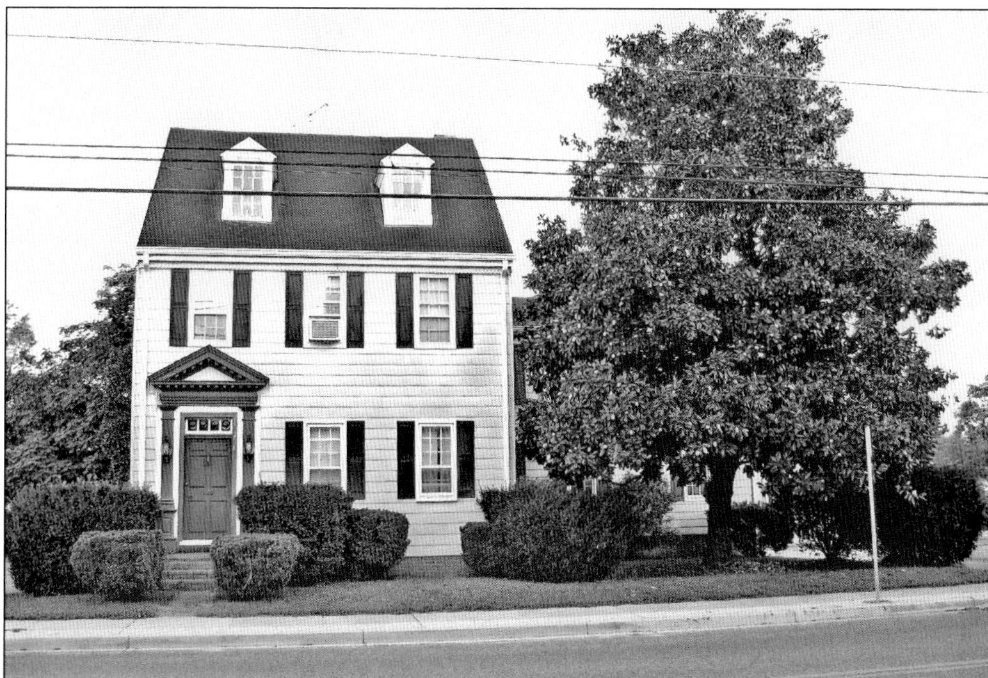

Shown here in 2007, the Massey/Boulais house has been expanded over the years and was remodeled and redecorated with Georgian details in the 1970s. The porch was removed during renovations, but the remainder of the structure remains true to its original construction. (Courtesy J. C. Reveal.)

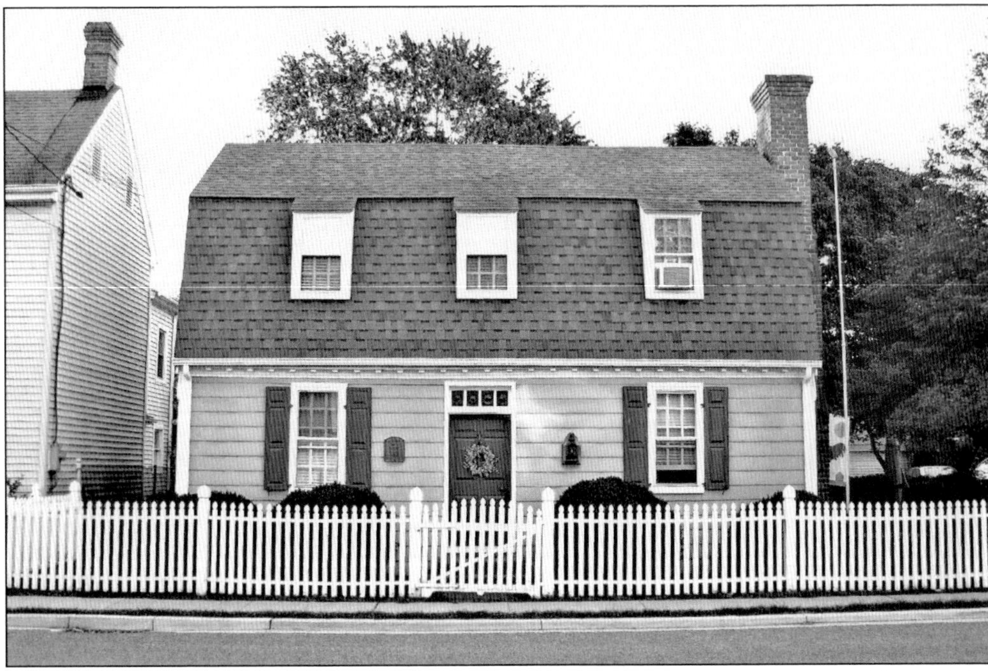

The lot for the Dr. Cook house was sold in 1784 to Dr. James Cook. A total rebuilding of this house on the original frame, including new siding, windows, doors, chimney, and so on, was done by Robert H. Taylor in the Williamsburg style, resulting in a drastic change from its original appearance. (Courtesy J. C. Reveal.)

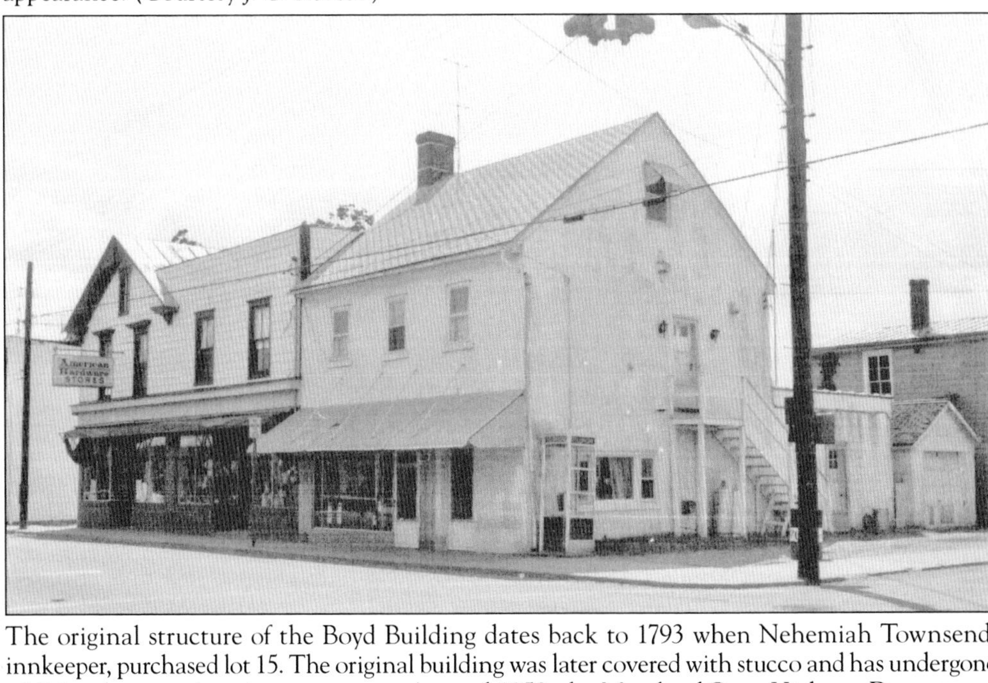

The original structure of the Boyd Building dates back to 1793 when Nehemiah Townsend, innkeeper, purchased lot 15. The original building was later covered with stucco and has undergone additional renovations in recent years. Around 1950, the Maryland State Highway Department widened Sunset Avenue; a long one-story wing that was part of the original building was removed at that time. (Courtesy the Maryland Historical Trust.)

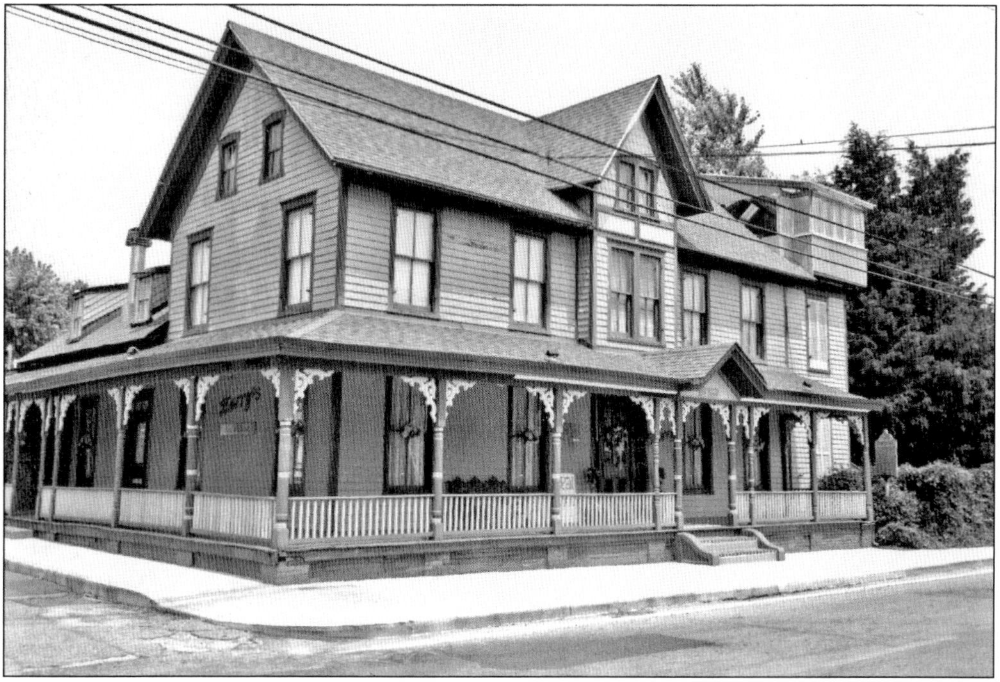

Peregrine Pratt sold the lot to William Turner in 1817; in 1837, Spencer Hitch bought the property, and in 1897, Dr. Griffin W. Goldsborough purchased the building for $2,000. Judge W. Laird Goldsborough, a grandson of G. W., bought the property in 1926. (Courtesy *Times Record* newspaper.)

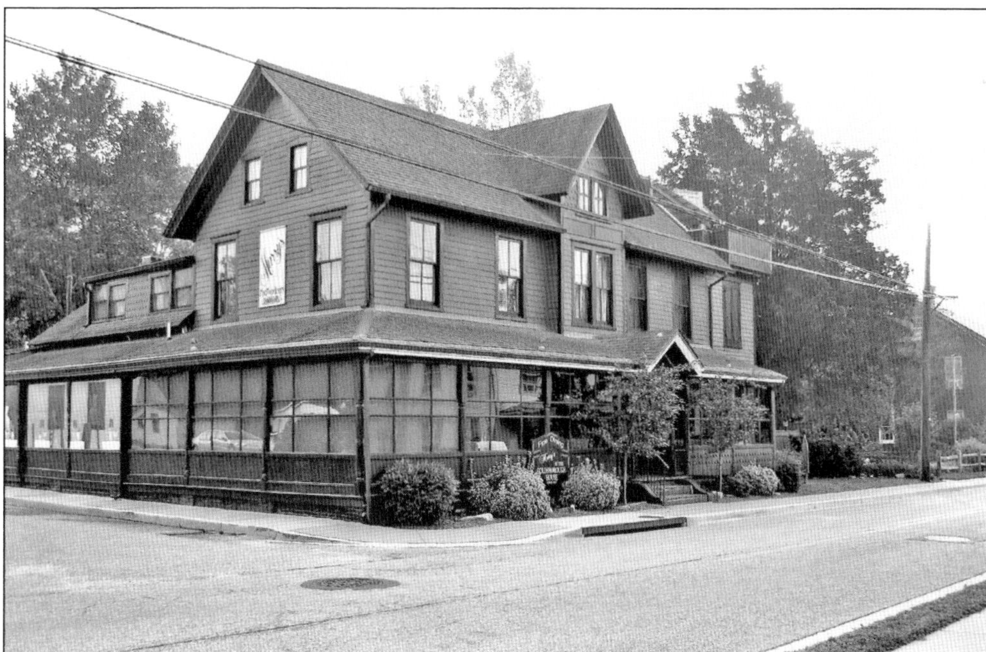

The Goldsborough House is one of the largest and least altered dwellings in Greensboro. Its conversion to a high-end restaurant has not affected its Victorian charm. (Courtesy J. C. Reveal.)

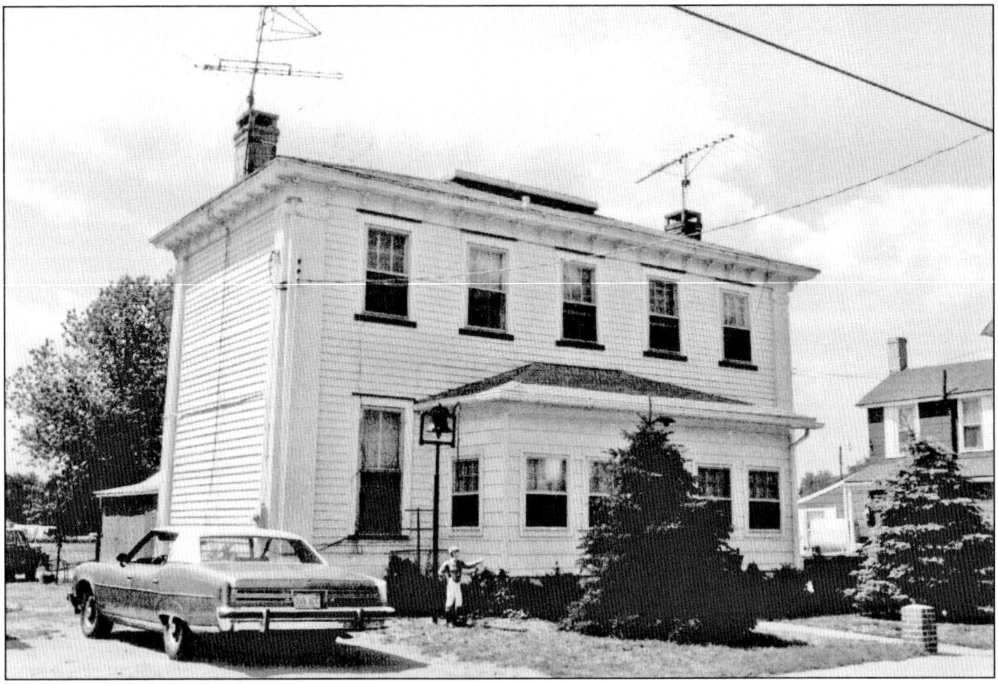

The *c.* 1860 Clinton Porter/A. B. Roe house is a fine example of an Italianate-style architecture from the mid-19th century. (Courtesy the Maryland Historical Trust.)

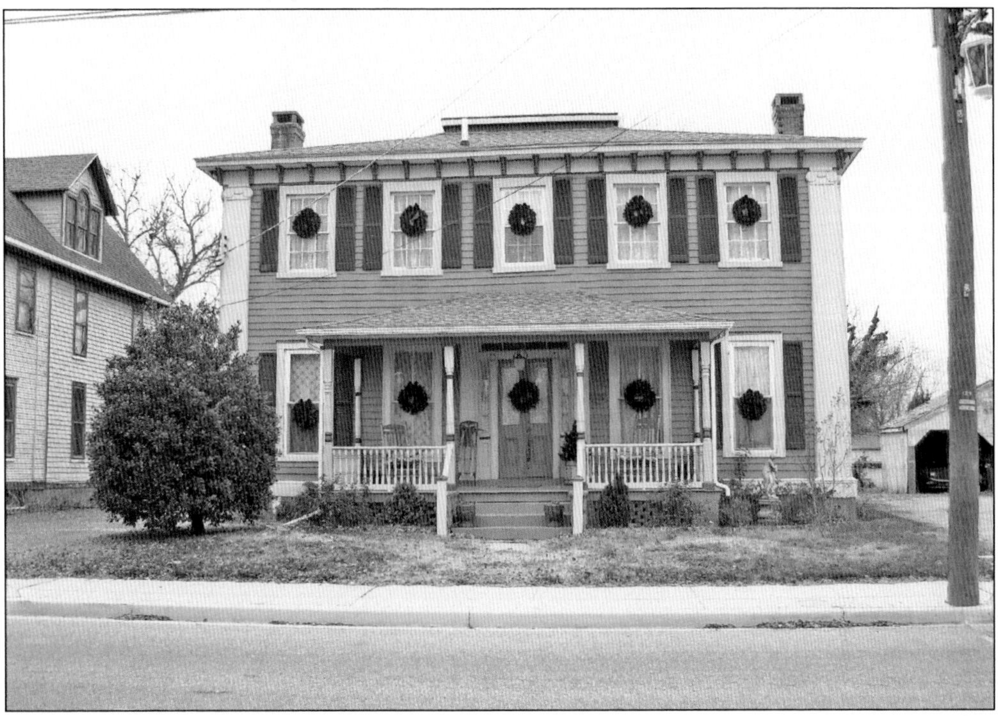

This is the Clinton Porter/Andrew B. Roe house as it appears today. A. B. Roe was involved in the fruit and vegetable packing business from 1872 to 1897 and served as Maryland state senator in 1882 and 1884. (Courtesy J. C. Reveal.)

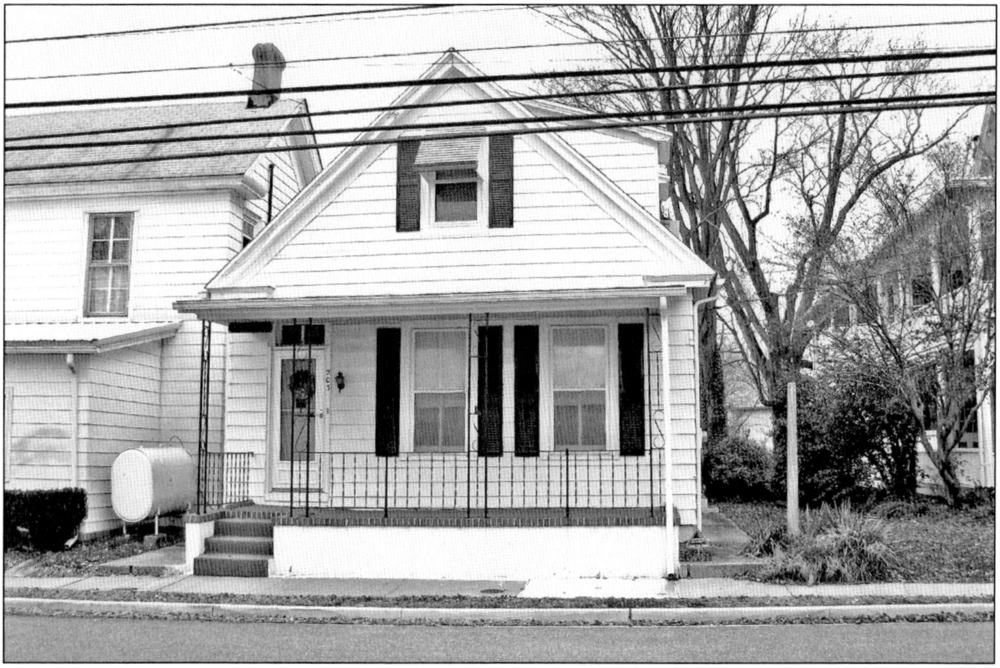

The significance of the 1860s McClyment/McGonigal house is that its structural form was constructed in the late 19th century and is closely related to the first forms and plans in the county. (Courtesy the Maryland Historical Trust/J. C. Reveal.)

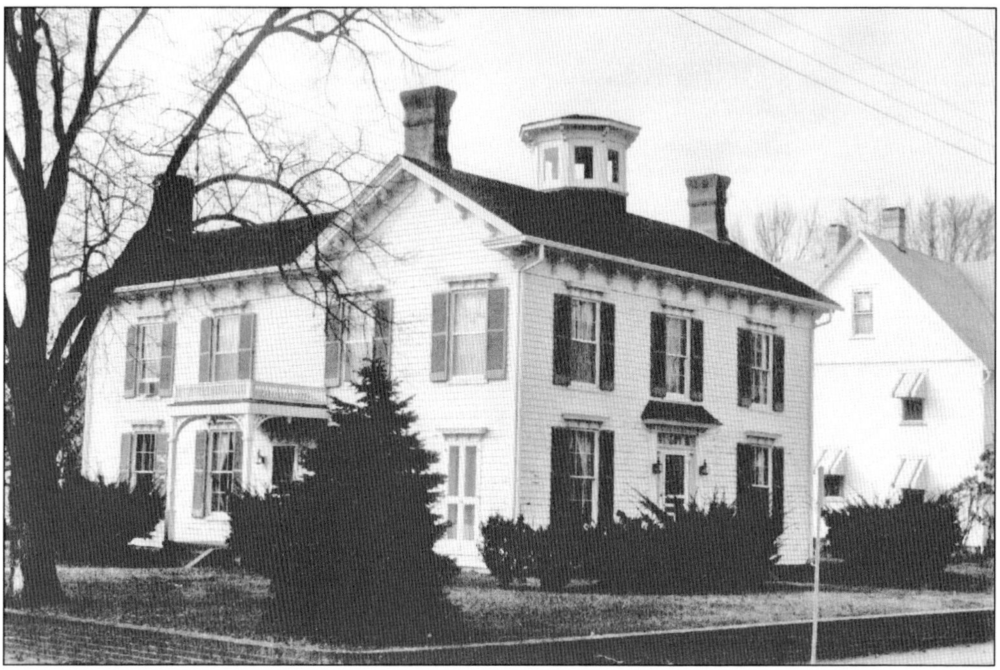

The M. K. Porter house was built between 1860 and 1870 in a style popular during that period. A porch probably extended around two sides of the house from the side door, and the outside kitchen has been removed; otherwise the house remains as it was originally constructed. (Courtesy the Maryland Historical Trust.)

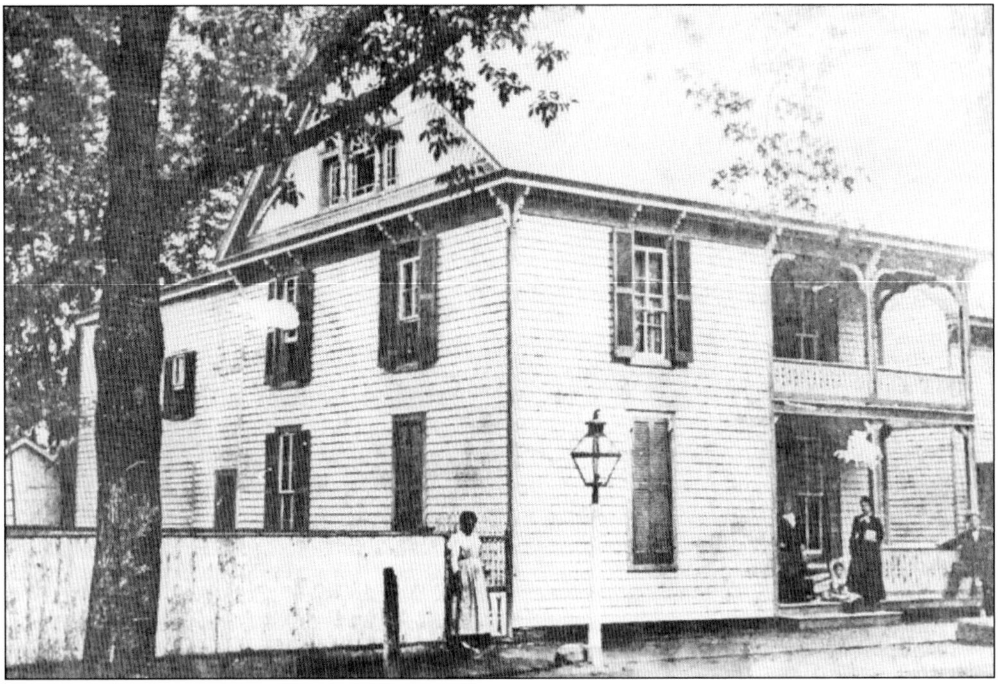

Here is the former home of Henry E. and Sally Jarrell on Main Street. On the porch, from left to right, are (seated) Ruth Plummer Taylor; (standing) Sally Jarrell, Effa C. Plummer, and Henry E. Jarrell sometime before 1900. (Courtesy Town of Greensboro.)

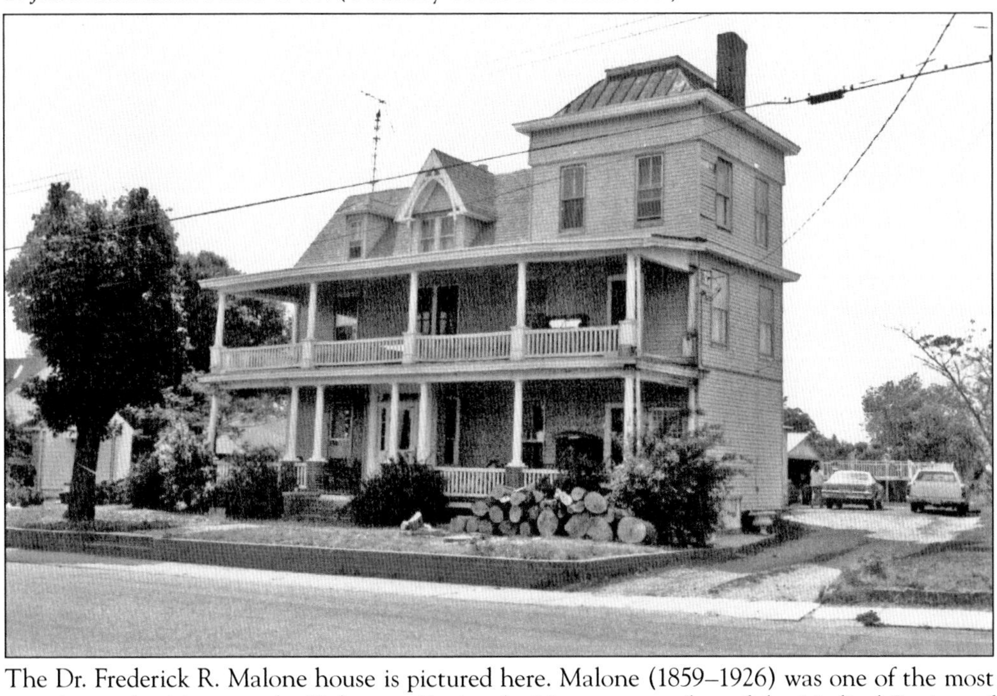

The Dr. Frederick R. Malone house is pictured here. Malone (1859–1926) was one of the most prominent physicians on the Delmarva Peninsula. He was a member of the Medical Society of Caroline County, a vestryman of Holy Trinity Protestant Episcopal Church, and an officer of the Caroline County Bank. (Courtesy the Maryland Historical Trust.)

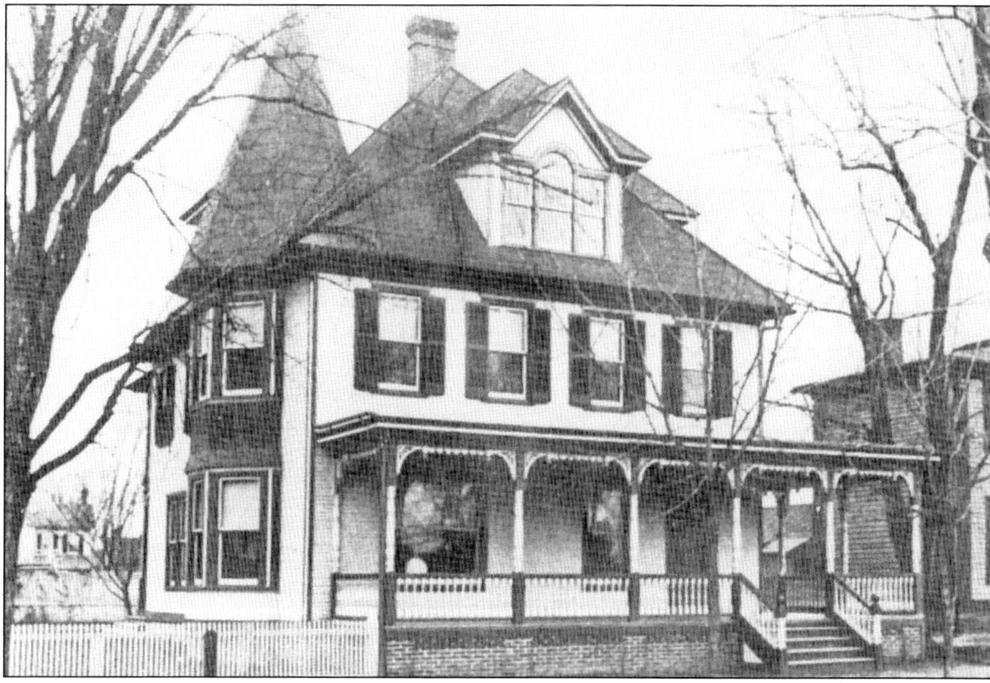

Fredrick P. Roe participated in the canning business from 1900 to 1941, when his cannery burned to the ground. His home is another fine example of Victorian architecture built in the town of Greensboro during the years of the canning boom. (Courtesy Town of Greensboro.)

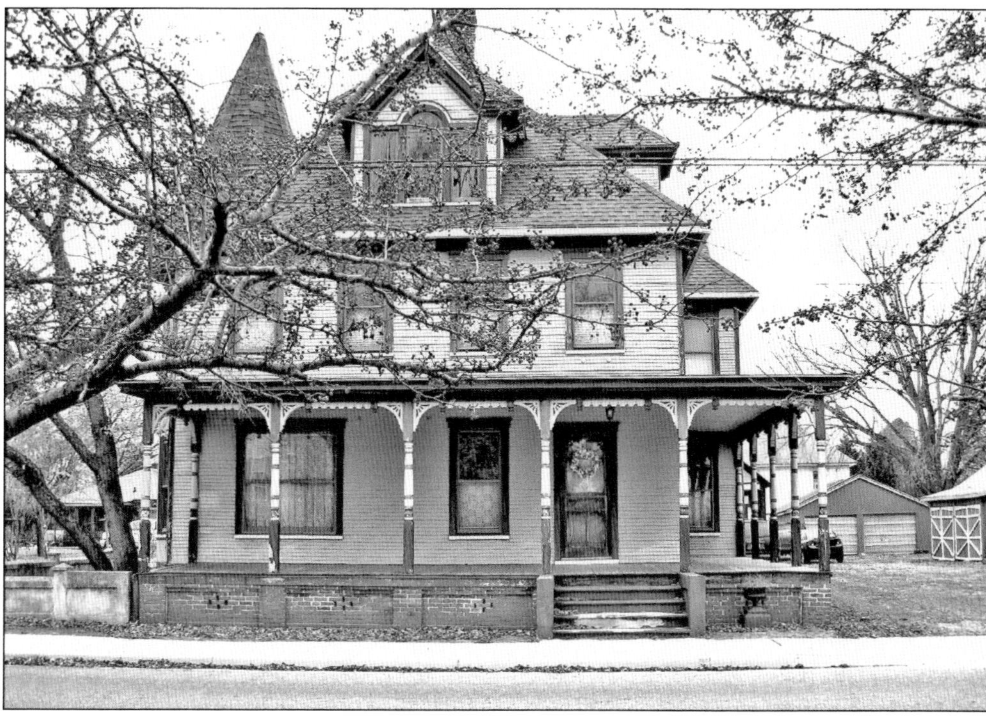

The F. P. Roe house, 118 South Main Street, as it looks today, has undergone few changes from its original appearance. (Courtesy J. C. Reveal.)

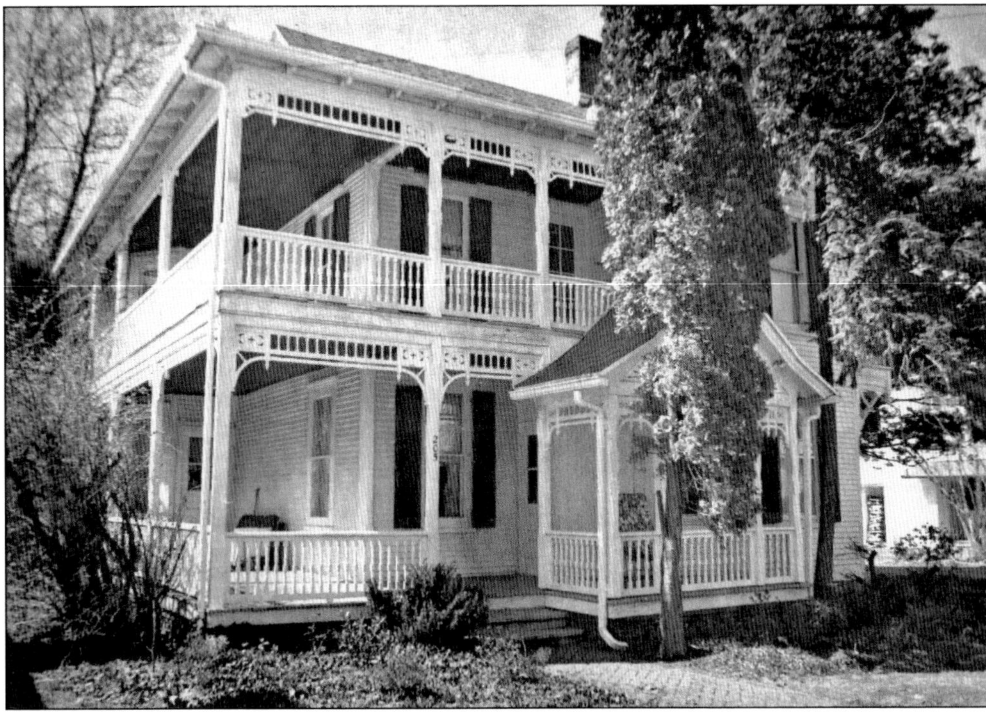

Clinton B. Jarman, a wealthy and influential resident and businessman of 19th-century Greensboro, built this Victorian home. Jarman also established the Riverside Hotel across the street using the old Roe cannery. (Courtesy Town of Greensboro.)

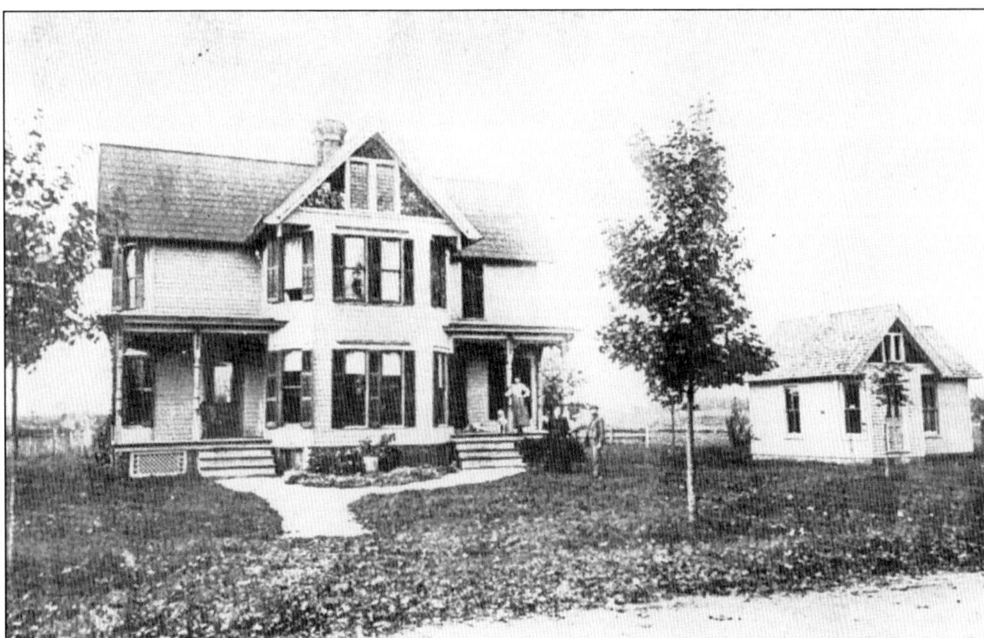

Situated on the south side of Greensboro on Maple Avenue, the Benjamin House/Harry Bastian home is a fine example of American farmhouse construction. (Courtesy Town of Greensboro.)

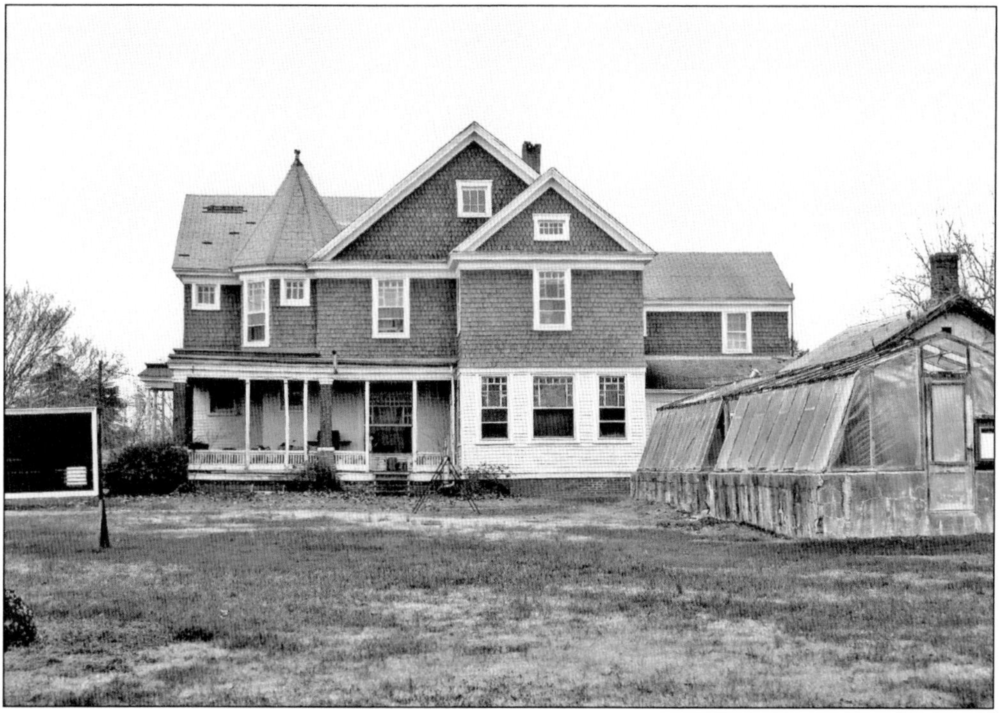

The Oscar Bernard house was built by Joseph H. Bernard, one of Greensboro's leading businessmen, for his son, Oscar. A florist's shop has been attached to this home since the late 1940s. (Courtesy J. C. Reveal.)

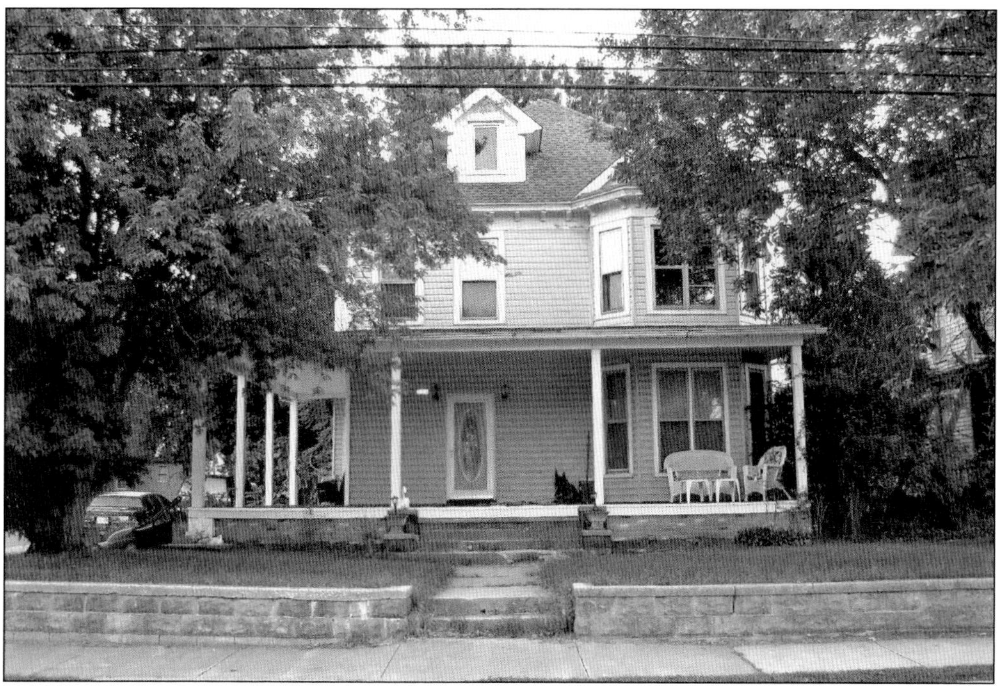

Nathaniel Horsey built this house in 1905. An active businessman for many years, Horsey also owned considerable acreage of fine farming land. (Courtesy J. C. Reveal.)

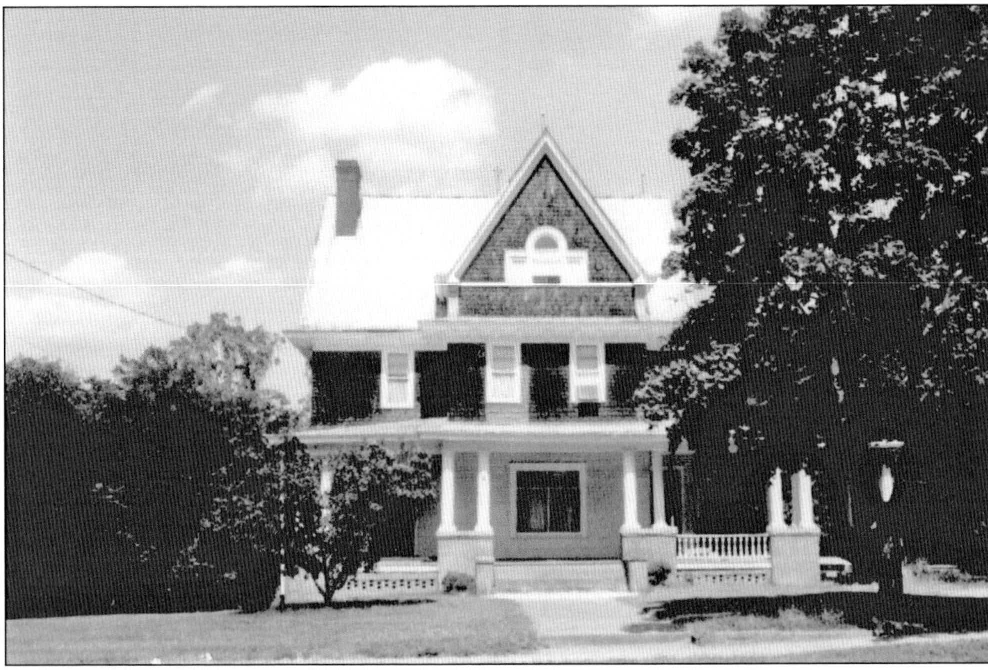

In 1902, Addison A. Christian built Riverdeen as a summer home for his family on a sizable portion of land on the east side of Greensboro. Christian worked as general manager of the Gimbel Brothers' Department Store in Philadelphia. The property was originally owned by the Satterfield family, and Christian purchased it at auction in 1900. (Courtesy the Maryland Historical Trust.)

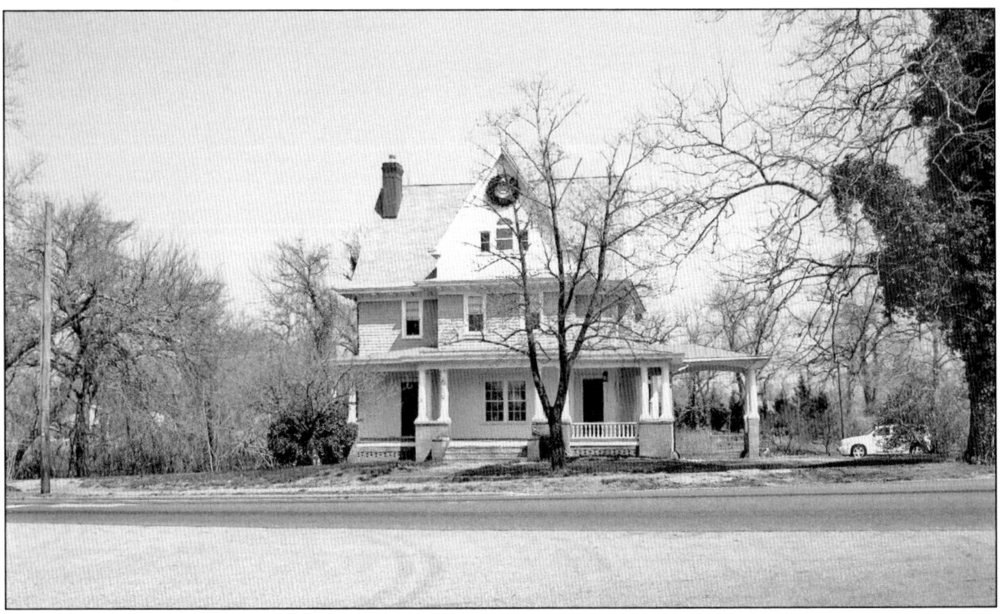

Christian had spent time in Greensboro as a youth and eventually married William Satterfield's daughter. It is reported that for a time during and after World War II the house was used as a maternity hospital. It has undergone numerous renovations, each staying true to the original structure. (Courtesy the Maryland Historical Trust/J. C. Reveal.)

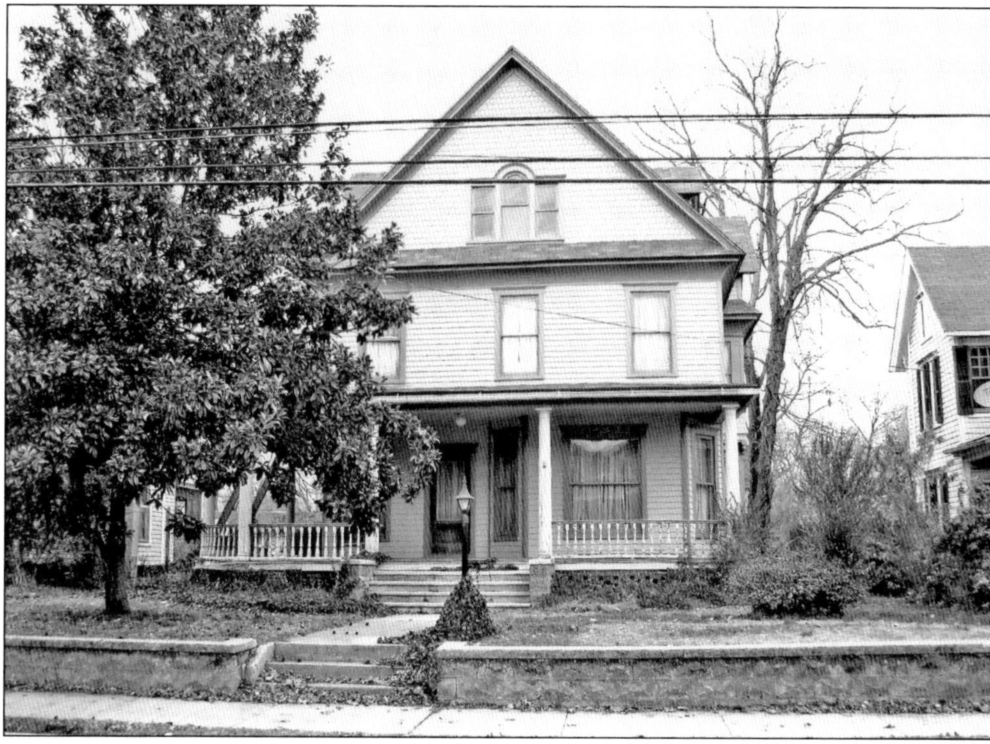

This house was built by Thomas Clayton Horsey around 1907. A Greensboro banker and businessman, Horsey served on the Board of the Caroline County Bank and as chairman of the Caroline County Democratic State Central Committee. (Courtesy J. C. Reveal.)

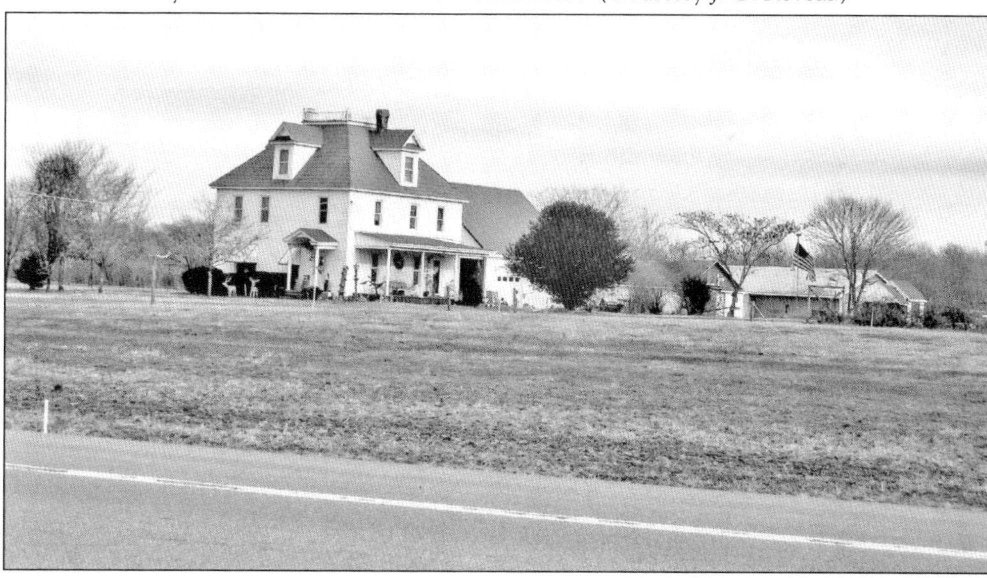

Addison A. Christian owned Greensboro Gardens, also known as the Dahlia Farm, around 1922, where he raised prize-winning dahlias. Christian also owned 10,000 acres in and around Greensboro under the Eglantine Farms name. His interest in poultry led to the raising of an internationally known, prize-winning white leghorn chicken known as "Lady Eglantine." This farm is located just north of the town limits. (Courtesy J. C. Reveal.)

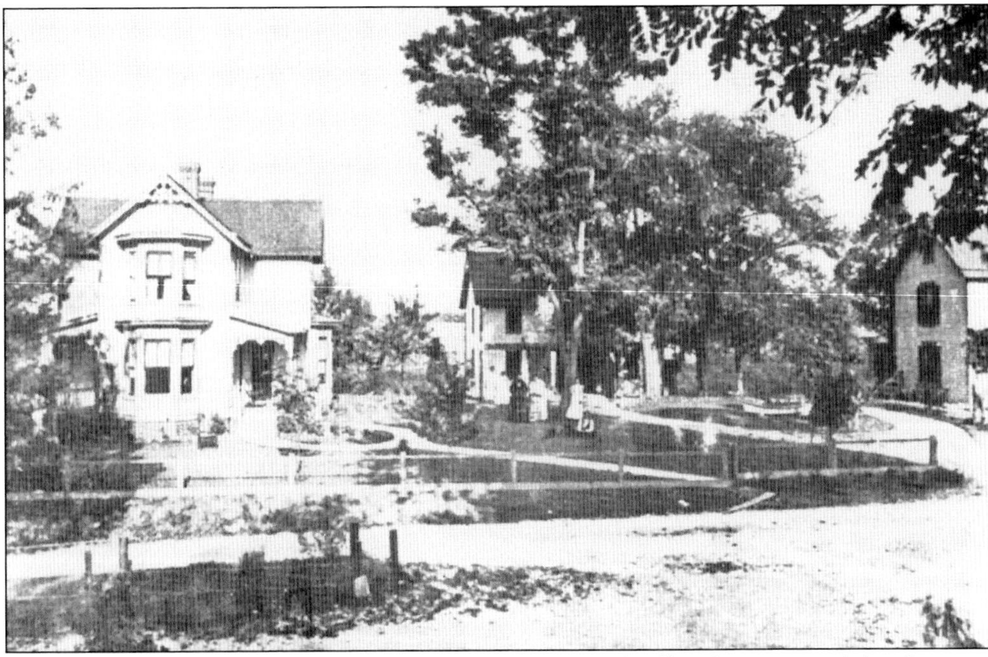

Capt. Daniel S. Brockway engaged in the transportation and milling business, with headquarters at Greensboro. In the late 1800s and early 1900s, he owned and operated a line of steamers that operated between Greensboro and Baltimore, two of which were the steamboat *Greensboro* and the steamboat *Brockway*. In 1904, Captain Brockway built a flour mill near his Choptank River steamboat wharf. (Courtesy Town of Greensboro.)

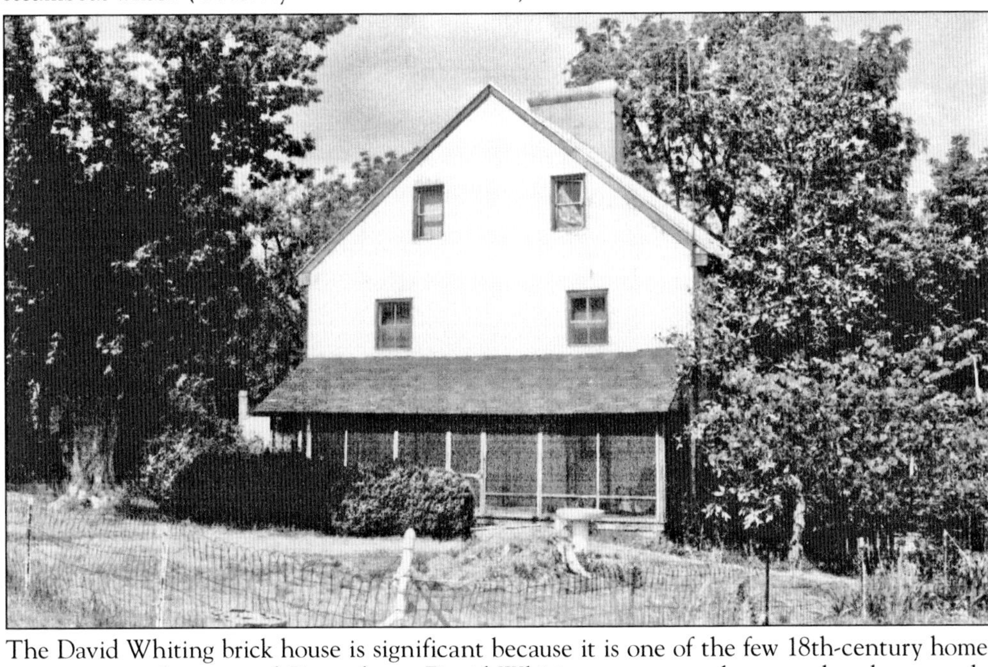

The David Whiting brick house is significant because it is one of the few 18th-century homes remaining in the town of Greensboro. David Whiting, a tanner who owned and operated a local tannery, leased this property in 1785 for a period of 99 years. (Courtesy the Maryland Historical Trust.)

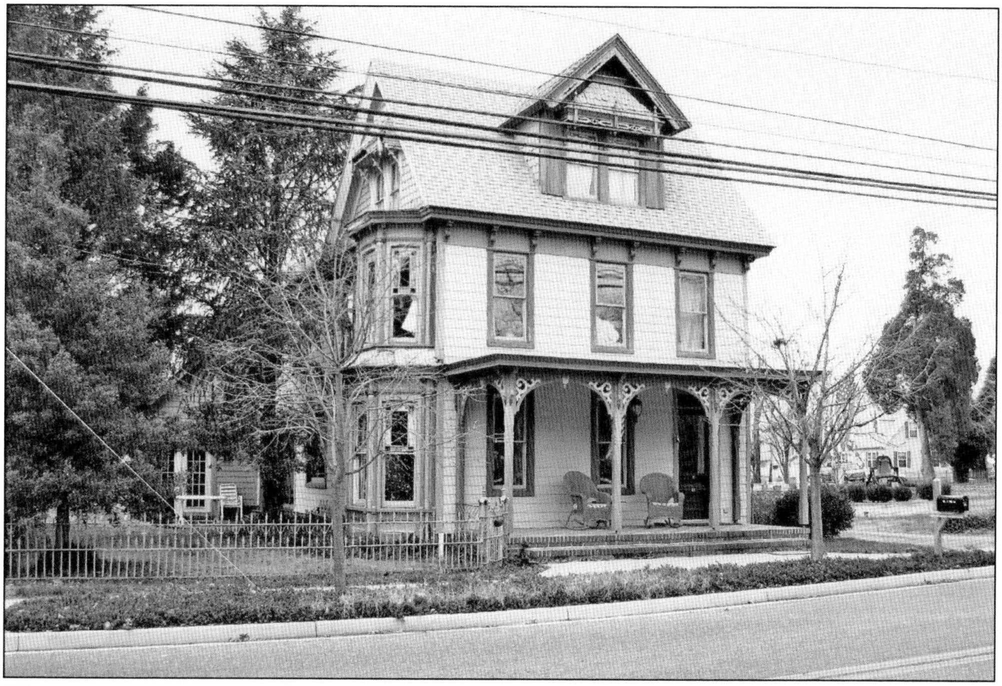

Thomas H. Jarman, a merchant and cabinetmaker, constructed this home in the mid-1800s. In 1880, he also established a hardware business on South Main Street in a building erected for that purpose. (Courtesy J. C. Reveal.)

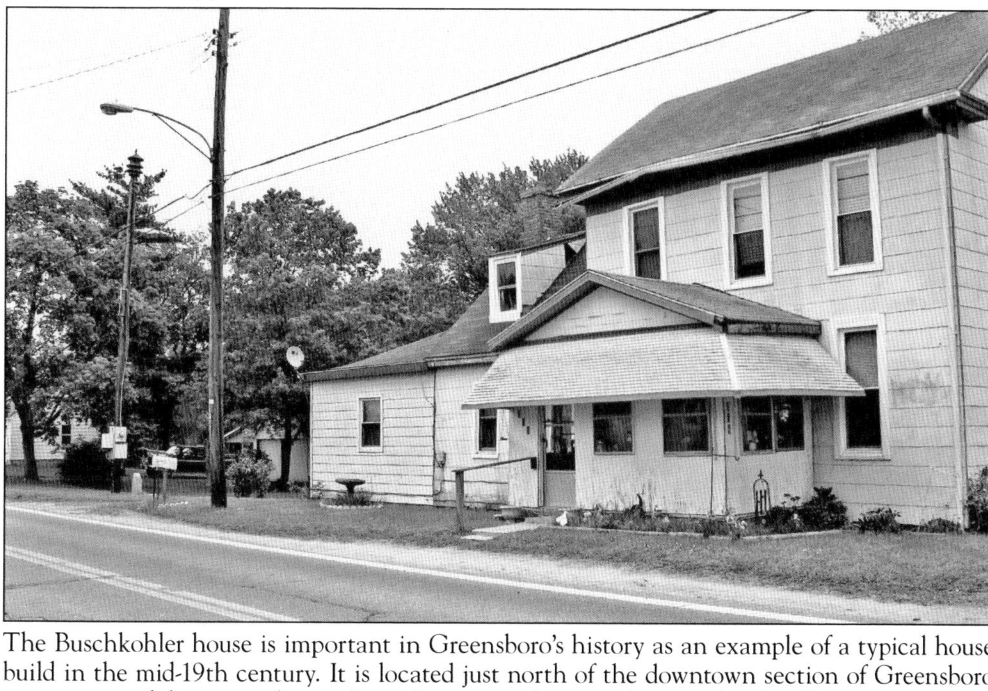

The Buschkohler house is important in Greensboro's history as an example of a typical house build in the mid-19th century. It is located just north of the downtown section of Greensboro next to one of the original town boundary stones bearing the initials of William Hughlett, an early town merchant and resident. The stone reflects the date of 1769. (Courtesy the Maryland Historical Trust.)

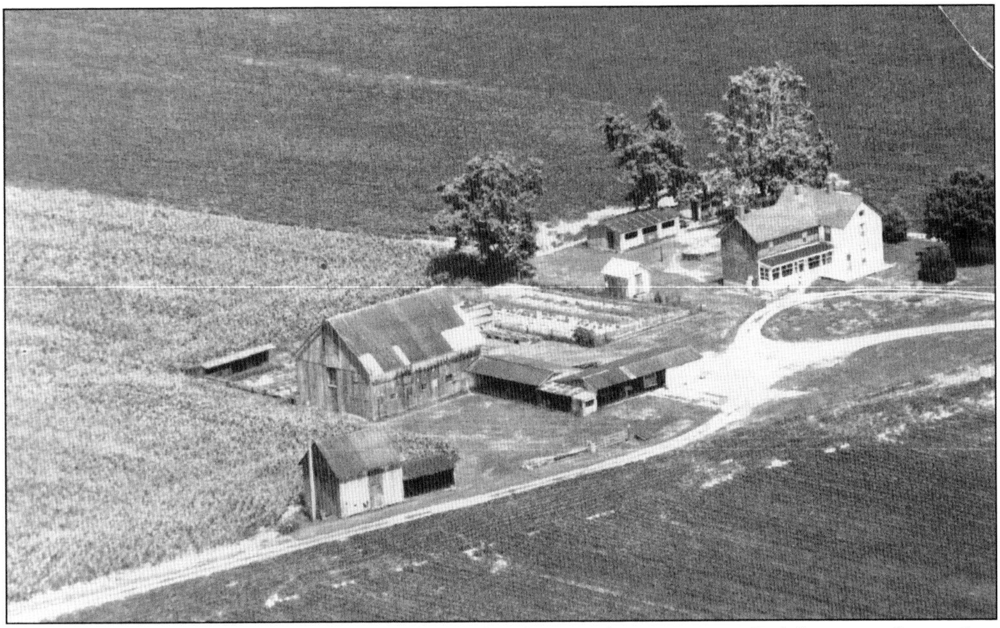

The Butler farm, located off Dukes Road outside of Greensboro, is typical of the many farms that dot the agricultural lands of the region. (Courtesy Joan Cesarini.)

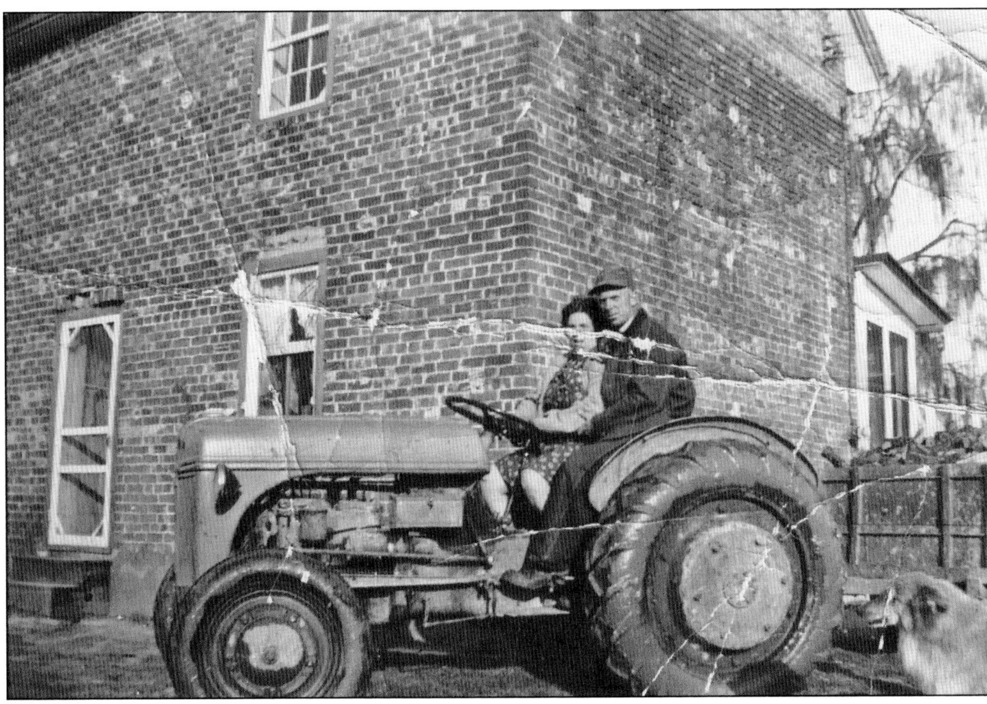

Ralph and Evelyn Dukes are on their tractor in front of the brick portion of their home that dated back to the early years of Greensboro. (Courtesy Joan Cesarini.)

Six

Greensboro's People and Social Activities

The people who have led Greensboro through over 200 years of success are many indeed, and this chapter attempts to look at those prominent merchants and professionals who have become the infrastructure upon which this town was built. Greensboro was a popular practicing point for physicians. Some of the more prominent doctors who have served the population (and the dates they set up shop) were Dr. William Sargent Kitteridge, 1760; Dr. Robert Cook, 1780; Dr. James Cooke, c. 1788; and Dr. Edward White, 1785. White proved instrumental in founding the Medical and Chirurgical Faculty in 1799. Dr. Joseph Price, 1798, was another founding member of the faculty. Dr. Henry Rousset (1785–1871) was originally from Breslau and Prussia; he fought at Waterloo as a sergeant general under Napoleon. He settled in Greensboro around 1860, where he practiced until his death in 1871.

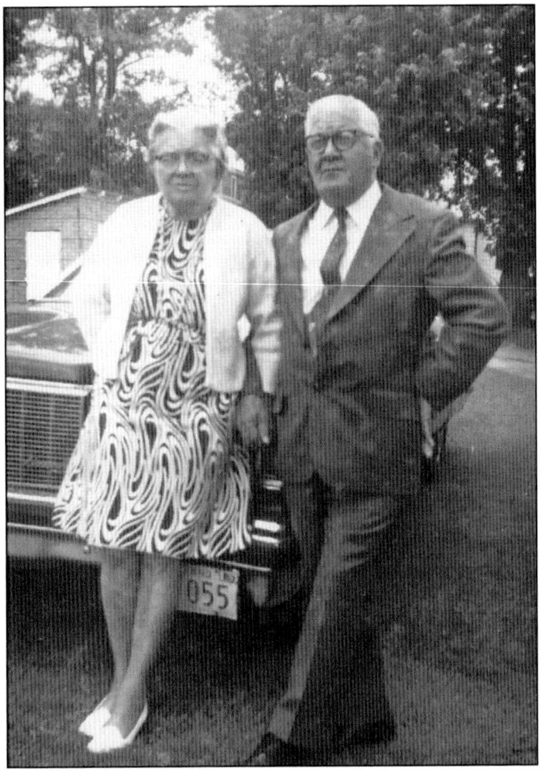

A discussion of the people of Greensboro would be remiss if it did not begin with Dr. Charles H. Stonesifer (1900–1978), who served the people of Greensboro well. On June 21, 1927, he registered with Caroline County as a physician and began his practice in Greensboro with Dr. W. W. Goldsborough and Dr. F. R. Everett. Dr. Stonesifer (seen in this photograph with his receptionist, Mabel Rich) spent much of his time making house calls at all hours. In spite of his busy practice, Dr. Stonesifer also found time for community service as president of the Caroline County Medical Society in 1935 and 1938. (Courtesy Joan Cesarini.)

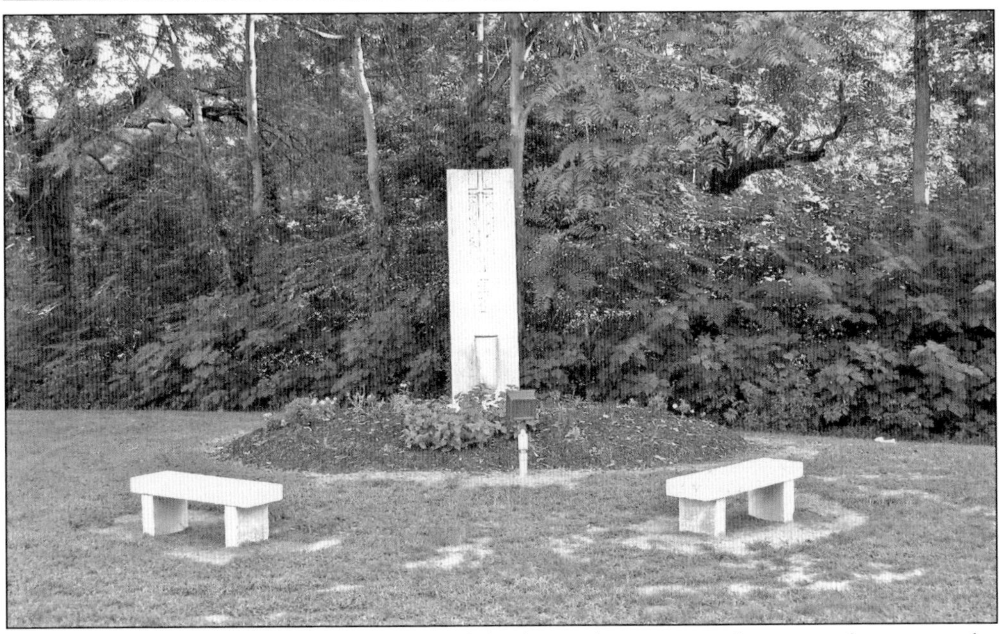

Dr. Stonesifer remained up-to-date on all of the latest therapies, medicines, and practices; he died of a disease that resulted from overexposure to X-rays. After his death, the town named a street Stonesifer Drive, and it erected a monument to him and his service. The inscription reads, "In Memory of our Beloved Doctor, C. H. Stonesifer, for 50 years of faithful service 1928–1978." (Courtesy J. C. Reveal.)

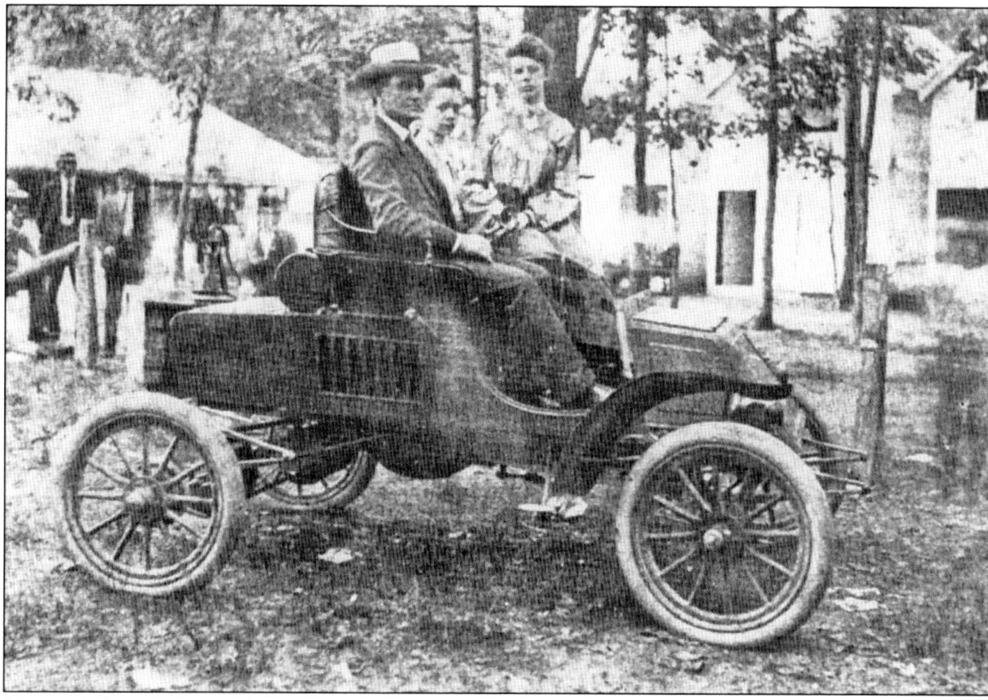

Henry Cohee was one of Greensboro's preeminent photographers, and many of his original images remain in the possession of local families. This photograph of Henry and his family was taken around 1910. (Courtesy Town of Greensboro.)

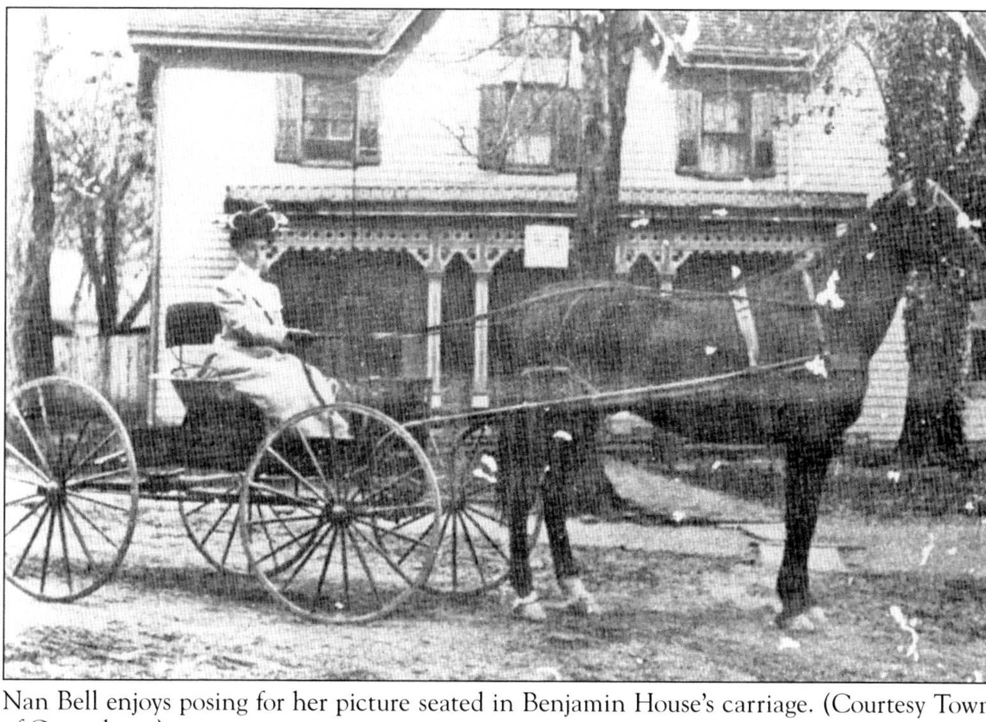

Nan Bell enjoys posing for her picture seated in Benjamin House's carriage. (Courtesy Town of Greensboro.)

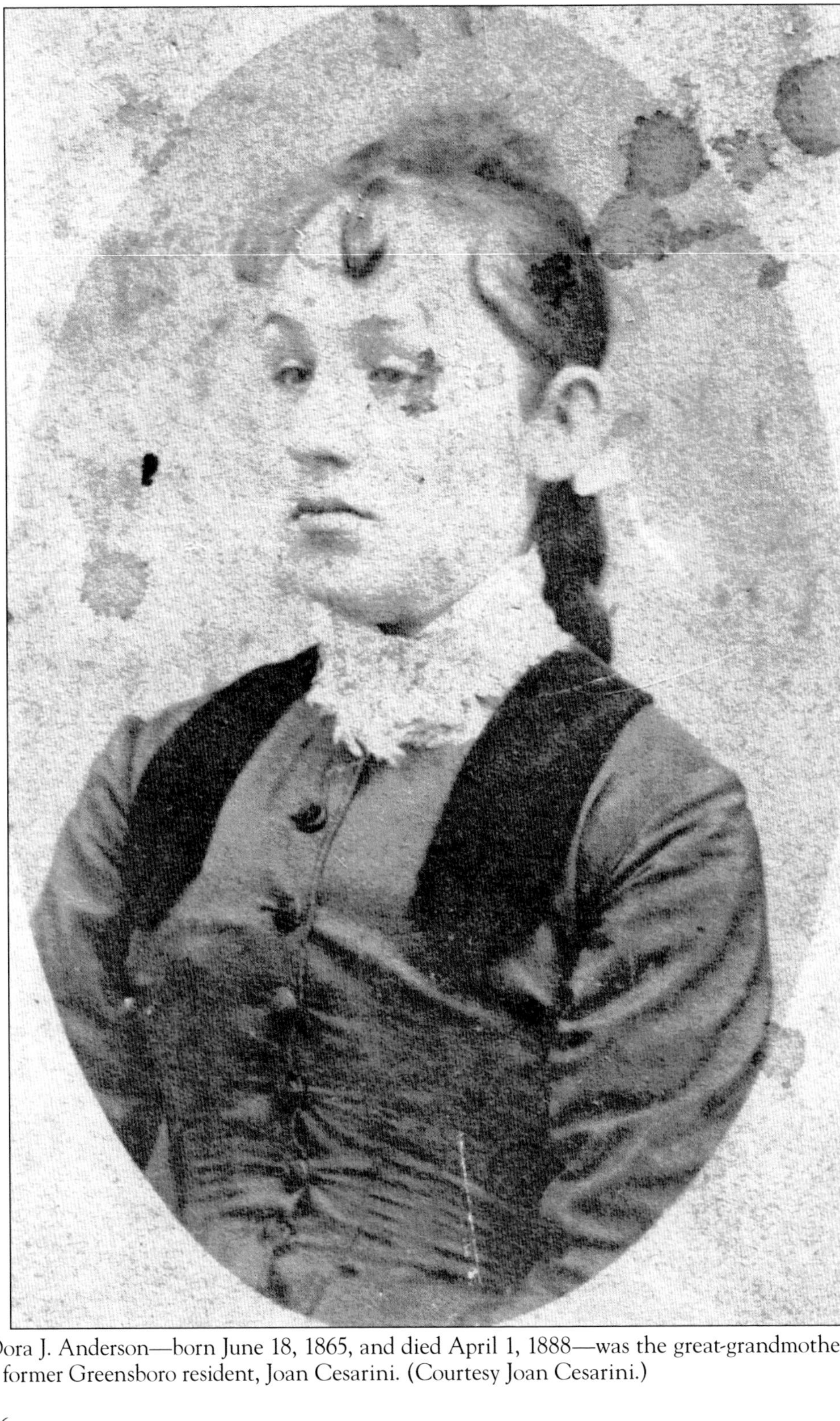

Dora J. Anderson—born June 18, 1865, and died April 1, 1888—was the great-grandmother of a former Greensboro resident, Joan Cesarini. (Courtesy Joan Cesarini.)

Remembrance cards were popular in the late 19th century as ways to keep loved ones near after their passing, reflected in this memorial for Dora J. Anderson. (Courtesy Joan Cesarini.)

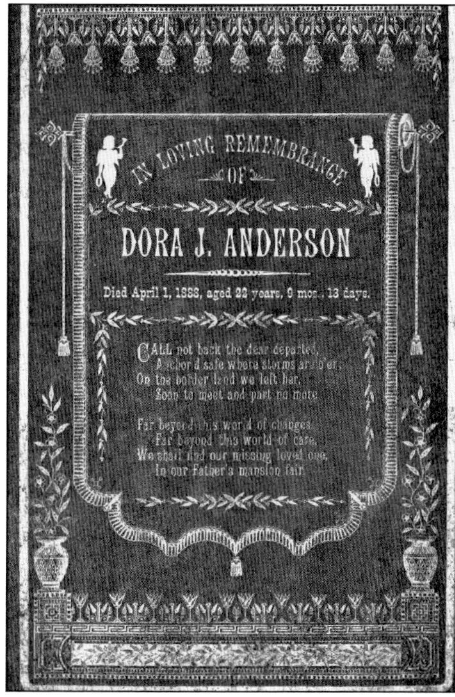

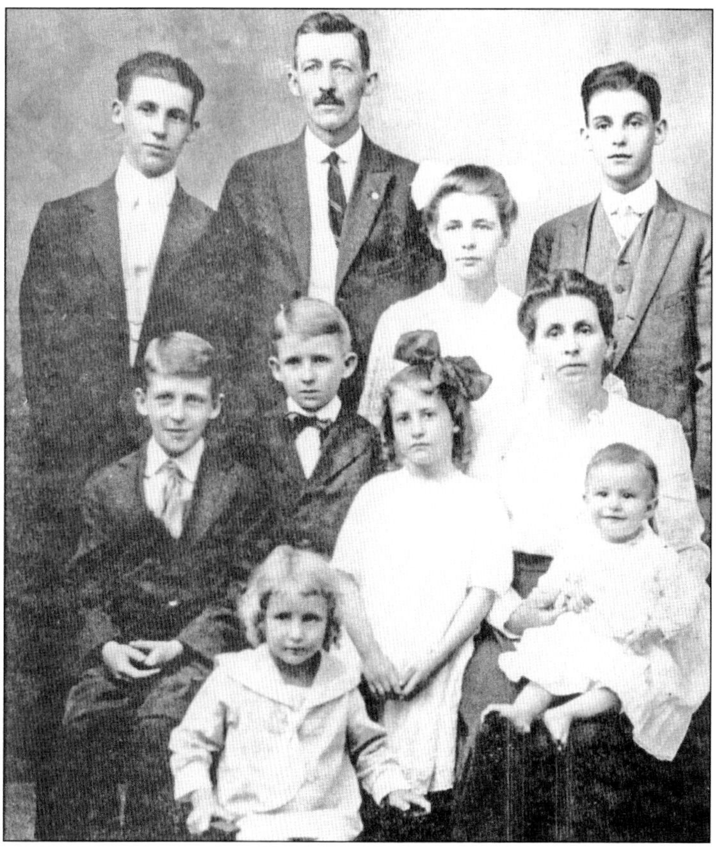

This portrait of the Linwood Riddleberger family shows the size of families in the 19th century. A successful businessman in the community, Linwood rented the Brockway Flour Mill and moved his family into the Brockway dwelling in 1916. His grandson, Tom Riddleberger, a contractor, served several terms as mayor in the 1990s through the turn of the 21st century. (Courtesy Tom and Mary Lou Riddleberger.)

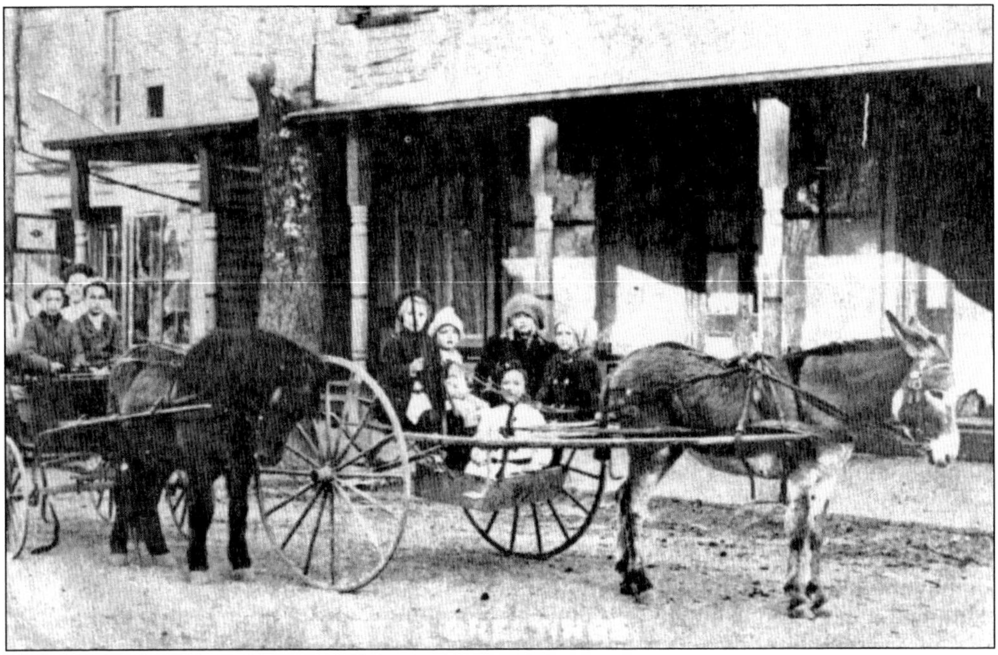

The Horsey Building was located on the east side of North Main Street between Sunset Avenue and Stonesifer Drive. The black pony belonged to the driver, Clinton Jarman Jr. Mae Pippin is in the back seat, next to Ed Willis's store. The mule and other passengers are in front of Hughes Millinery, next to Turpin Drug Store, which was eventually purchased by W. W. Goldsborough for his pharmacy. (Courtesy Town of Greensboro.)

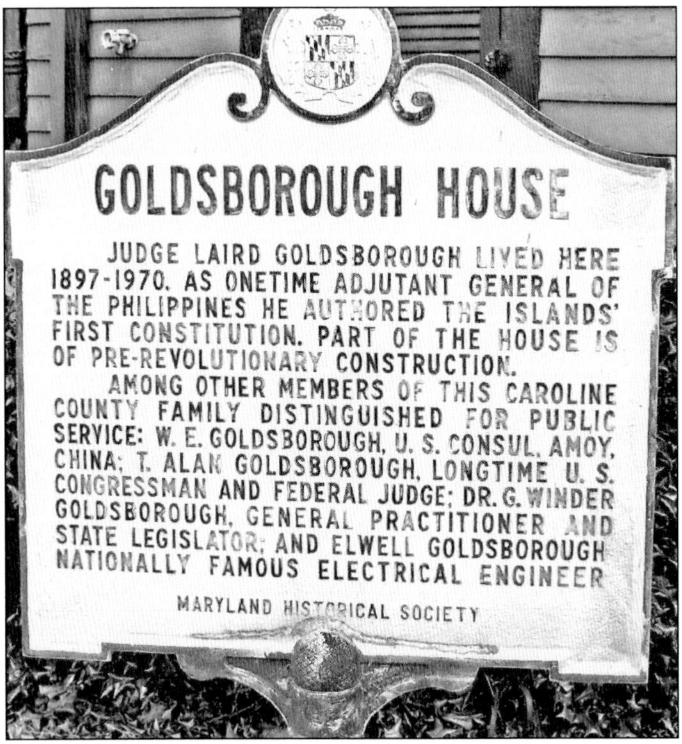

The third of the Maryland Historical Society plaques to recognize Greensboro's contribution to Maryland's history is located at the Goldsborough House and provides insight into the efforts of Hon. Laird Goldsborough and the Goldsborough family on behalf of the town. (Courtesy J. C. Reveal.)

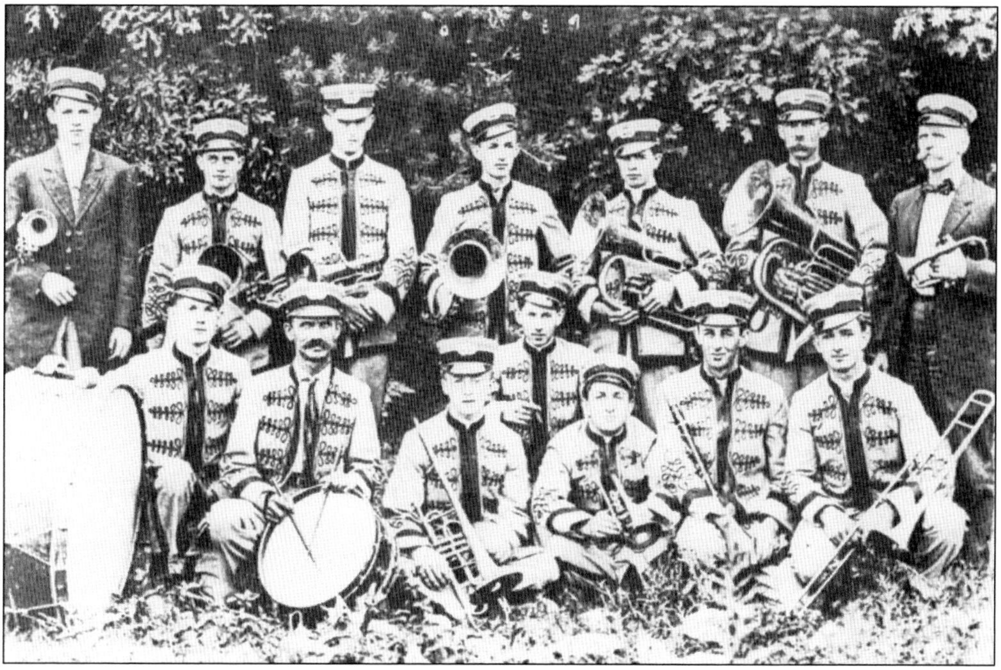

The people of Greensboro participated in social activities in a variety of ways. This is the Greensboro band around 1920. (Courtesy Town of Greensboro.)

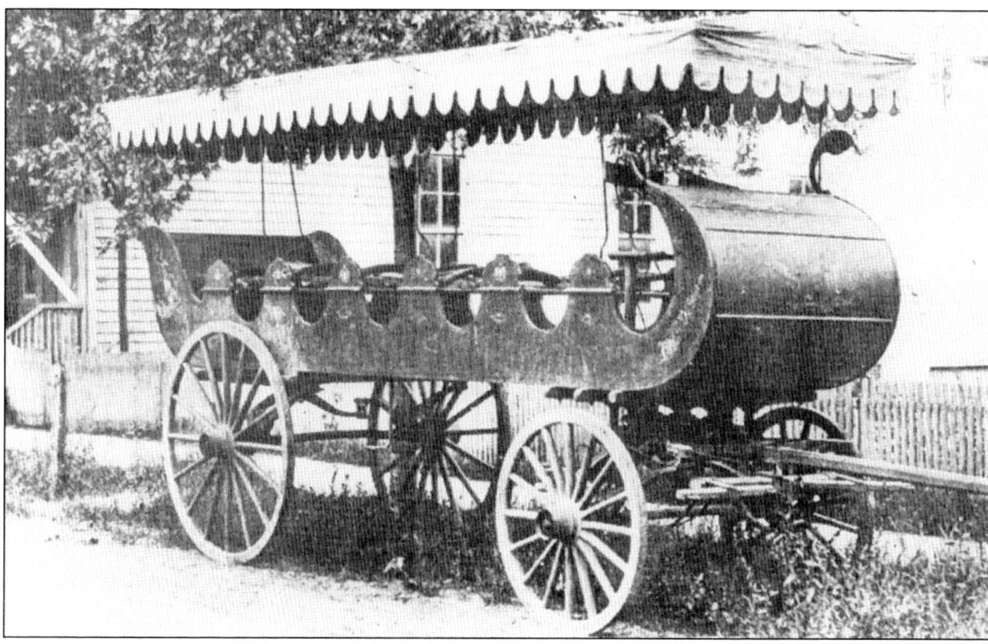

The band traveled in style from one performance to the next in this 1908 bandwagon. What a show it would have been to see the band, all decked out in their fine costumes, riding to their next event. (Courtesy Town of Greensboro.)

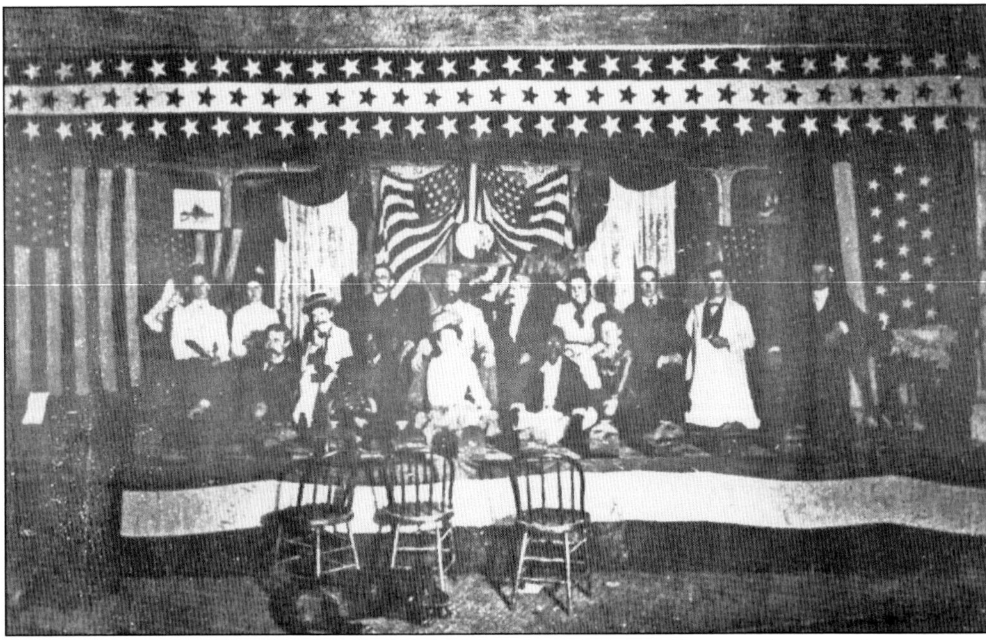

Local talent tripped the light fantastic in the variety of plays and musical events that occurred at Mozart Hall. This *c.* 1900 presentation was put on by a local group. (Courtesy Town of Greensboro.)

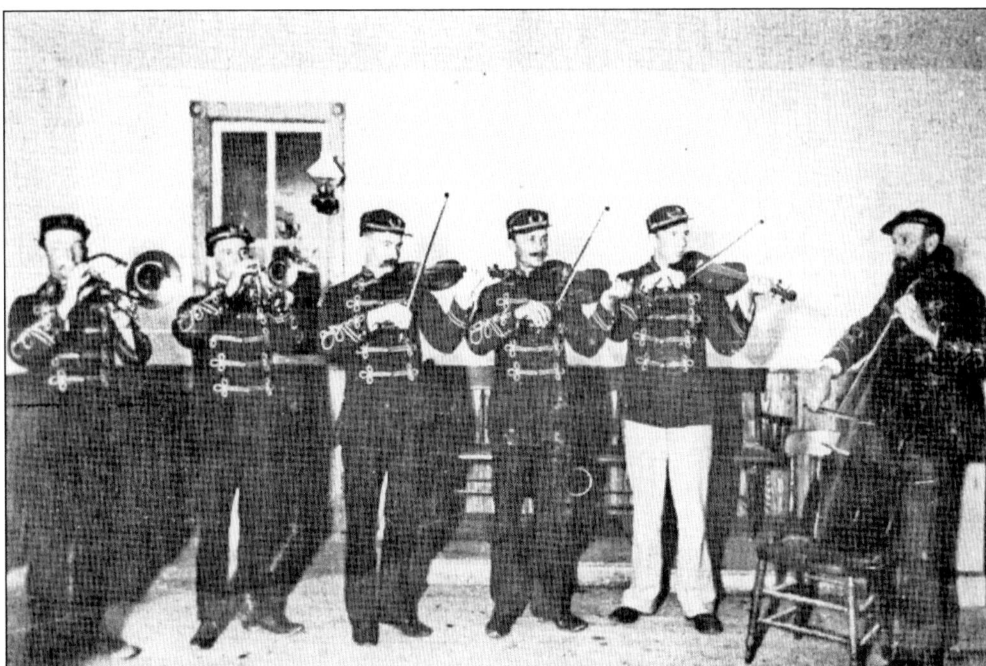

Members of the Greensboro band practice for a live performance around 1900. Pictured from left to right are Harvey Coursey, Clarence Jackson, Ollie Jackson, Harry Karcher, Nat House, and Benjamin House. (Courtesy Town of Greensboro.)

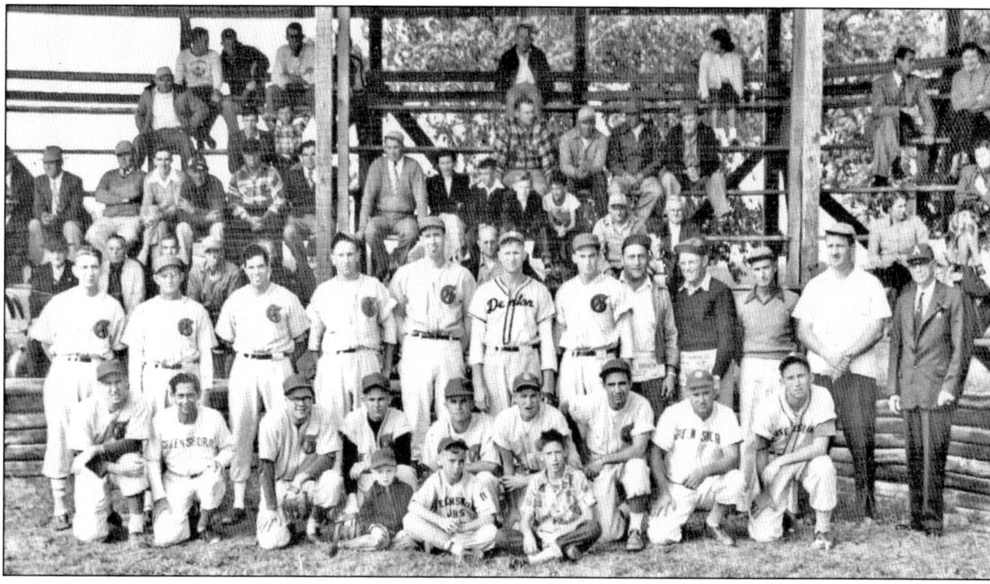

Sports, especially baseball, were and remain a favorite with town residents. The 1950–1951 Greensboro baseball team thrilled the crowd. From left to right are (first row) two unidentified bat boys and Alan Boyd; (second row) Duke Kinnamon, Calvin Butler, Sonny Henry, Junior Walls, Eddie Dill, Jake Usilton, Joe Scurto, Zeth Cox Weaver, and Tommy Dulin; (third row) Tom Smith, Paul Dill, Tony Gianninoto, Tinker Todd, Lanky Bilbrough, Granvill Diffie, John Mundt, Eddie Schmidt, Frank Usilton, Eddie Walls, Tom Hill, and Harry Butler. (Courtesy Tony Gianninoto.)

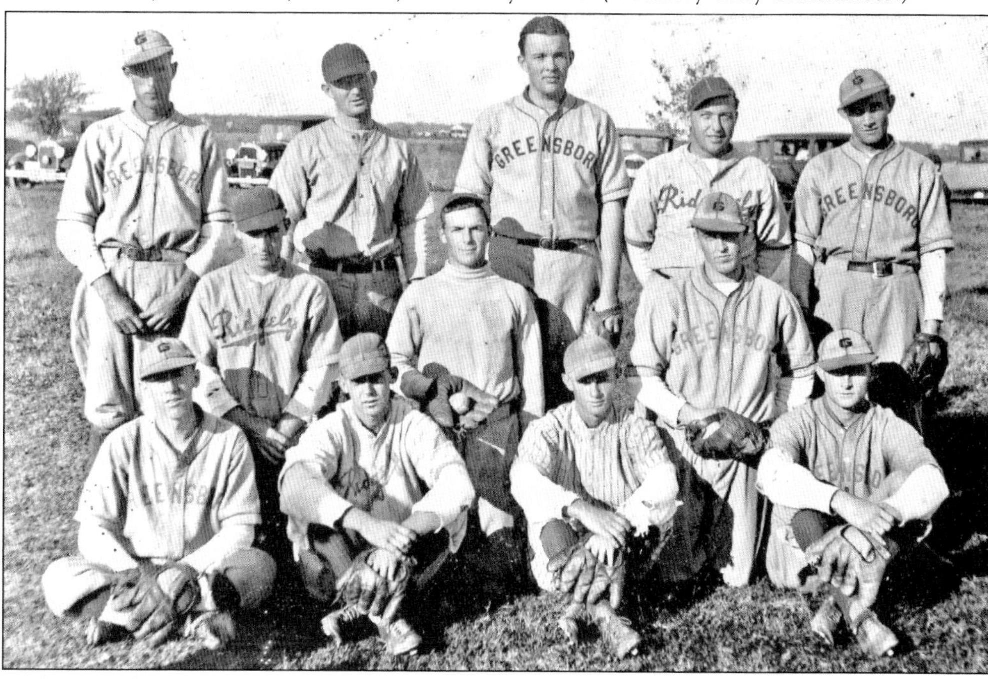

Unfortunately many of the names of this 1933 Greensboro baseball team are lost to history. From left to right are (first row) Pete Beumont, Weaver Jones, and two unidentified; (second row) three unidentified; (third row) Eddie Walls, Woody Dill, Charlie Bilbrough, "Nuts" Glockston, and Paul Dill. (Courtesy Tony Gianninoto.)

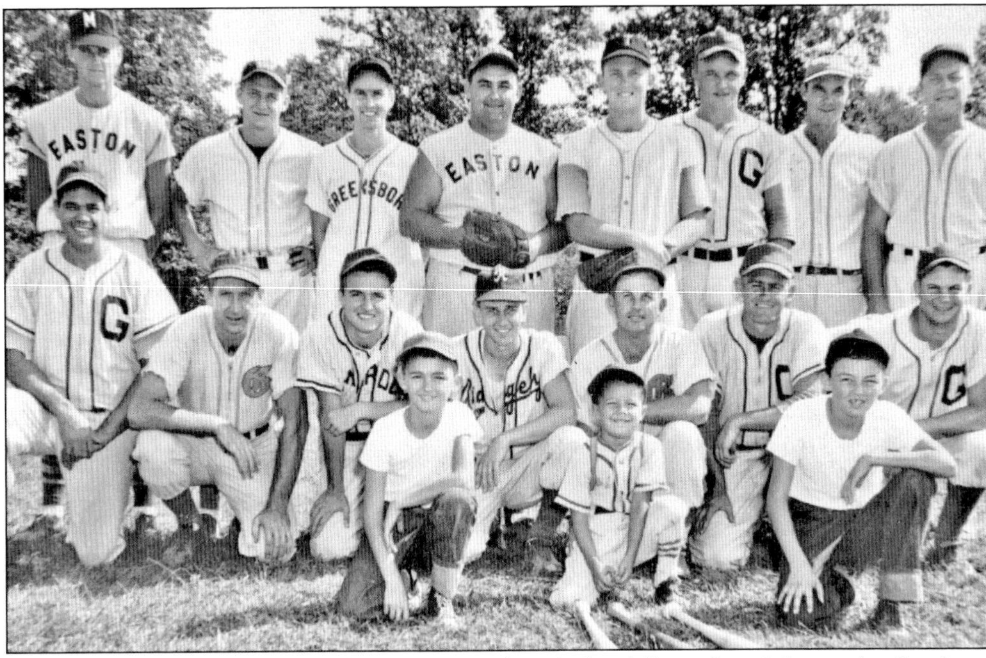

The Greensboro baseball team of 1957–1958 is identified as follows, from left to right: (bat boys) Jack Jarrell, Tony J. Gianninoto, and Henry Jarrell; (second row) Tony Gianninoto, Buddy Bennett, ? Nickerson, Chuck King, Eddie Dill, Duncan Weber, and Alvin Simpson Jr.; (third row) ? Wilson, Wayne Tribbett, Lenny Tribbett, B. Caulk, Tommy Dulin, Jesse Chance, Med Shorts, and Joe Simpson Sr. (Courtesy Tony Gianninoto.)

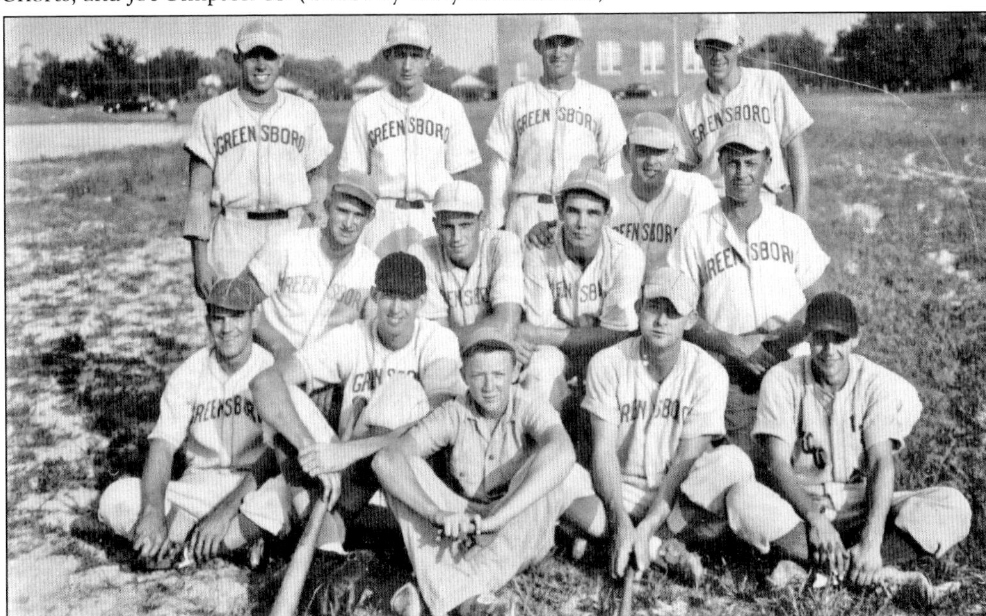

Greensboro's baseball team of 1941 included, from left to right: (first row) Bob Roberts, Lanky Bilbrough, bat boy Bob Kirwan, Woody Dill, and unidentified; (second row) Zeth Weaver, two unidentified, Charlie Bilbrough, and Joe Simpson; (third row) unidentified, Buck Downes, Paul Dill, and Leon Spence. (Courtesy Tony Gianninoto.)

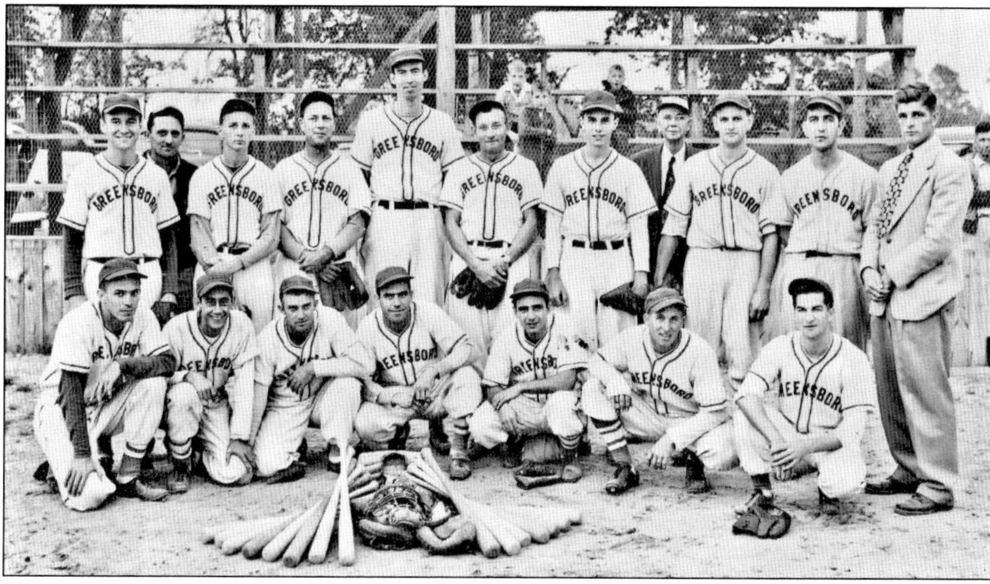

The winners of Greensboro's 1951 League Championship are, from left to right, (kneeling) Gus Granden, Calvin Butler, Zeth Weaver Jr., Bob Roberts, Joe Scurto, Howard Tribbett, and unidentified; (standing) Eddie Kietrick, unidentified, Eddie Hollingsorth, Eddie Van Deusen, Joe Simpson, Bob "Lanky" Bilbrough, unidentified, H. F. Butler, unidentified, Tom Smith, and ? Griffin. This picture was taken at the Greensboro Grandstand of the Charles Bilbrough Baseball Park, just outside of the town limits. (Courtesy Tony Gianninoto.)

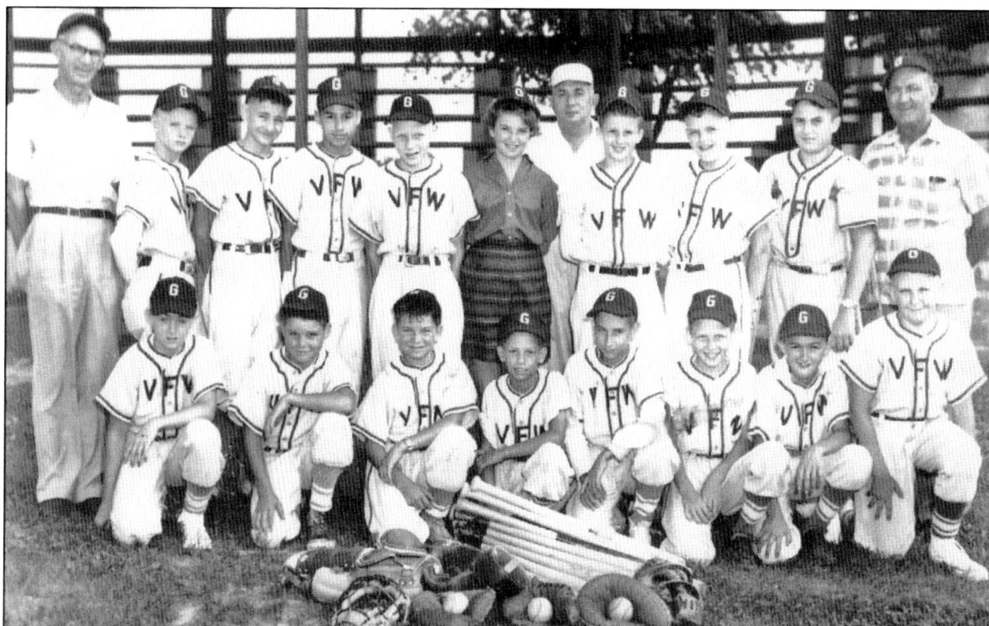

The 1958 Greensboro Maryland Little League Champions were, from left to right, (first row) Joe Smith, Francis Wothers, Irving Ober Jr., Karl Kendall, Dicky Pursley, Harold Shaffer, Jack Jarrell, and Harry Michael Koch; (second row) coach Mike Pursley, Fred Wothers, Bob Bickling, Robert Toth, John Berger, Dottie Stirn (scorekeeper), coach Jim Bilbrough, Dennis Schurman, Alan Holsinger, Jimmy Bilbrough, and manager Harry Koch. (Courtesy Tony Gianninoto.)

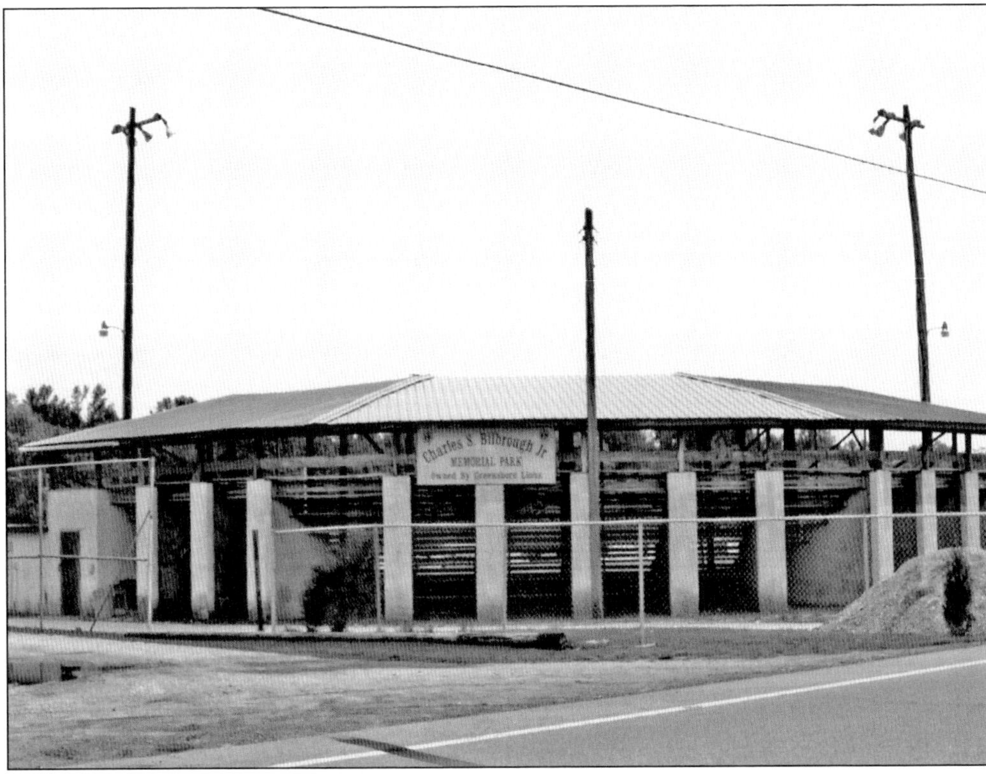

Greensboro residents have enjoyed "America's sport"—baseball—at the Charles Bilbrough Baseball Park for several generations, and the park remains a favorite place throughout the season. (Courtesy J. C. Reveal.)

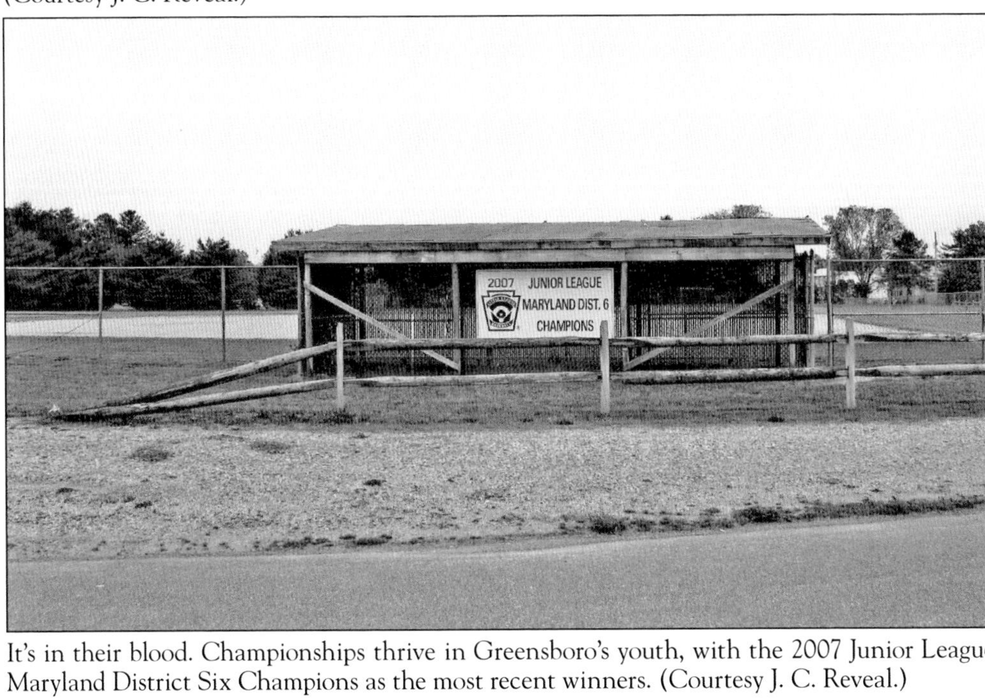

It's in their blood. Championships thrive in Greensboro's youth, with the 2007 Junior League Maryland District Six Champions as the most recent winners. (Courtesy J. C. Reveal.)

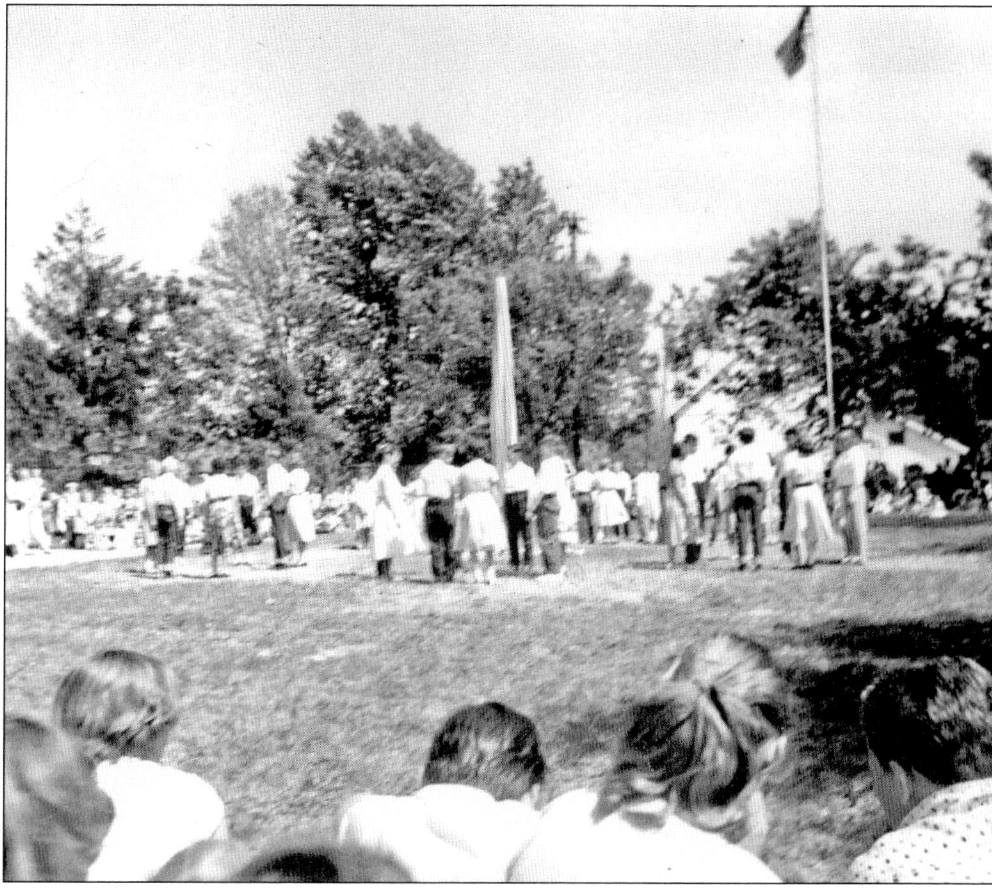

The beginning of spring brought many celebrations, such as the May Day celebration of 1957, which got under way at the Greensboro School. (Courtesy Virginia Bishop Jones.)

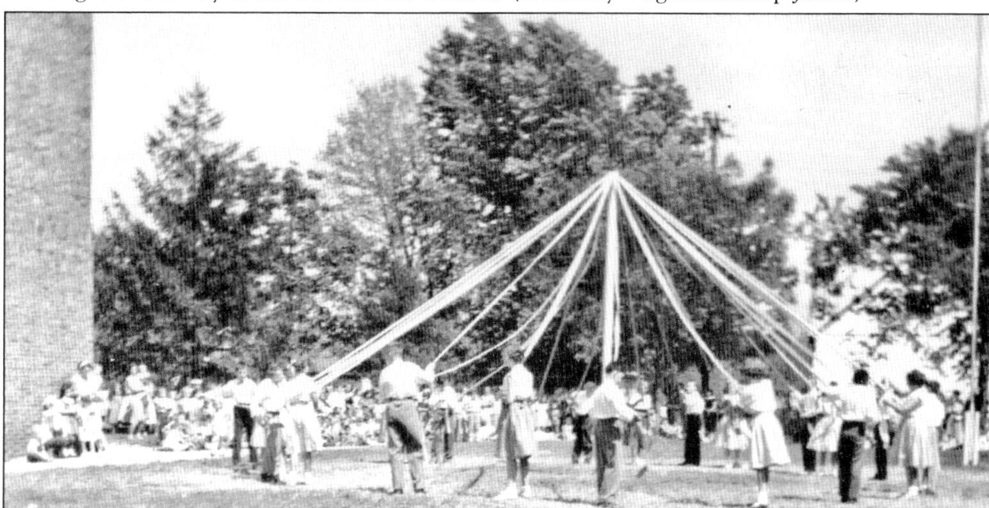

The May Day celebration of 1957 centered on the maypole at the Greensboro School. (Courtesy Virginia Bishop Jones.)

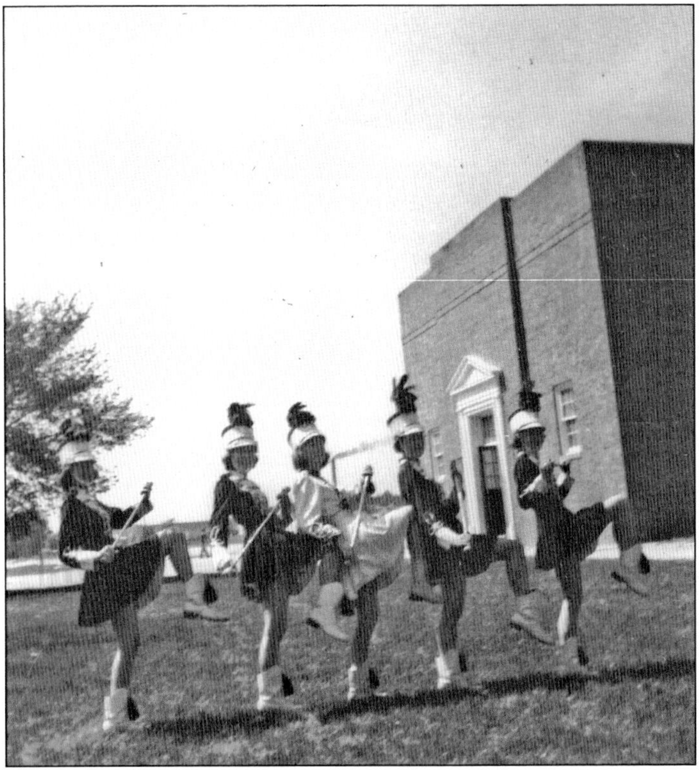

School celebrations included demonstrations by Greensboro School cheerleaders around 1957. (Courtesy Virginia Bishop Jones.)

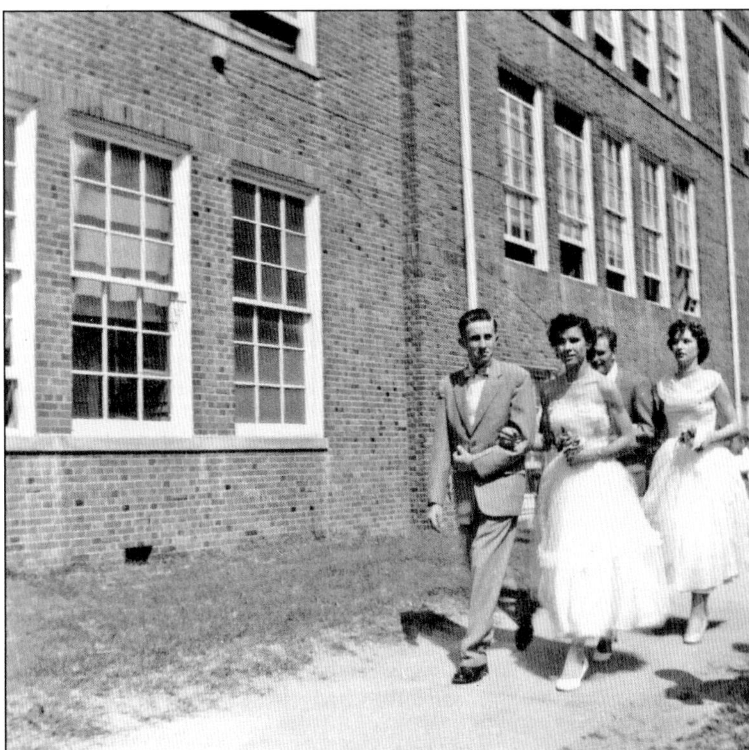

George Weaver, Virginia Bishop, Steve Nemith, and Charlotte Simpler enjoy the formal march around Greensboro High School at the annual May Day festivities. (Courtesy Virginia Bishop Jones.)

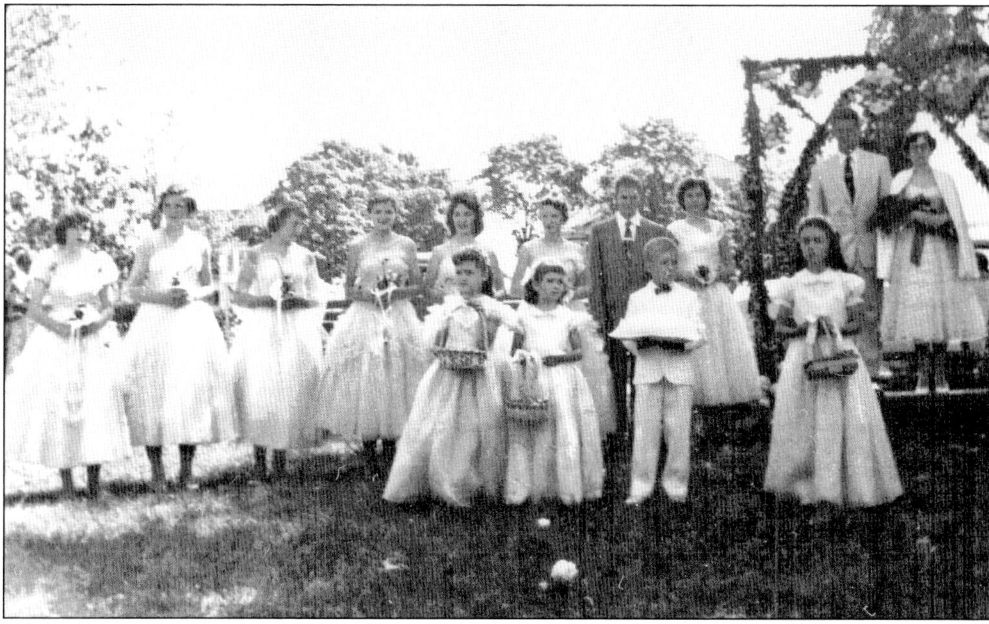

May Day would not be complete without the reigning court, with students of all ages and classes represented. Pictured here is the *c.* 1957 court. (Courtesy Virginia Bishop Jones.)

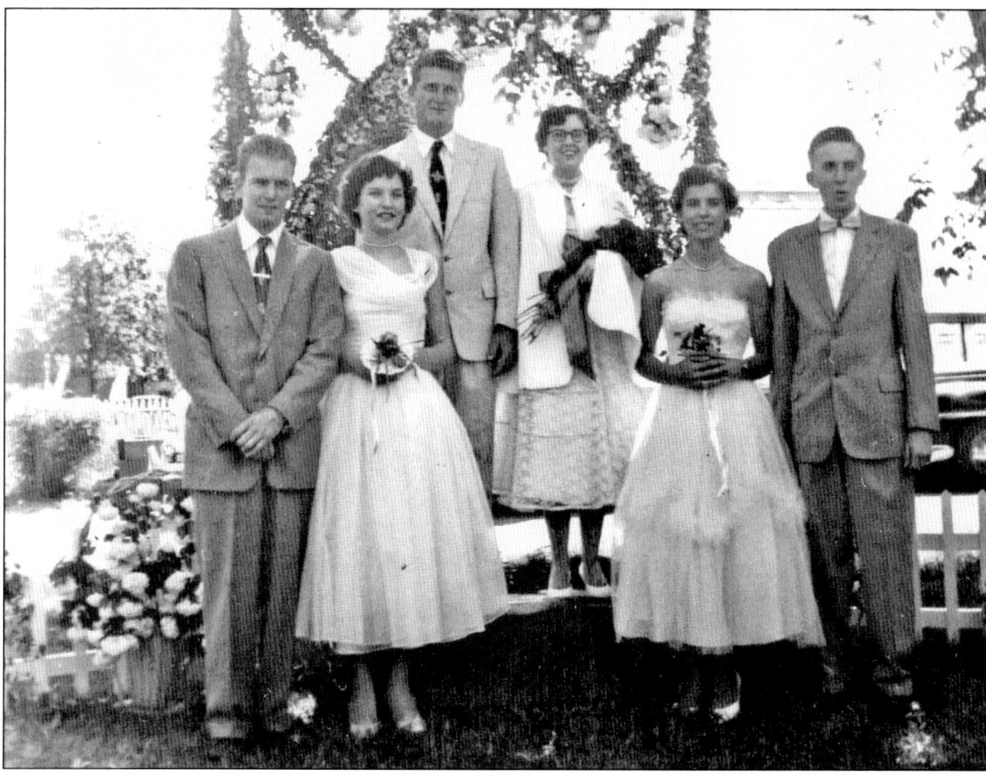

May Day 1957 was well represented by the high school court. King Wayne Tribbett and Queen Connie Monroe (second row) are surrounded by their attendants, Steve Nemith, Charlotte Simpler, Virginia Bishop, and George Weaver. (Courtesy Virginia Bishop Jones.)

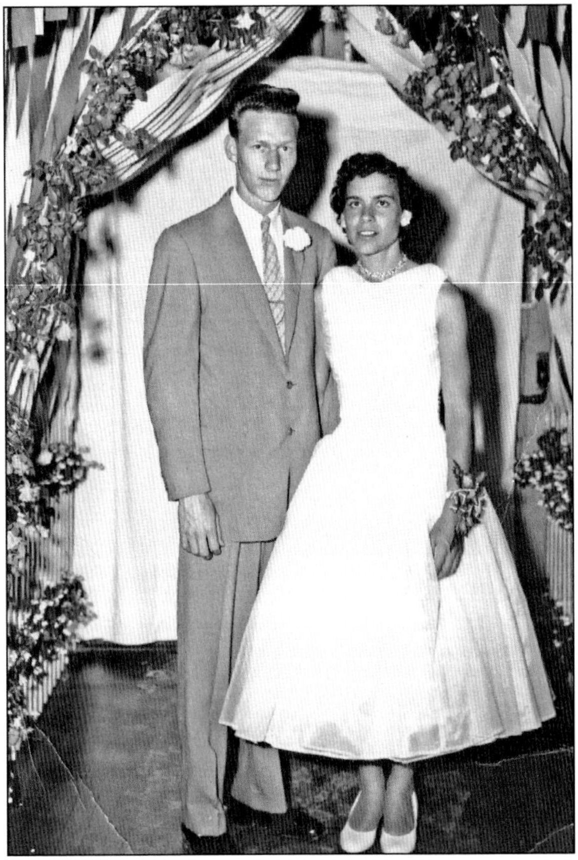

Bill Jones and Virginia Bishop enjoy the annual Greensboro High School prom. (Courtesy Virginia Bishop Jones.)

Social events in Greensboro include tractor pulls and lawn mower pulls, which are performed at venues such as the Fireman's Annual Carnival, much to the enjoyment of both adults and children alike. (Courtesy Cheryl Jones.)

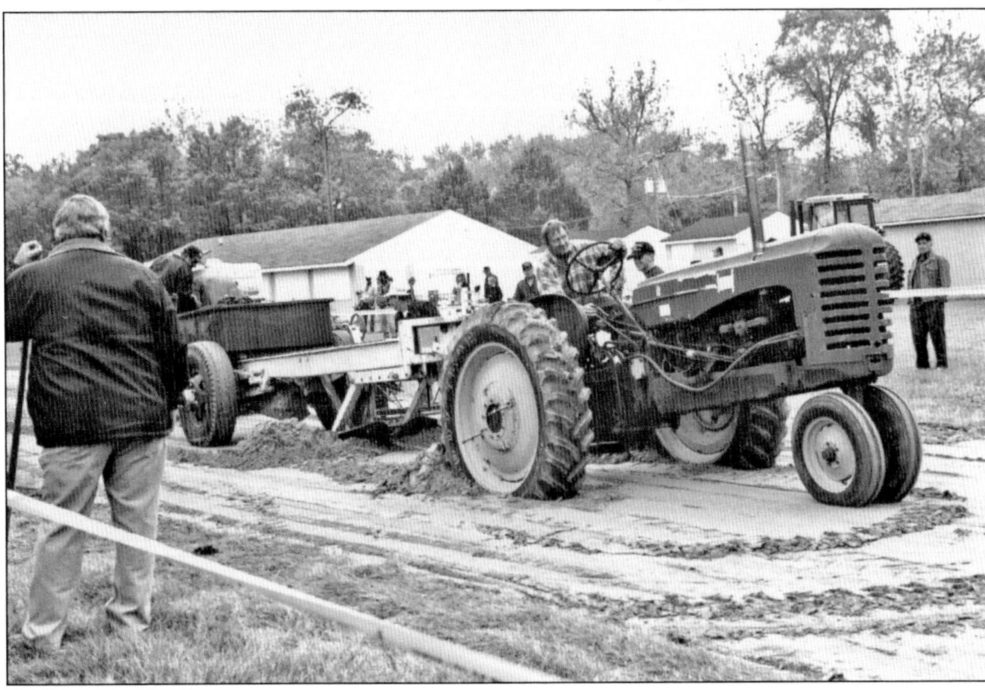

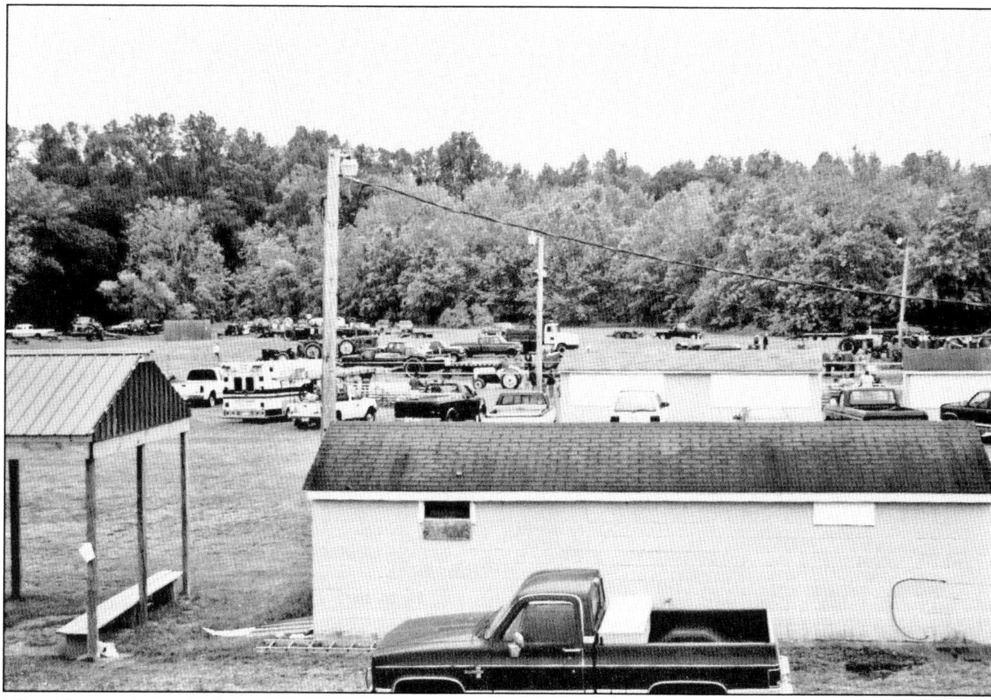

The Greensboro Volunteer Fire Department owns and operates the Carnival Grounds for the enjoyment of all citizens. Events throughout the year include the Fireman's Annual Carnival and Founder's Day, as well as ongoing events such as yard sales. (Courtesy Cheryl Jones.)

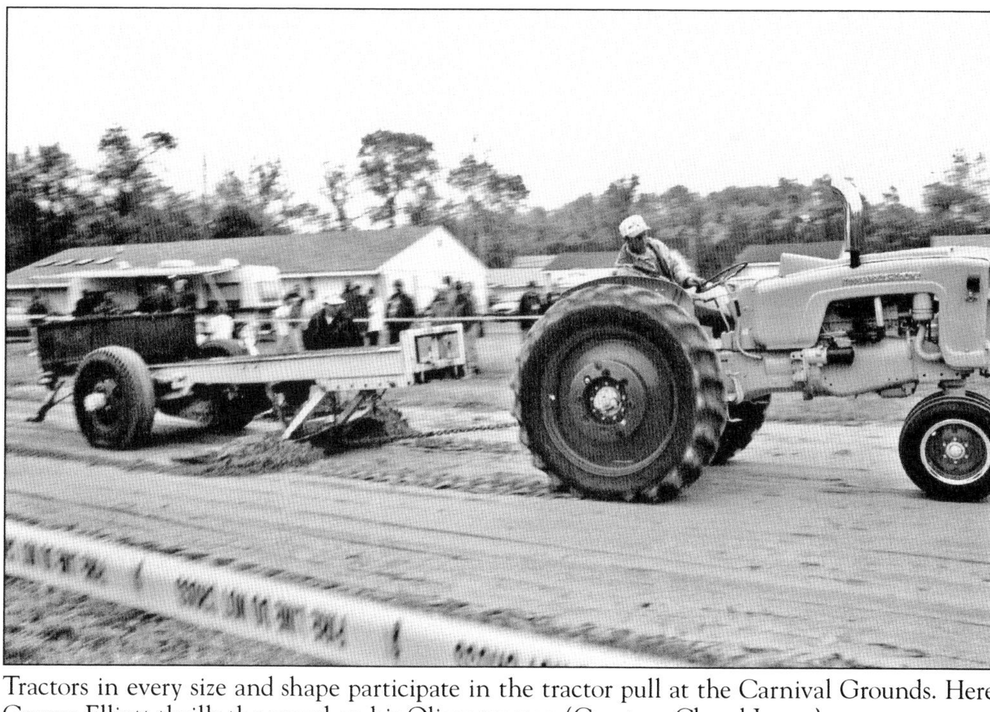

Tractors in every size and shape participate in the tractor pull at the Carnival Grounds. Here George Elliott thrills the crowd on his Oliver tractor. (Courtesy Cheryl Jones.)

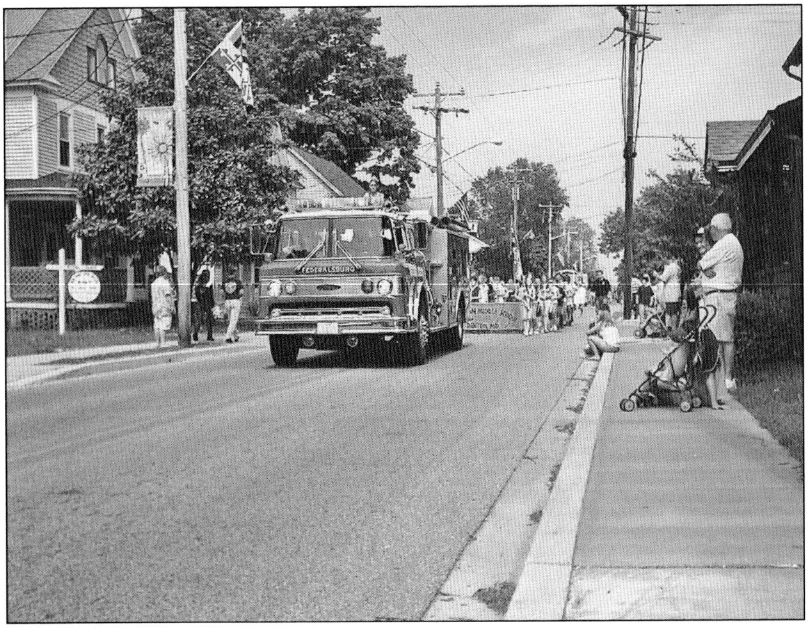

Current-day celebrations center on the annual Founders' Day event. It starts with a parade from West Sunset Avenue led by the fire department through town to the Carnival Grounds at Choptank Park. (Courtesy J. C. Reveal.)

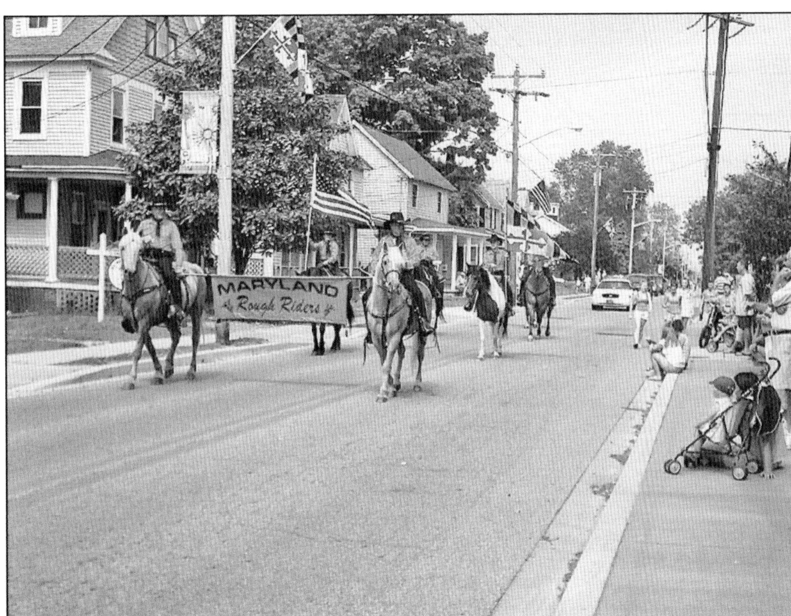

The popularity of the Maryland Rough Riders remains high, and this group is invited to participate in the parade each year. (Courtesy J. C. Reveal.)

Seven

Industry in Greensboro

In 1773, Caroline County was cut from the lands of Dorchester and Queen Anne's Counties. The proceedings and acts of the General Assembly of 1748–1751 states that in 1749, the "Justices of Queen Anne's County are hereby empowered [*sic*] . . . by the last day of August next, to the contracting for building a Warehouse at Choptank Bridge." The journal of the 1784–1789 State Council records that in "August of 1783, His Excellency William Smallwood Esquire . . . [issued] commissions to [Peter Harrington] appointed Inspector(s) Caroline County . . . [of] Choptank Bridge Warehouse." By 1902, Greensboro enjoyed a thriving commercial community with 29 businesses ranging from cabinetmakers to blacksmiths, from canners to druggists and general merchants. Although not large by today's standards, many of these industries were substantial to the growth and development of this community.

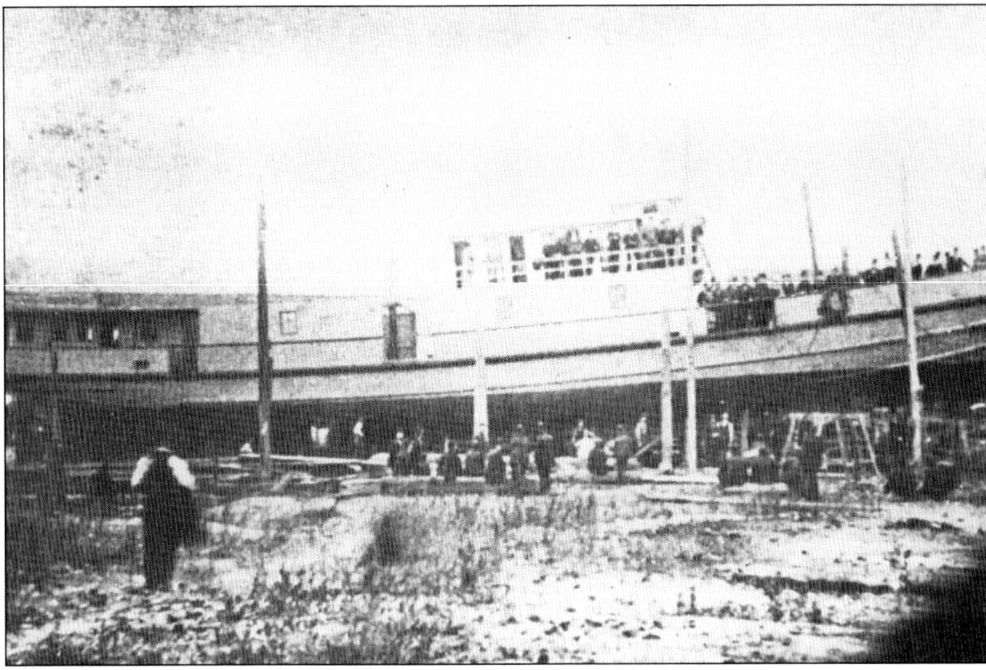

Shipbuilding was a primary industry and means of employment in Greensboro. This picture, taken prior to 1880, shows workers at Satterfield shipyard near the old bridge, building the SS *Greensborough*. (Courtesy Town of Greensboro.)

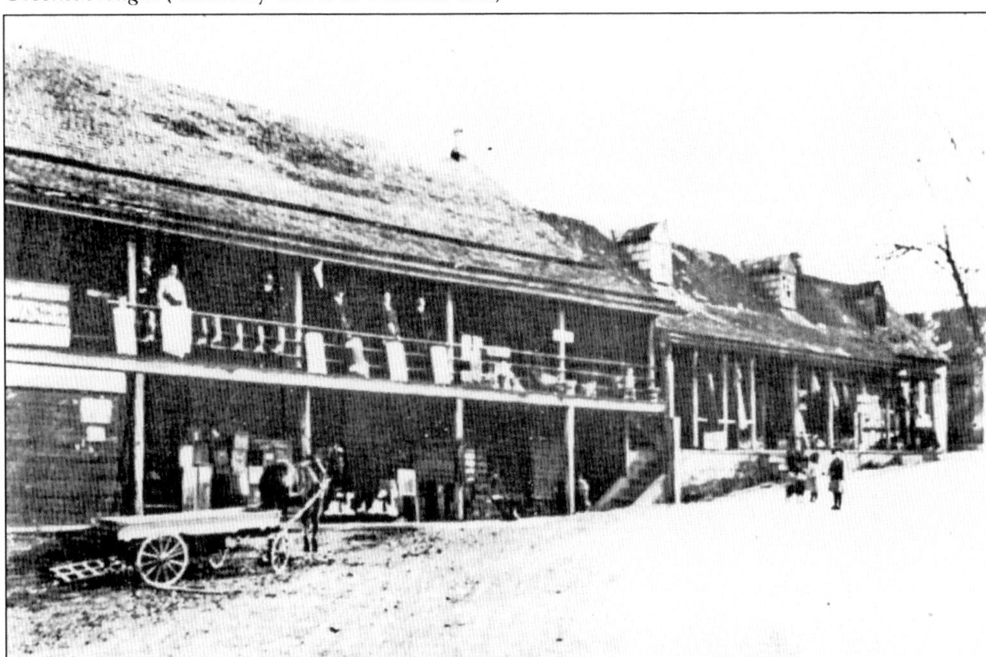

The firm of Satterfield and Moore, pictured around 1903 with the Peter Rich house behind to the right, built numerous ships, including the *Sarah Fort* in 1865. The A. *Denicke* (1874), *W. Churchman* (which sank in 1921), the *Dexter* (a bay schooner), the *Olive Davis*, and the *Greensboro* were all built in the 1870s. (Courtesy Town of Greensboro.)

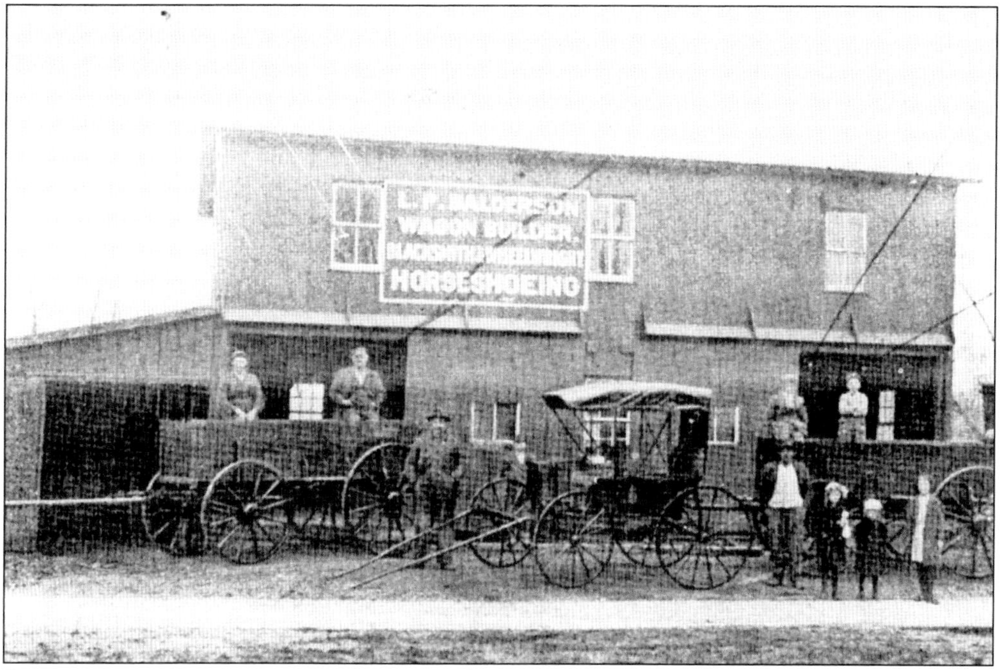

Even as improvements in transportation and agriculture were made, blacksmithing remained a strong, profitable industry. Employees, customers, and their families posed in 1912 at the Balderson Blacksmith Shop on Sunset Avenue at the river while waiting for their carriage. (Courtesy Town of Greensboro.)

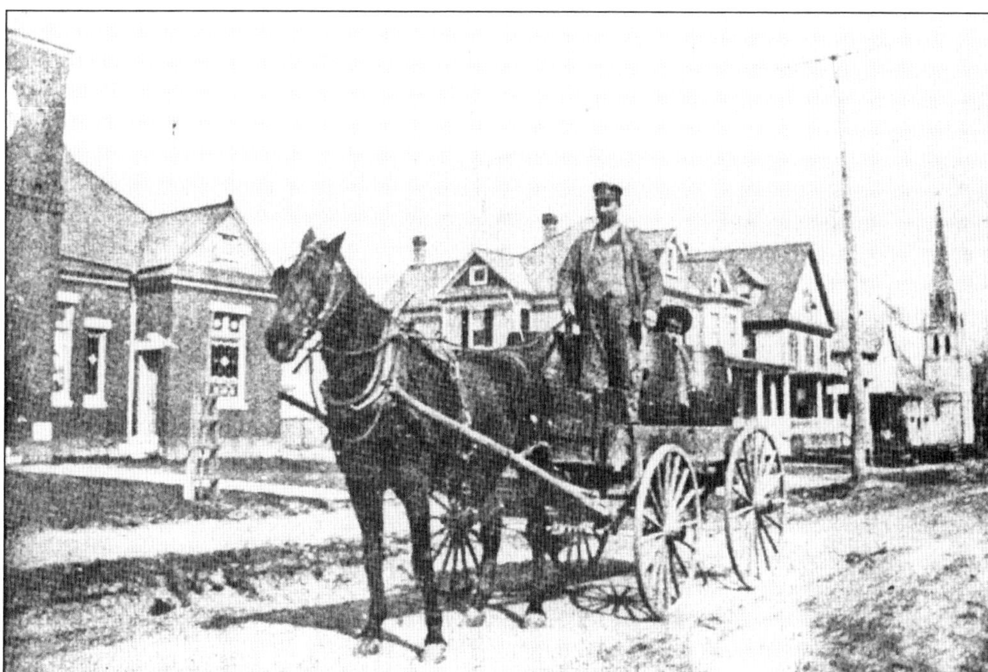

Horse and buggy were a common sight delivering products throughout the town. (Courtesy Town of Greensboro.)

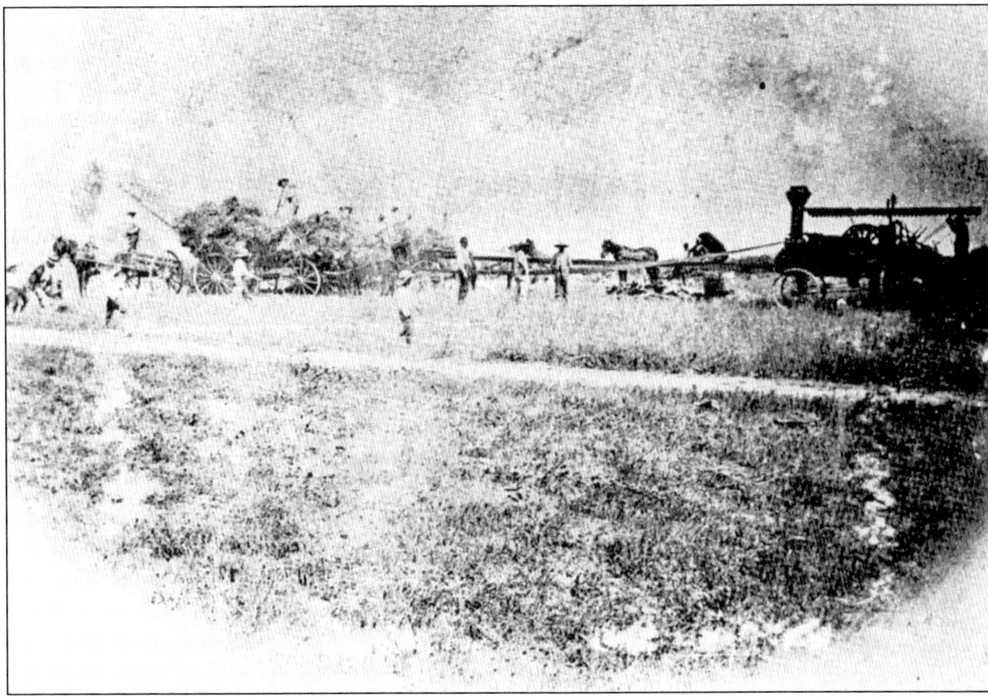

From its beginnings, the area around Greensboro has seen agriculture as a primary industry. This 1880 picture reflects the struggles of wheat threshing at this time. (Courtesy Town of Greensboro.)

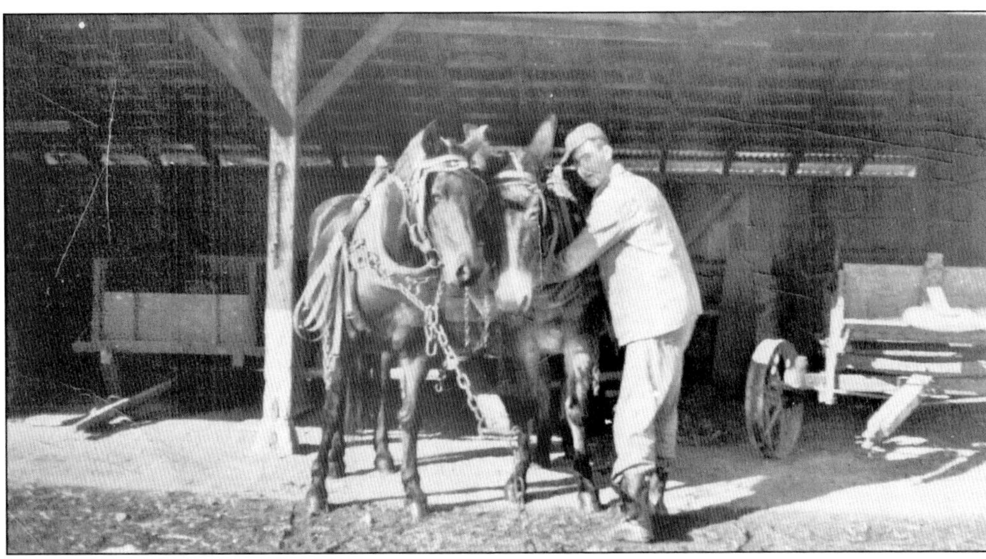

Junior Dukes feeds his horses and prepares for a day in the fields around 1940. (Courtesy Joan Cesarini.)

Planting and sowing, the old-fashioned way, with horses pulling the wagon, continued well into the 20th century. (Courtesy Joan Cesarini.)

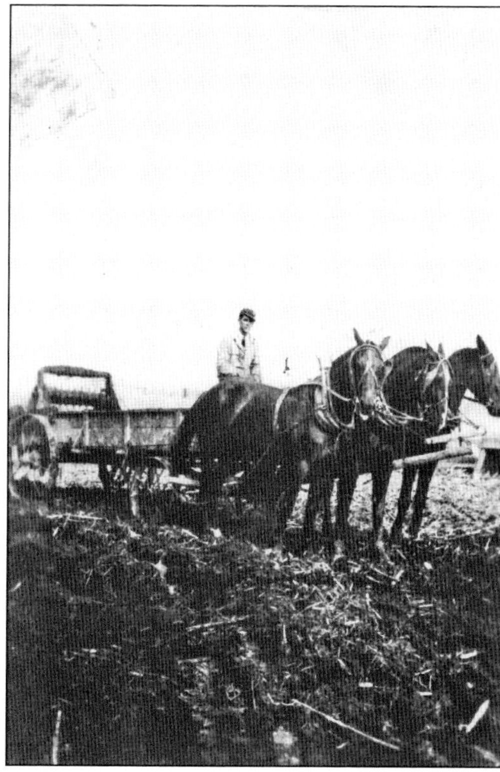

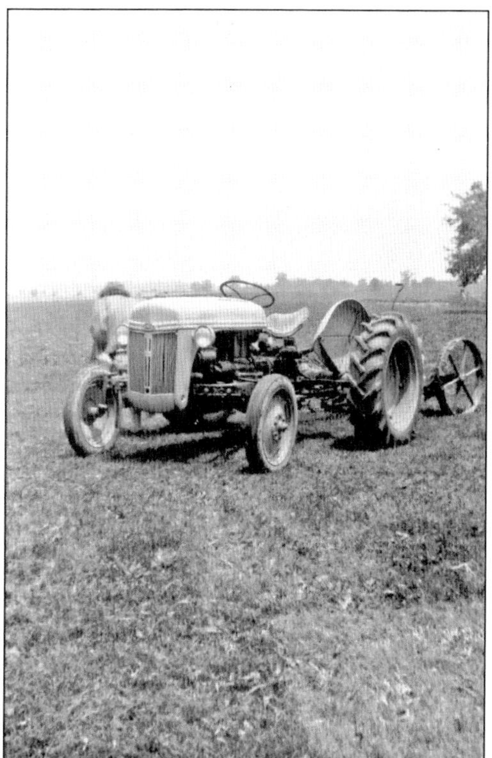

Ralph Dukes, a local farmer shown around 1940, moved into the 20th century with his tractor. (Courtesy Joan Cesarini.)

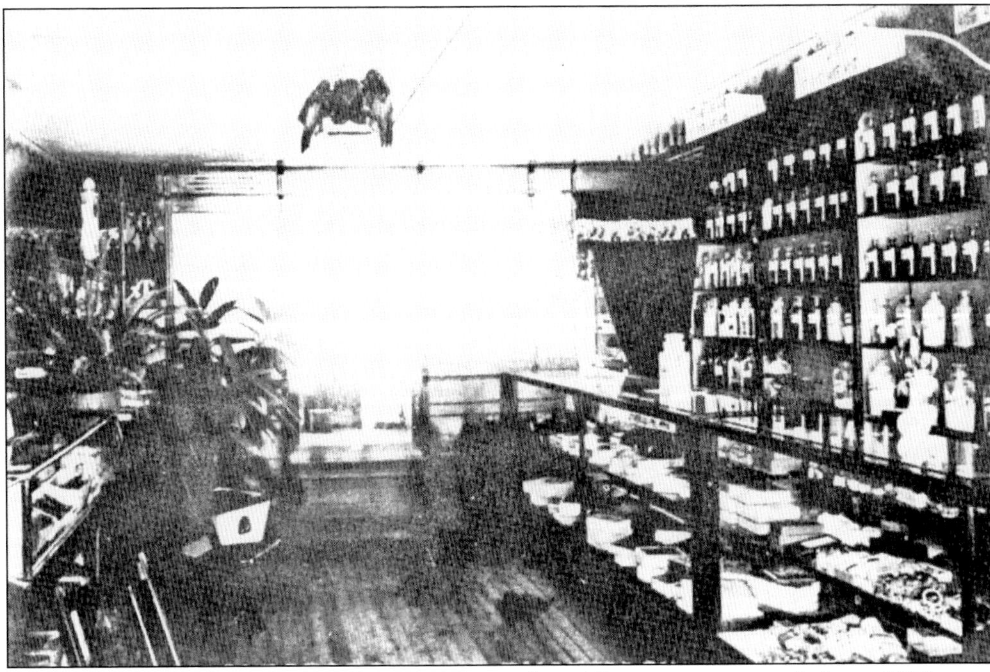

General merchandise stores such as the Greensboro Pharmacy, pictured about 1900, were cornerstones to the survival of the community. (Courtesy Town of Greensboro.)

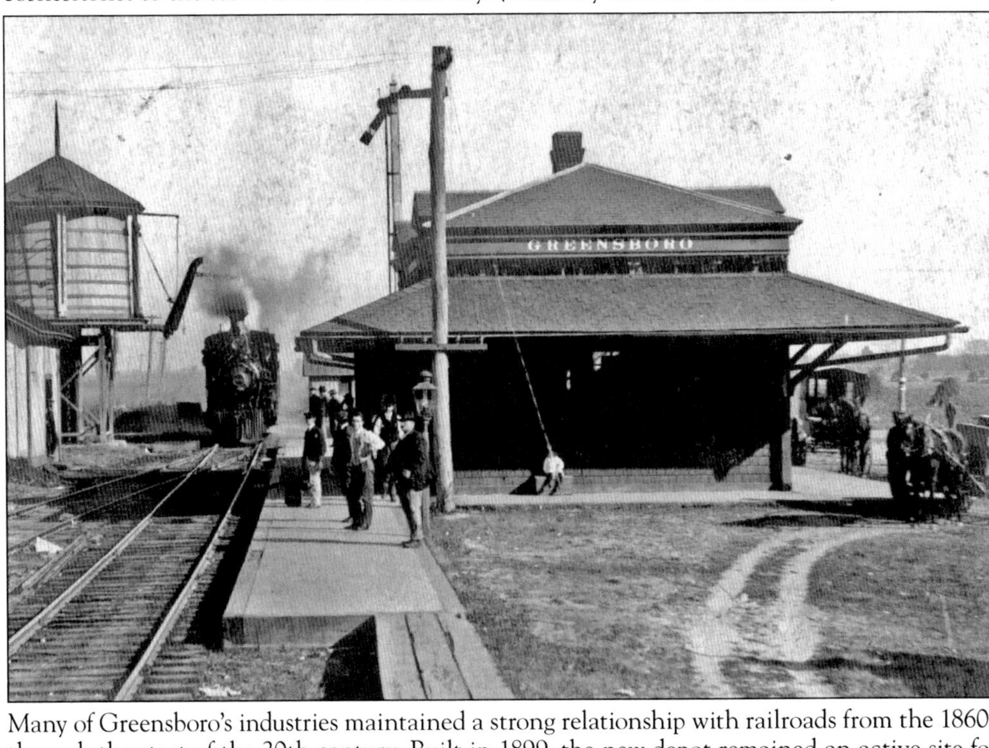

Many of Greensboro's industries maintained a strong relationship with railroads from the 1860s through the start of the 20th century. Built in 1899, the new depot remained an active site for train transportation throughout the area. This photograph was taken around 1908. (Courtesy Town of Greensboro.)

General merchandise stores remained popular through the mid-20th century. Burt Hobbs stands in front of his general store (right), which was located at Sunset Avenue and Granby Street. But the citizens had to shop early, as Burt had no lights in his store at all. The building was destroyed by fire in 1952. (Courtesy Town of Greensboro.)

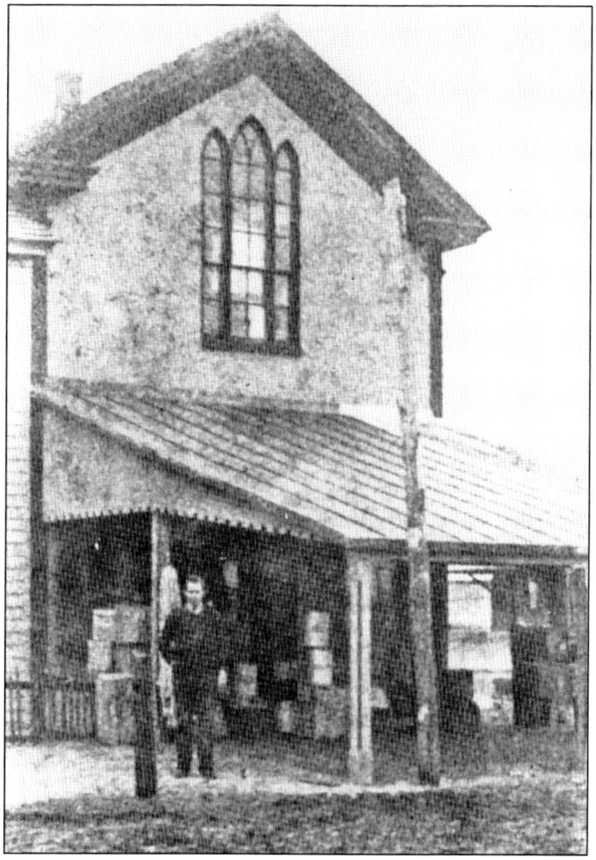

This commercial building below was constructed by Dr. John E. Lobstein in 1878 to house a drugstore and a hardware store. The second floor of this building contained a theater known as Mozart Hall, which was used for stage plays and for other functions of various community organizations. The A. W. Brumbaugh Department Store occupied the building from 1910 to 1966, followed by Gray's Appliances and Gray's Gas. (Courtesy J. C. Reveal.)

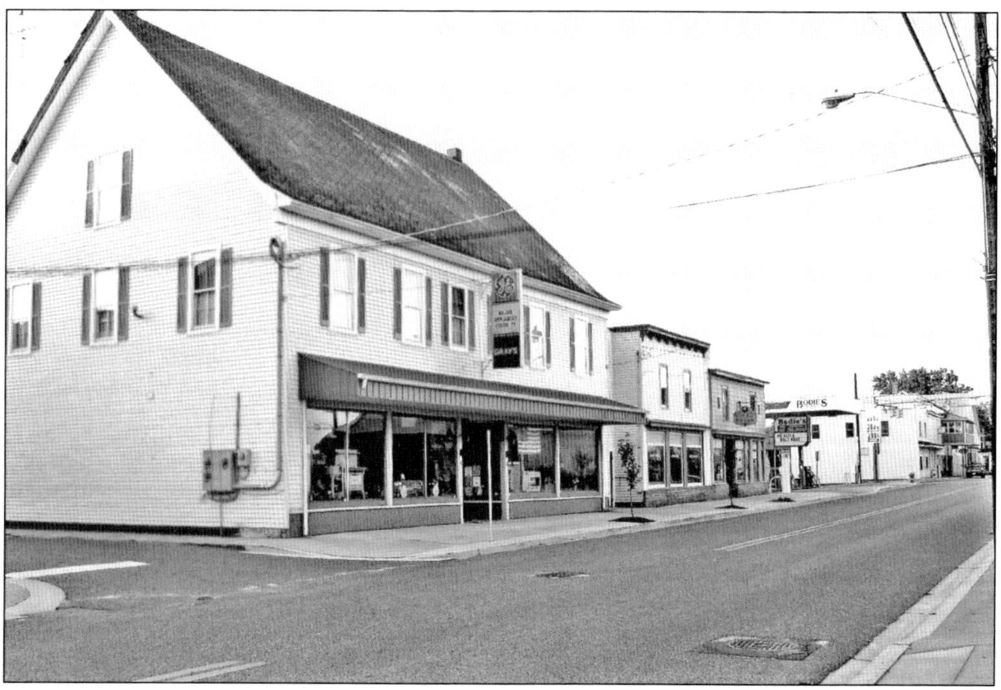

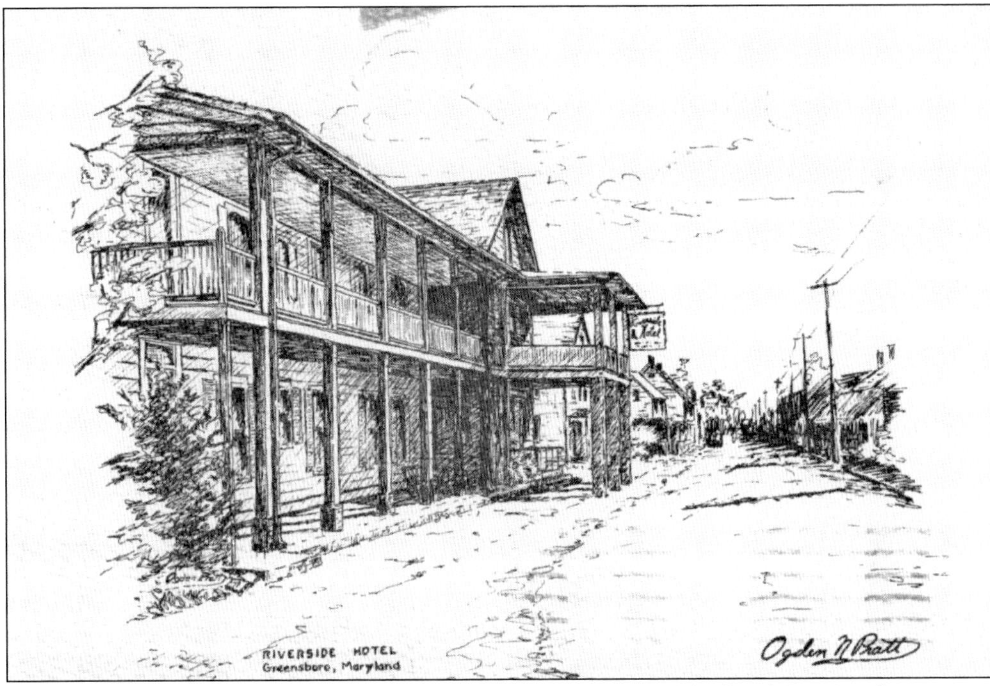

The Riverside Hotel stationery provides a glimpse into the history of this hotel. Bea Czuchrey, owner, used this piece of stationery to write a letter to the *Times Record* explaining the circumstances of the hotel closing during periods when tourism was down. (Courtesy *Times Record* newspaper.)

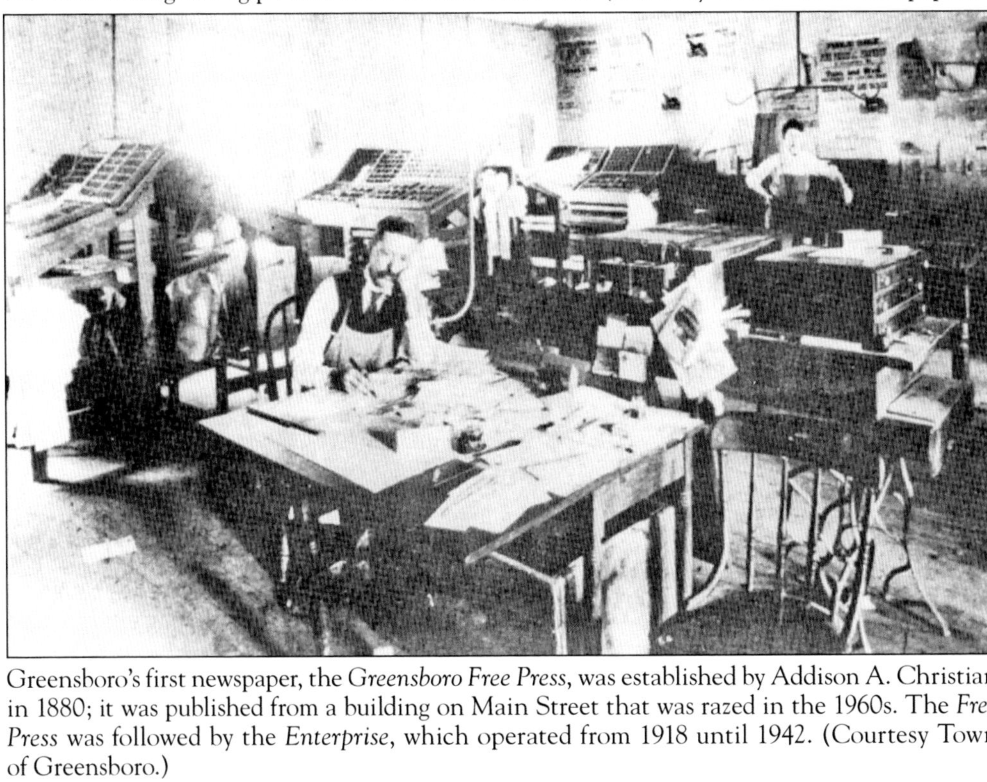

Greensboro's first newspaper, the *Greensboro Free Press*, was established by Addison A. Christian in 1880; it was published from a building on Main Street that was razed in the 1960s. The *Free Press* was followed by the *Enterprise*, which operated from 1918 until 1942. (Courtesy Town of Greensboro.)

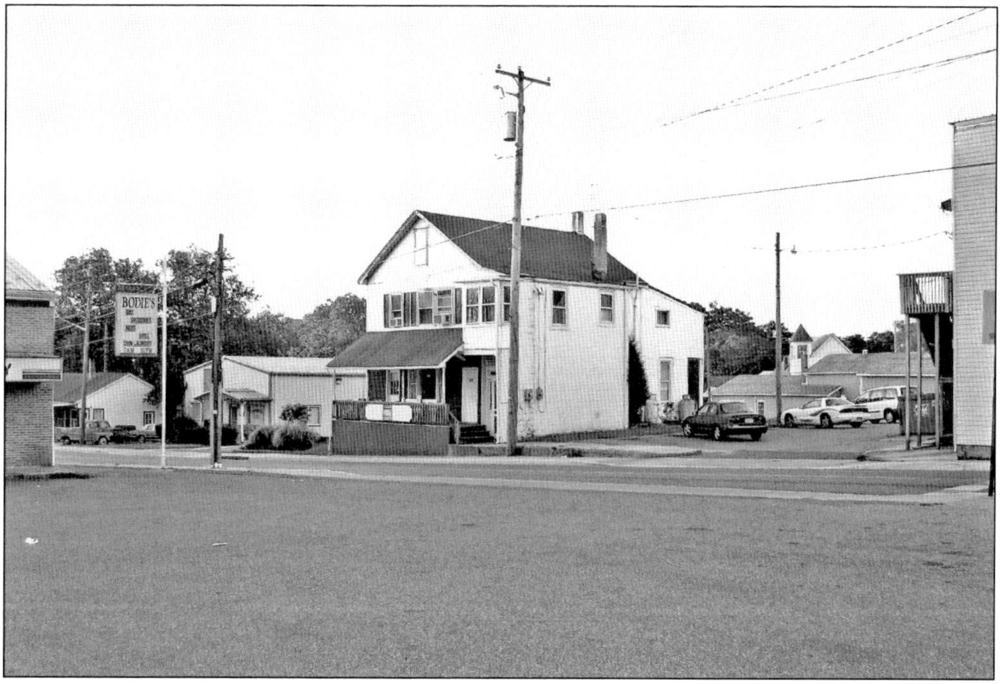

This building, on Sunset Avenue just east of Four Corners, originally served as one of the newspaper offices. As the newspaper business moved away from Greensboro, this building experienced a variety of uses, including a local florist's shop. (Courtesy Town of Greensboro.)

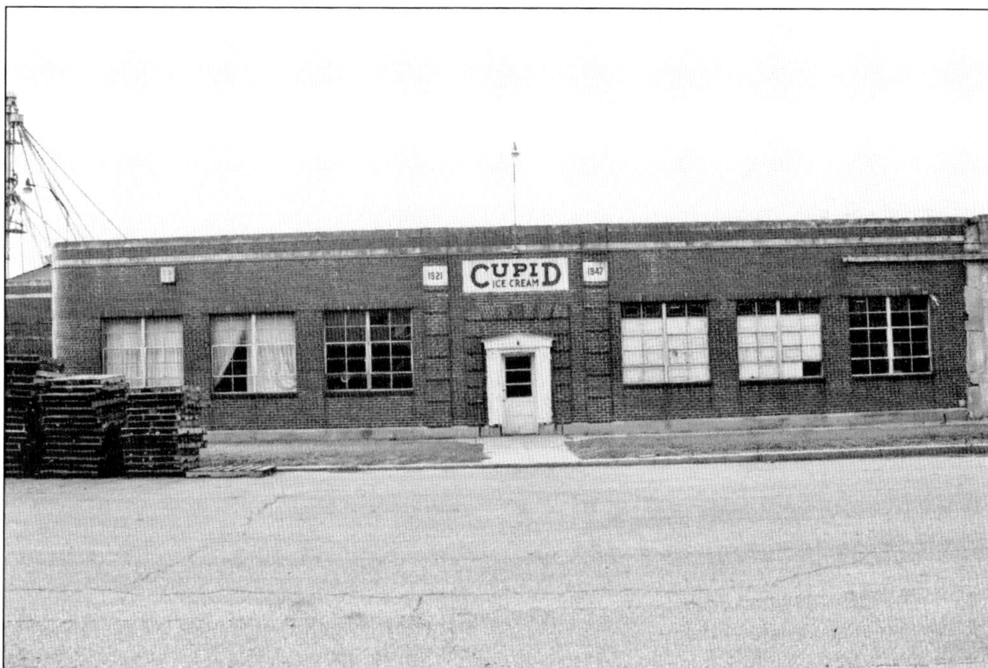

Cupid Ice Cream Company served the residents of Greensboro from 1921 until 1947. Although the company closed many years ago, the building remains in the West Greensboro Industrial Park. (Courtesy Cheryl Jones.)

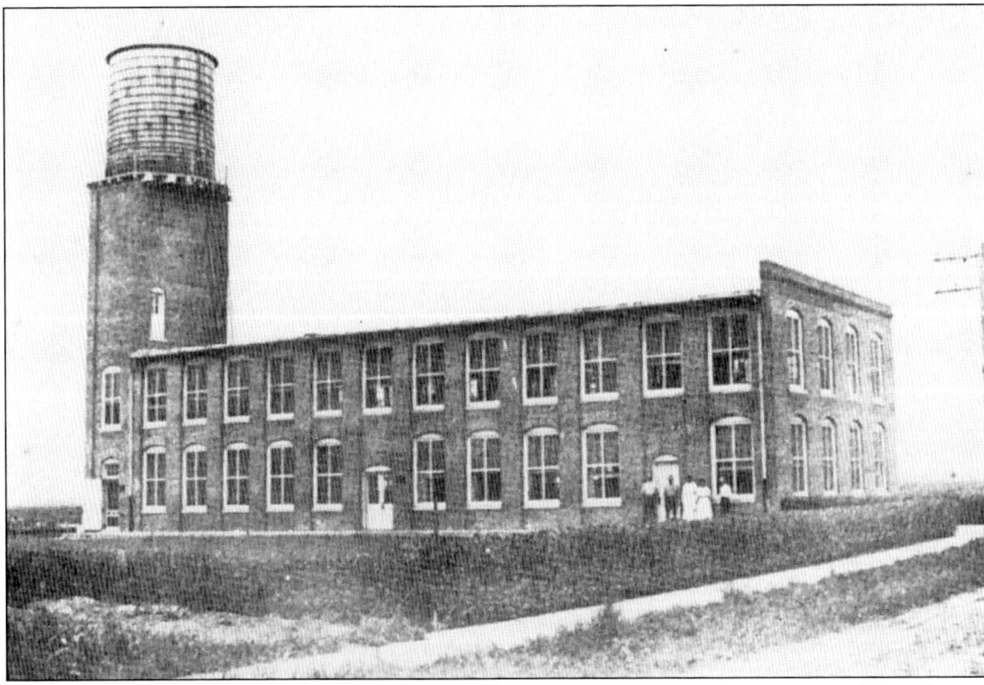

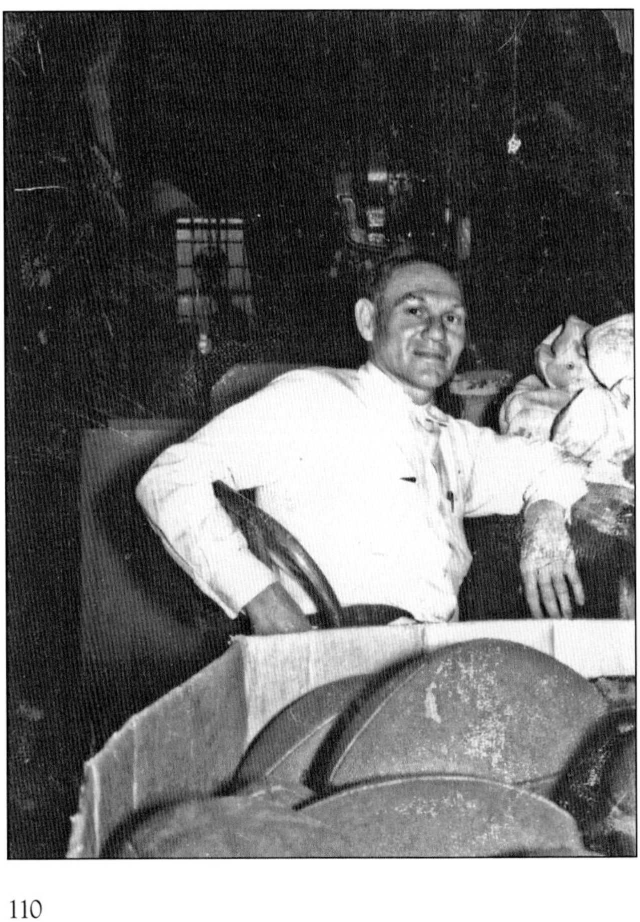

The glove factory (above), Allgreen Manufacturing Company, was located on Cedar and Church Streets. It later became George A. Reach Sporting Goods Company—a sporting goods manufacturer that produced a variety of major sports equipment, such as baseball gloves, baseballs, and basketballs. This building has undergone several renovations and changes in ownership. The building remains much the same as it is seen in this picture. (Courtesy Town of Greensboro.)

Resse Bickling enjoys a break from making official footballs at the George A. Reach Sporting Goods Company. (Courtesy Jean Gardner Warren.)

Pete Beumont provided quality control and is seen here checking official baseball gloves made at the George A. Reach Sporting Goods Company. (Courtesy Jean Gardner Warren.)

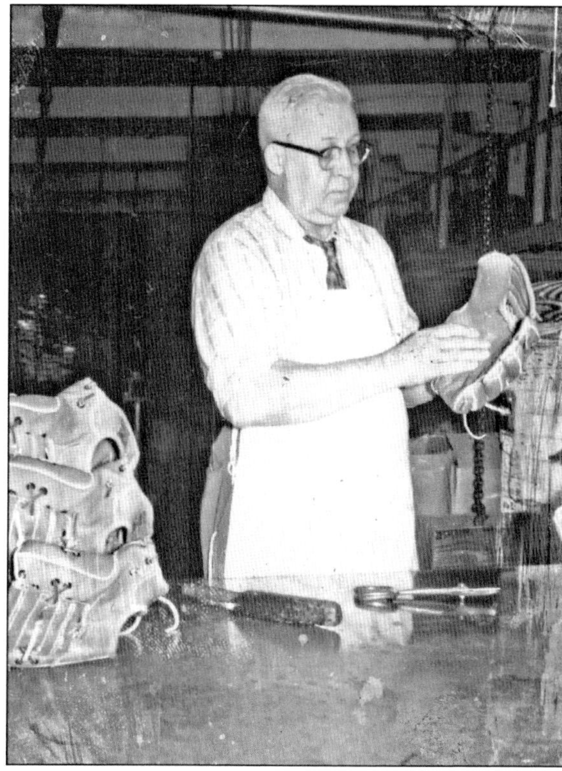

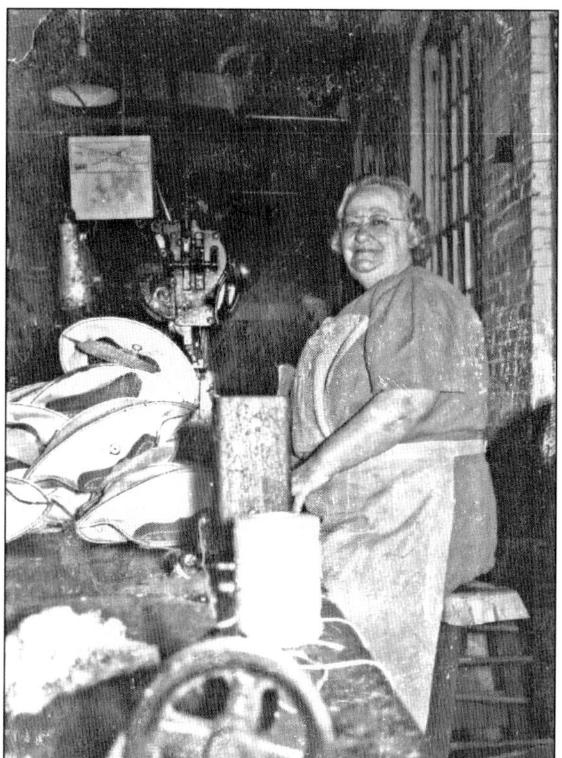

Florence Thornton works at the George A. Reach Sporting Goods Company, a business that provided employment for many of Greensboro's residents. (Courtesy Jean Gardner Warren.)

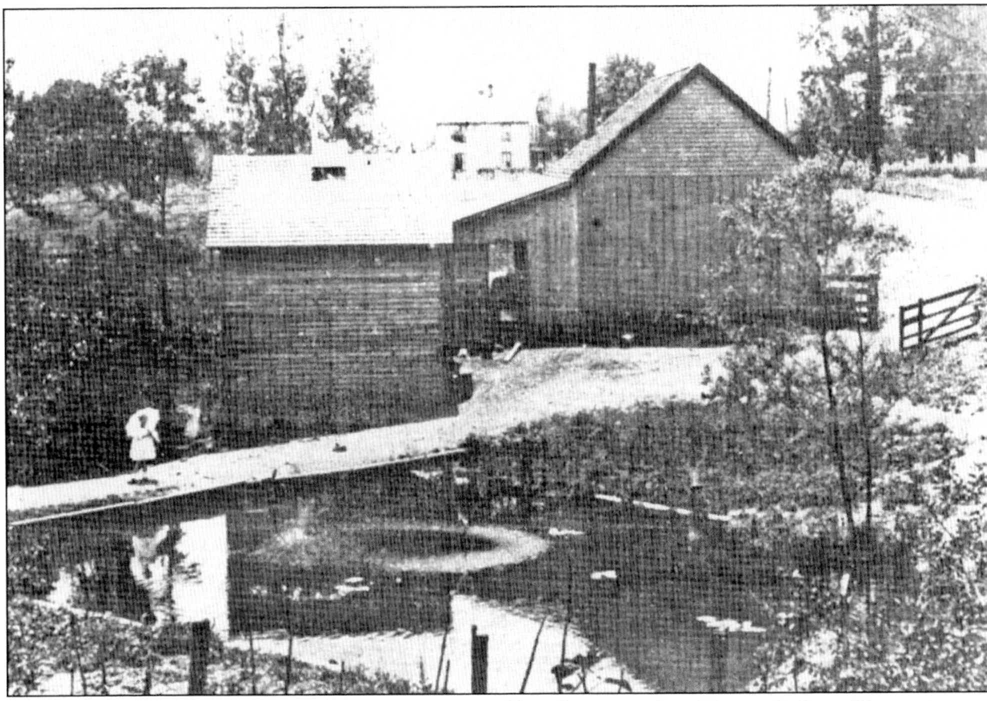

This ice pond and adjacent icehouse were owned by photographer Henry Cohee. He cut ice out of the pond during the winter and stored it in the icehouse to sell during the hot summer months. (Courtesy Town of Greensboro.)

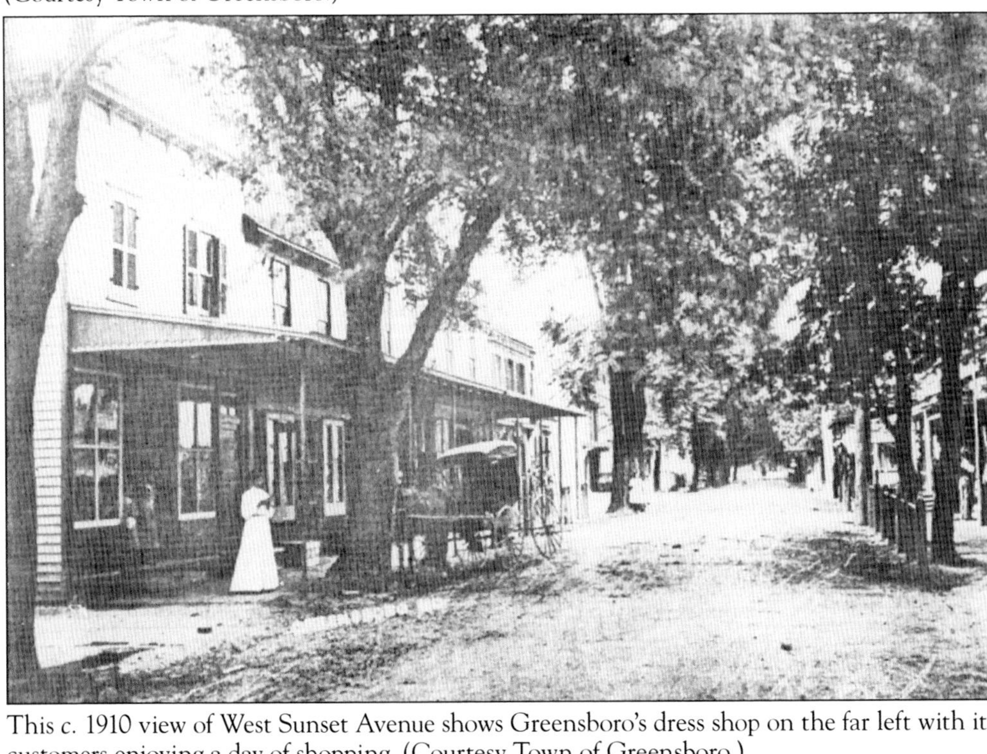

This c. 1910 view of West Sunset Avenue shows Greensboro's dress shop on the far left with its customers enjoying a day of shopping. (Courtesy Town of Greensboro.)

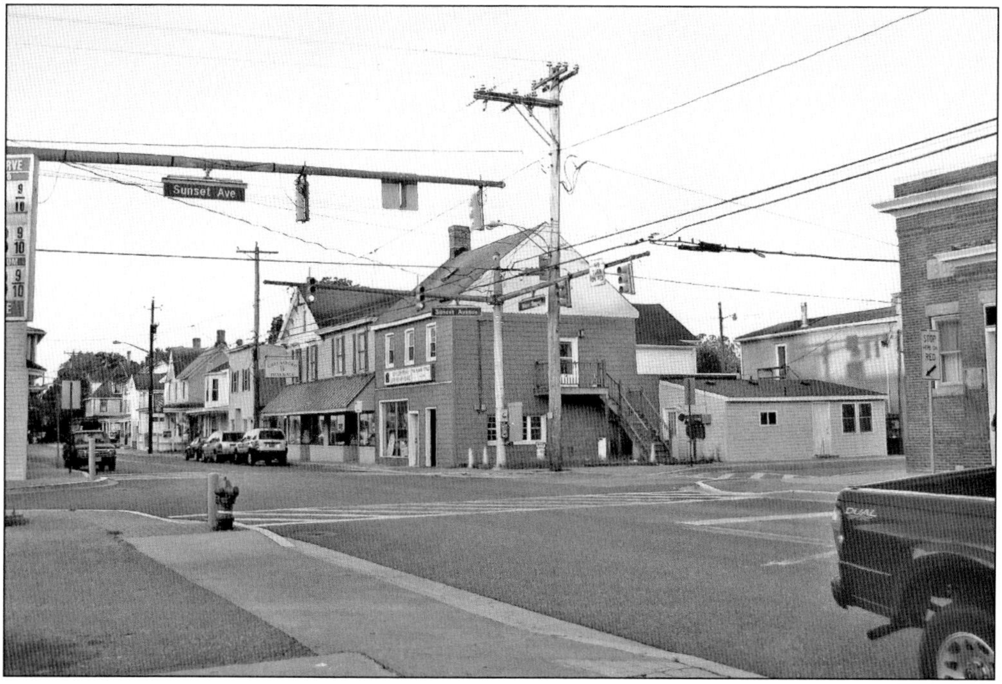

In 1793, this town lot (center) was sold to Nehemiah Townsend, an innkeeper and future major in the War of 1812. The remaining portion of the building possibly dates from Townsend's period. This building, also referred to as the Boyd Building, also served as the Farmers and Merchants Bank of Greensboro, the town's first bank. (Courtesy J. C. Reveal.)

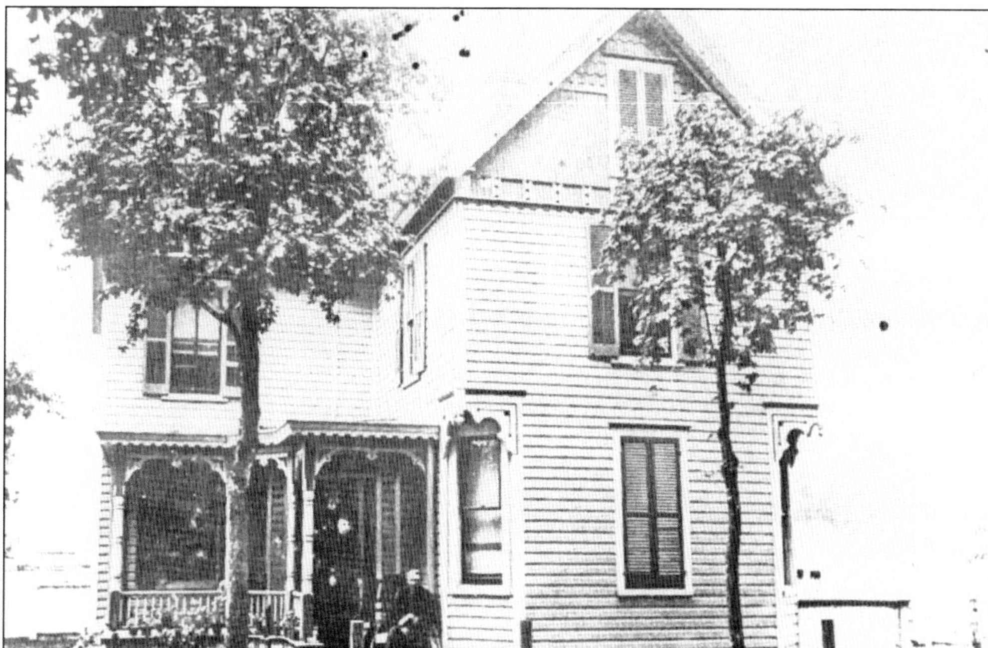

The M. M. Andrews house on Sunset Avenue was also the business of the local undertaker and cabinetmaker. (Courtesy Town of Greensboro.)

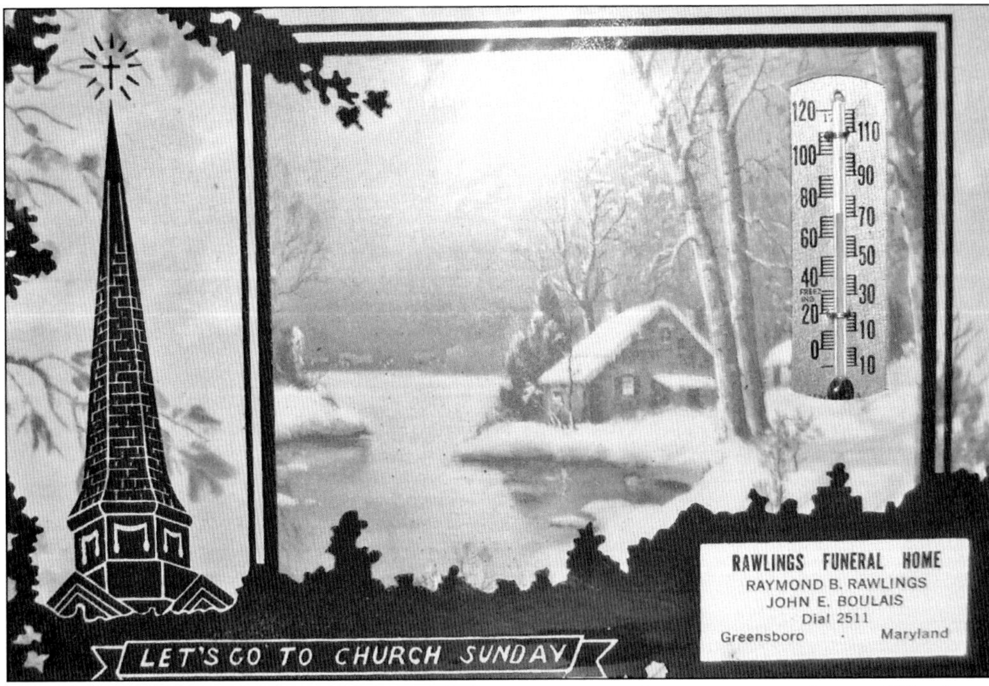

This gift from the Rawling–Boulais Funeral Home was a popular memento and can still be found in many homes around the area. Note the telephone number has no area code or exchange. (Courtesy Mary Kinnamon Jones Raughley.)

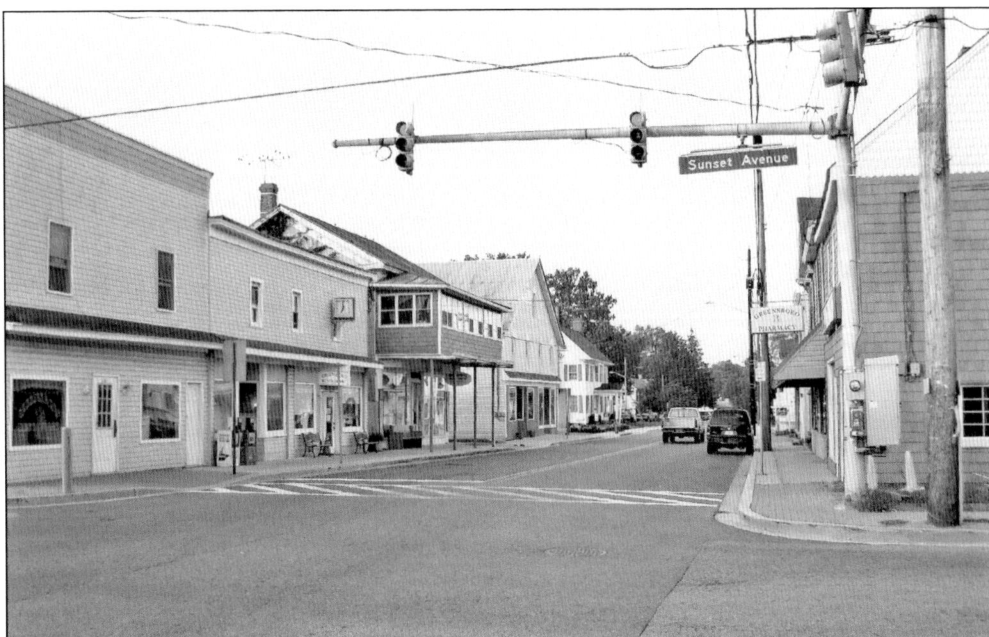

Four Corners today looking south on Main Street reflects a prosperous business community with the Greensboro Restaurant, Greensboro Trading Company, and town hall on the left, and the historic Boyd Building and Greensboro Pharmacy on the right. (Courtesy J. C. Reveal.)

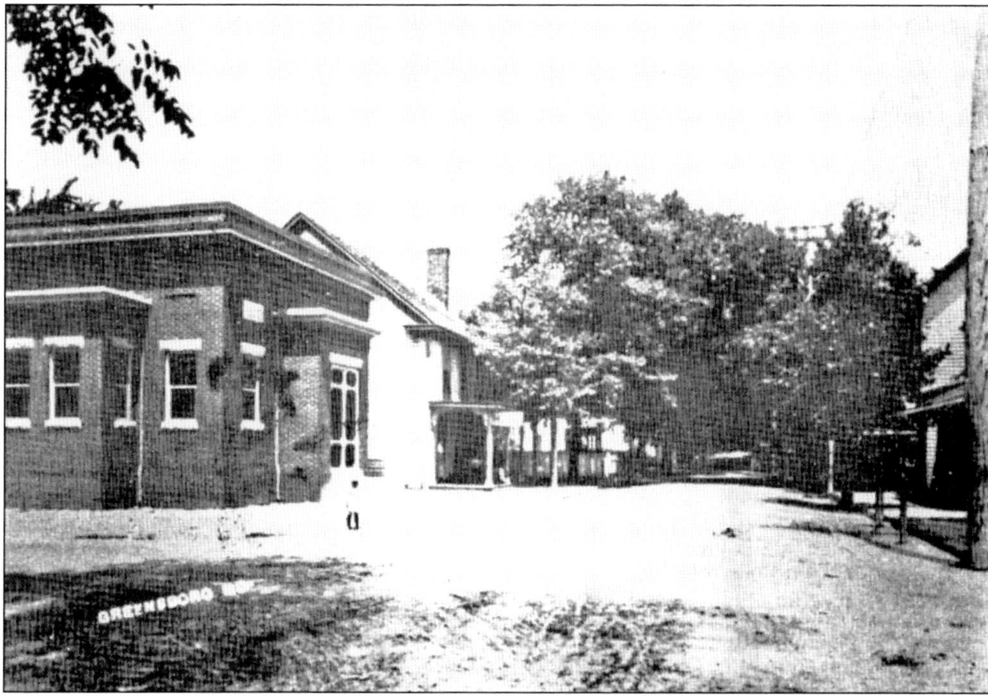

Caroline County Bank is pictured in 1906. Although the bank has undergone numerous changes, the original building remains much the same as it is seen in this picture. (Courtesy Town of Greensboro.)

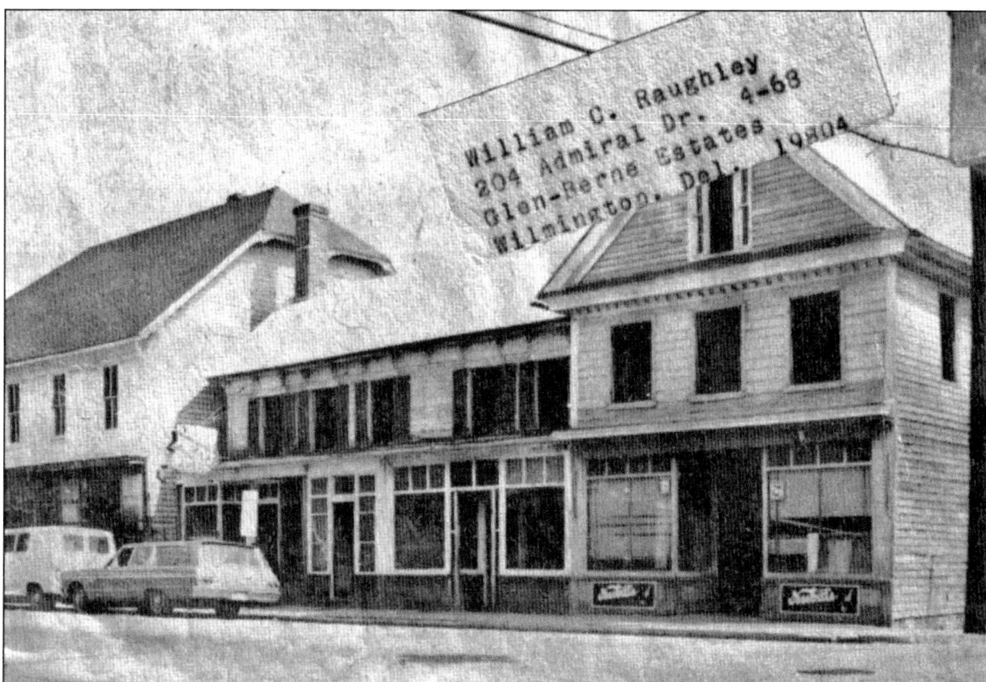

Urban renewal in Greensboro occurred on October 4, 1967. This picture shows the buildings at the northeast corner of Four Corners prior to their demolition. (Courtesy Cheryl Jones.)

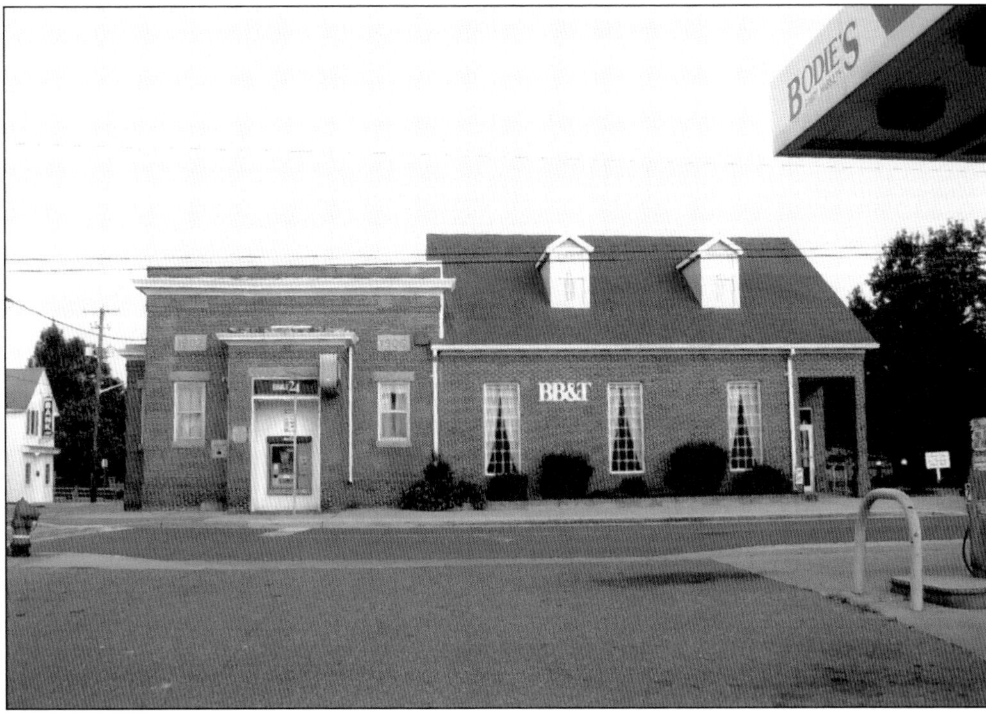

Branch Bank and Trust is seen here as it appears today. The original Farmers and Merchants Bank was the original portion of the building, on the left. (Courtesy J. C. Reveal.)

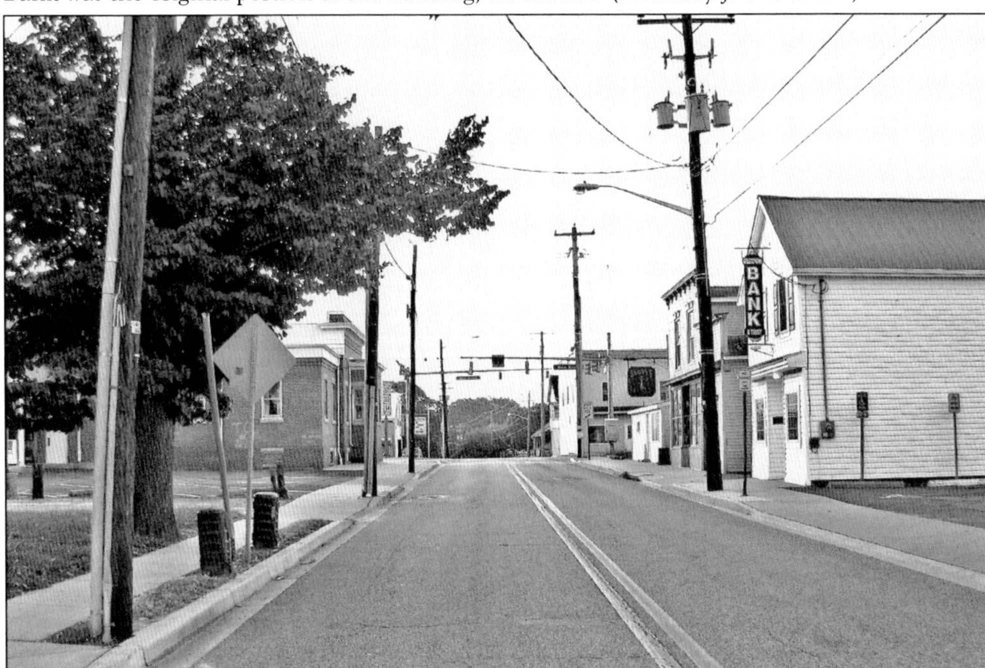

As Greensboro continues to appeal to both young families and retirees, new businesses have entered the marketplace. The Greensboro Bank and Trust recently opened its doors as the second bank to find a home in Greensboro. (Courtesy J. C. Reveal.)

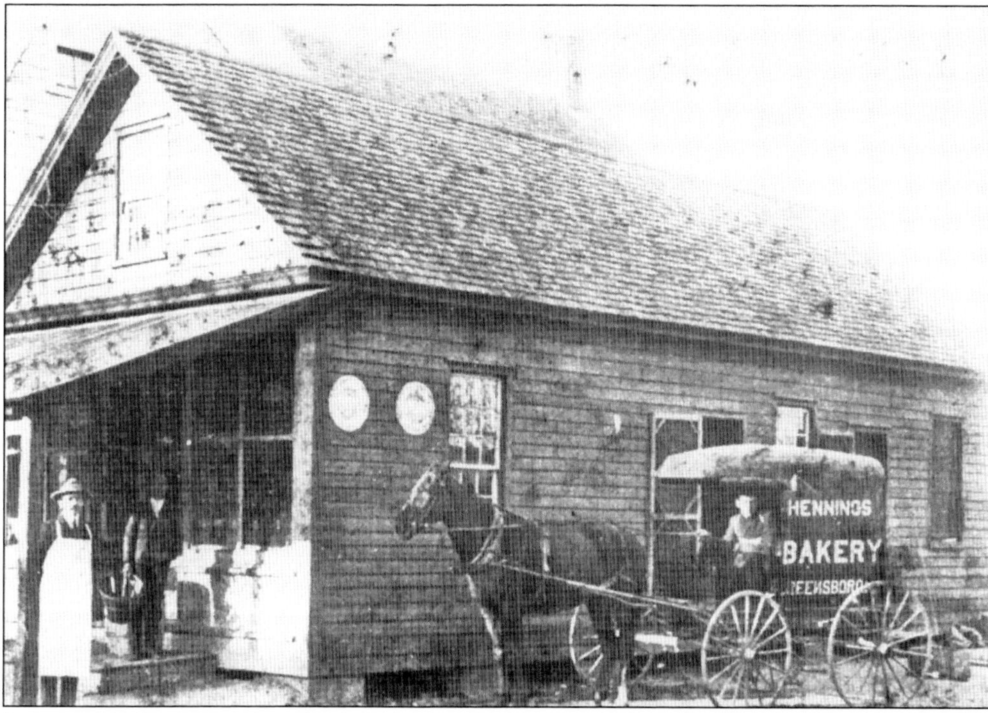

Hennings Bakery was a popular store in Greensboro. Mack Mitchell is in the carriage, with Fred Hennings to the left in the white apron. Note the spelling of "Greensboro," with the backward "N" on the side of the delivery wagon. (Courtesy Town of Greensboro.)

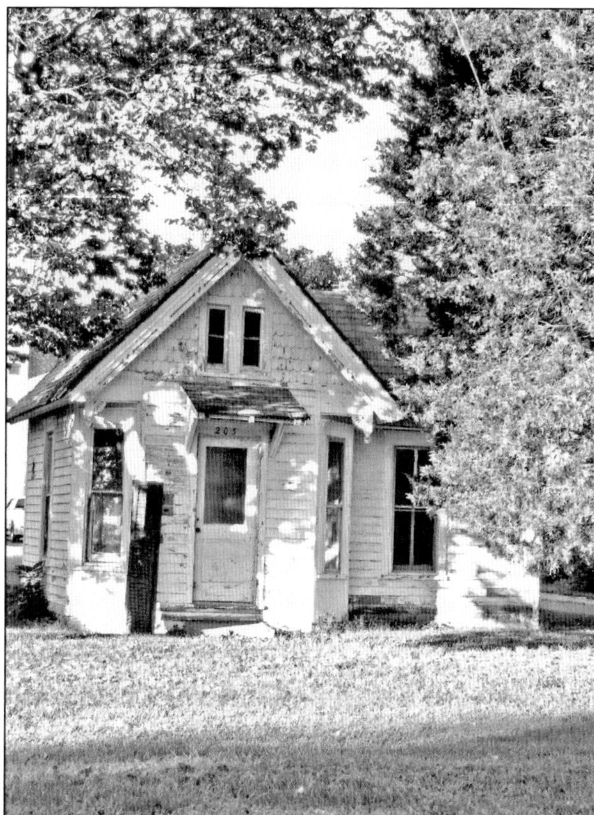

This small building was constructed by Benjamin House as his separate business office and eventually became a photography studio. It is being renovated and moved to the Curtis Harvey Memorial Park by the river, where it will become a tourism kiosk and meeting place for local groups and organizations. (Courtesy J. C. Reveal.)

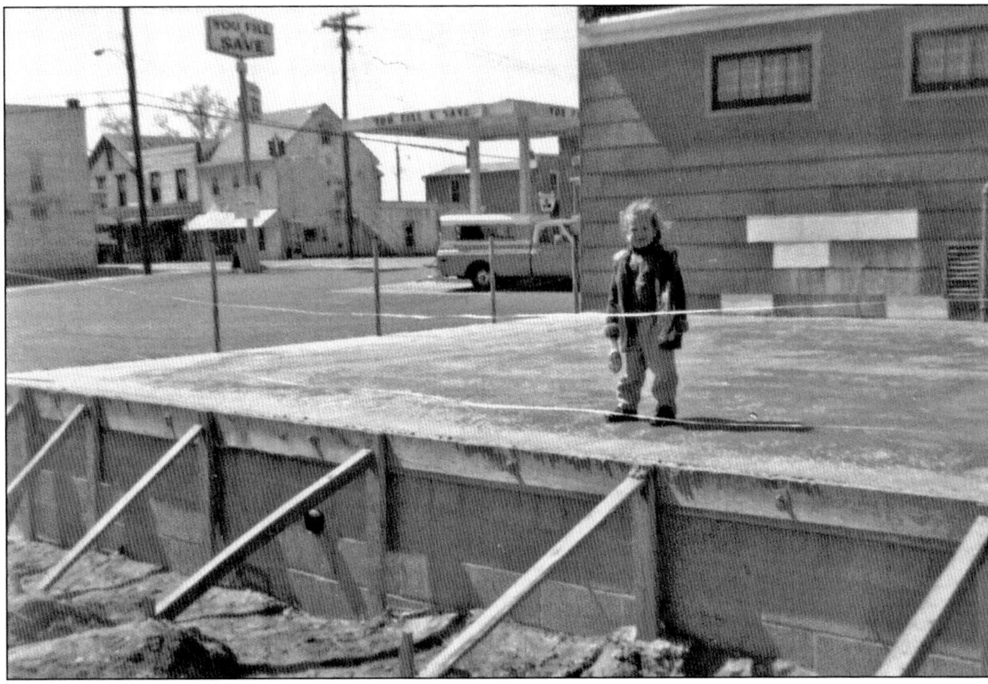

As communities grow, their faces change. In 1976, Mary Jones stands on the new loading dock being built at Four Corners. (Courtesy Cheryl Jones.)

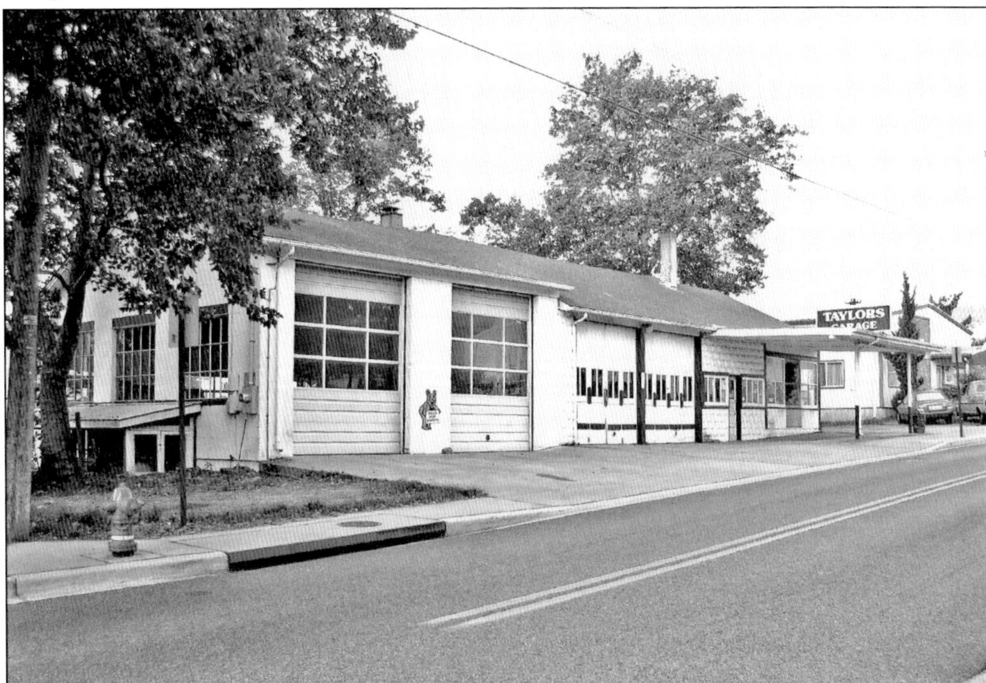

Some businesses in Greensboro have enjoyed a long life and support from residents, both newly settled and long-term. One of those is Taylor's Garage, which has been servicing automobiles since 1919 and continues to thrive with a devoted following. (Courtesy J. C. Reveal.)

Eight

GOLDSBORO
OUR FRIEND AND NEIGHBOR

Just three miles north of Greensboro on State Route 313 sits the quiet community of Goldsboro. Incorporated in 1906, the town of Goldsboro actually dates its beginnings farther back, to 1867. Originally named Oldtown, it was renamed Goldsboro in honor of Dr. G. W. Goldsborough, who was a prominent physician and landowner in the area. From the second half of the 19th century, when the Delaware and Chesapeake Railroad traveled through the town, and through the early part of the 20th century, Goldsboro enjoyed a thriving business community, including a cannery, a milk processing plant, and a feed mill among its major employers. Although major industry no longer exists, the town enjoys a strong government and a religious community and sees growth on its doorstep as citizens from across the Chesapeake Bay seek life on Maryland's Eastern Shore in serene and peaceful communities such as Goldsboro. Many of Greensboro's residents share religious and family ties with Goldsboro.

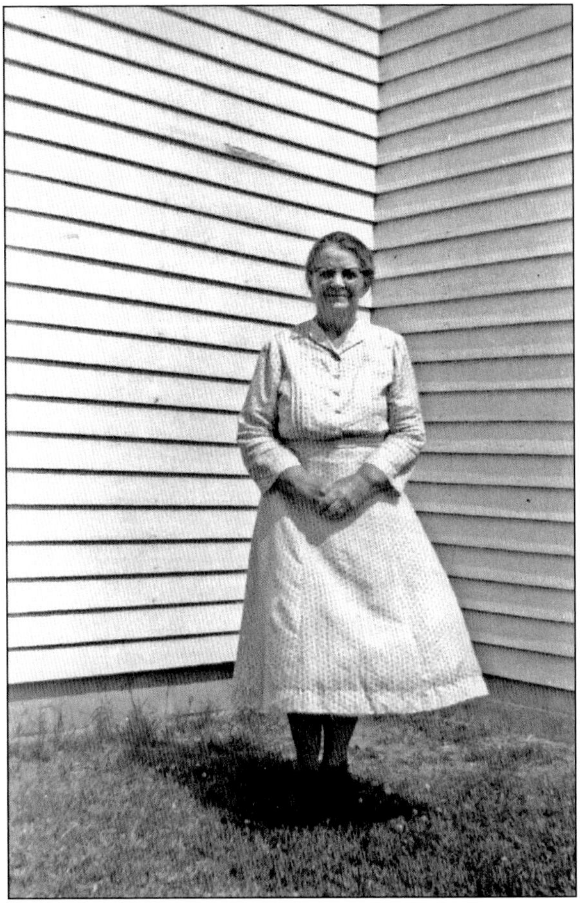

Rev. Mary Garrett stands at the Bethel Pilgrim Holiness church at Goldsboro in 1959. Garrett served the church from 1933 through 1939. She left for Cape Charles, Virginia in 1955 and she was recalled to Maryland where she worked to reestablish the Cedar Grove Church while serving the Bethel Pilgrim Holiness Church at Goldsboro. (Courtesy Virginia Bishop Jones.)

The *c.* 1955 Goldsboro Bible School class poses below at the Pilgrim Holiness church of Goldsboro. (Courtesy Virginia Bishop Jones.)

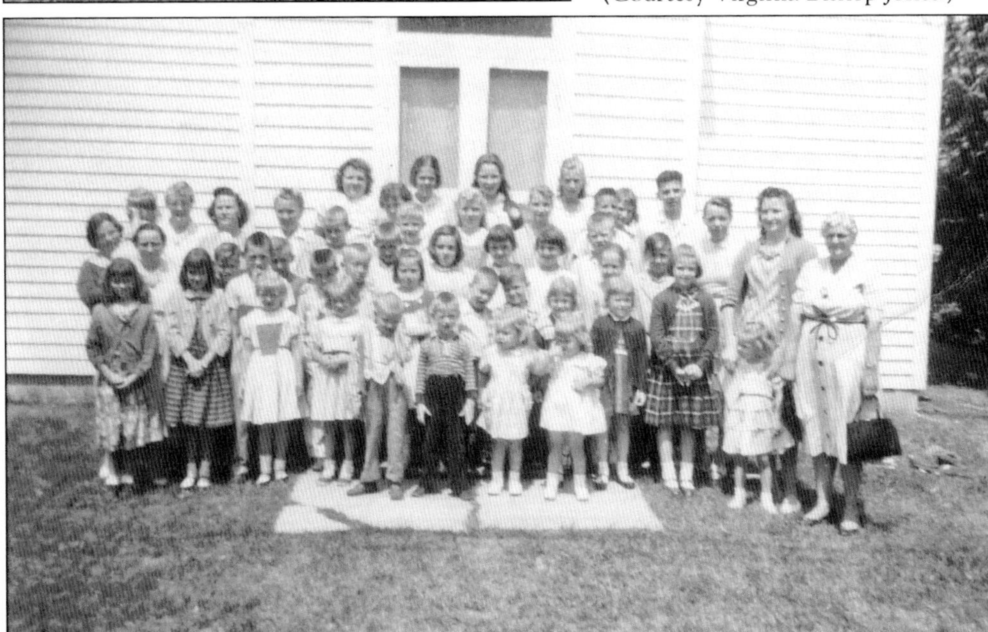

The Goldsboro Methodist church in November 1961 weathers one of the few major snowstorms that have come through the area. (Courtesy Mary Kinnamon Jones Raughley.)

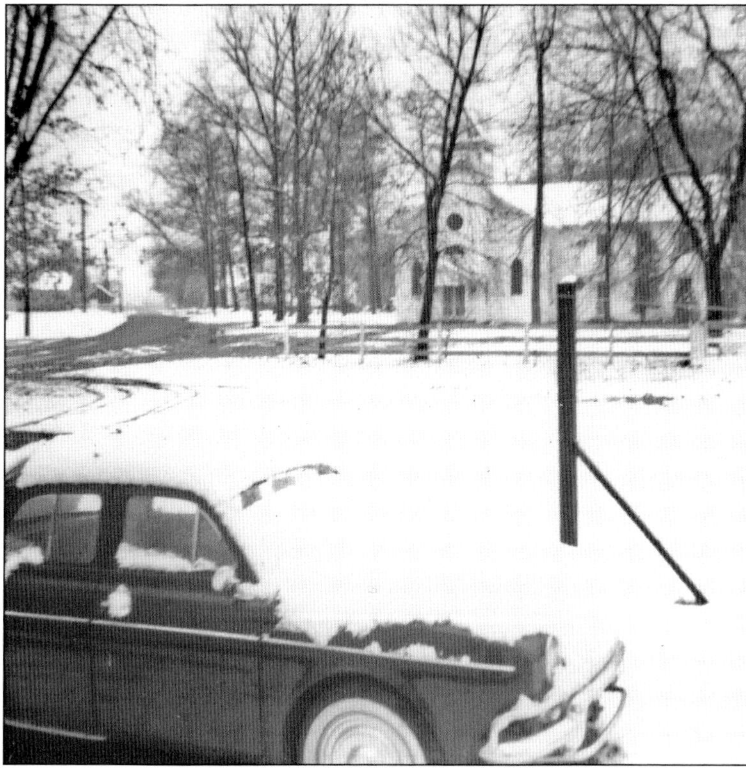

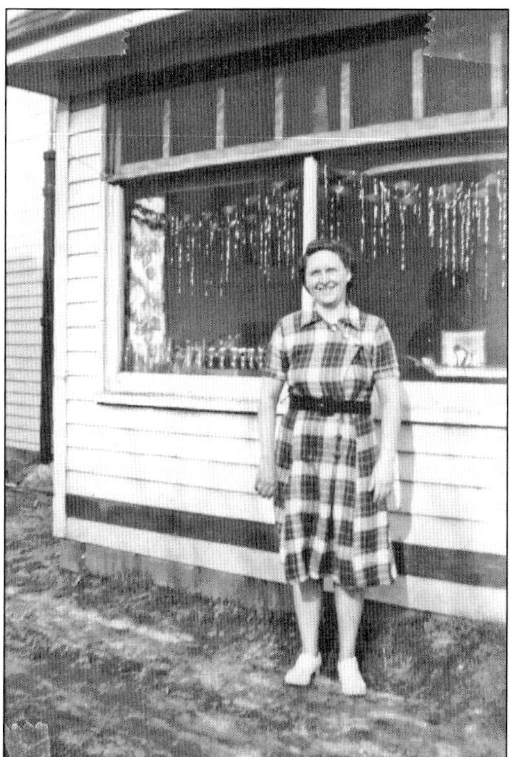

In 1948, Mary Kinnamon Jones poses in front of her restaurant, the Goldsboro Restaurant, a favorite haunt of locals and out of towners alike. Small business thrived in Goldsboro. (Courtesy Mary Kinnamon Jones Raughley.)

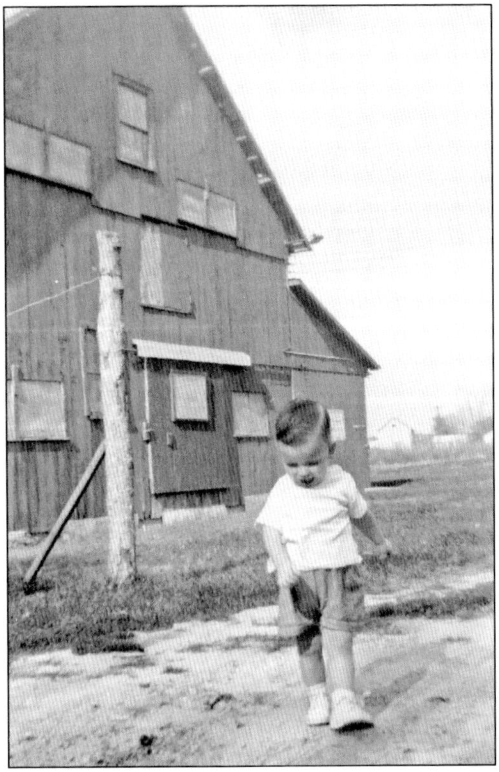

In Goldsboro, Jimmy Raughley plays in front of the DeWitt Cannery building in March 1957. By this time, canneries had become a thing of the past, leaving only the skeleton of their previous successful life. (Courtesy Mary Kinnamon Jones Raughley.)

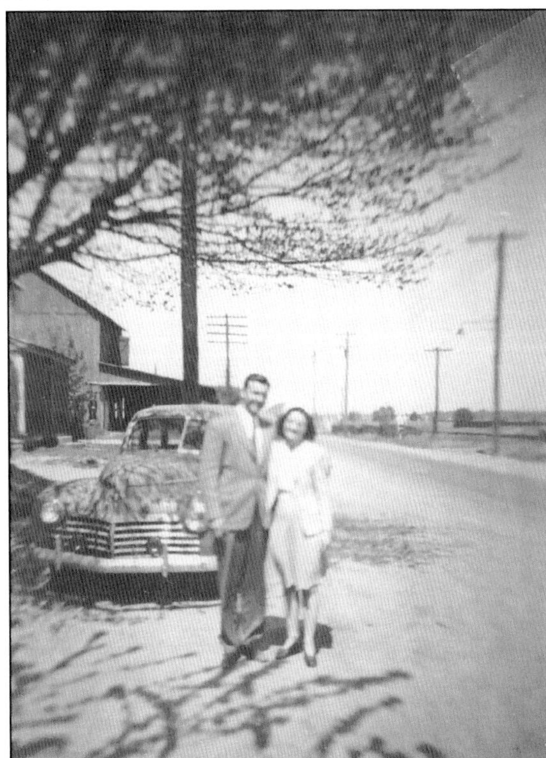

During the late-19th and early-20th centuries, canneries were a way of life on the Eastern Shore. This photograph, taken during World War II, shows Helen Murray and a male visitor who worked at the shipyard standing in front of the DeWitt Cannery, which thrived in Goldsboro at the time, providing employment for many residents. (Courtesy Mary Kinnamon Jones Raughley.)

Cooklyn Milk Plant trucker Norris Williamson poses in front of his truck in Goldsboro. This milk plant, like the Helvetia/Pet Milk plant in Greensboro, prospered during the middle of the 19th century. (Courtesy Mary Kinnamon Jones Raughley.)

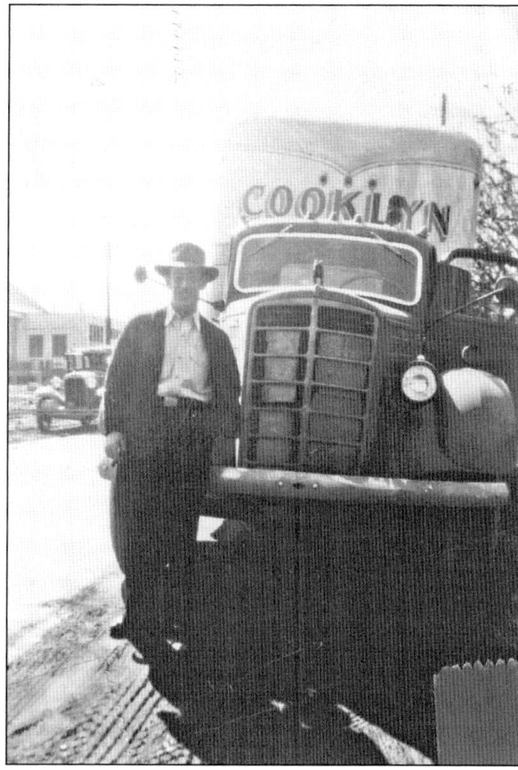

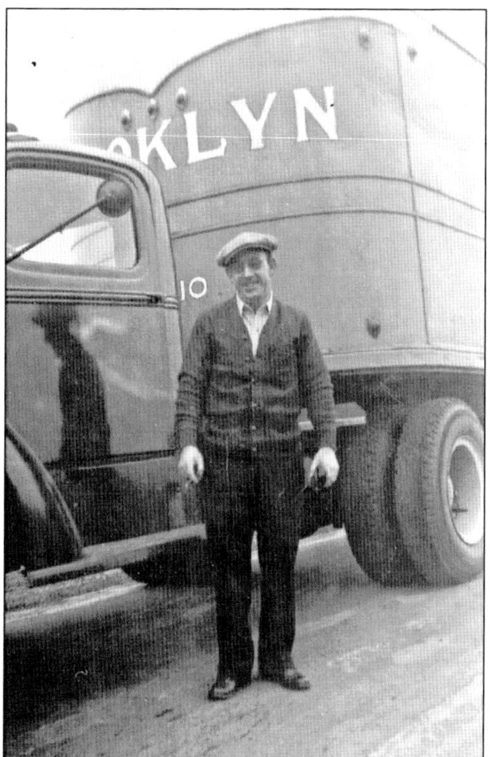

Milk plants experienced a brief life on the shore, with Helvetia/Pet Milk in Goldsboro and Cooklyn Milk Plant in Greensboro. Here trucker Norris Williamson stands in front of a Cooklyn Milk Plant delivery truck in the 1930s. (Courtesy Mary Kinnamon Jones Raughley.)

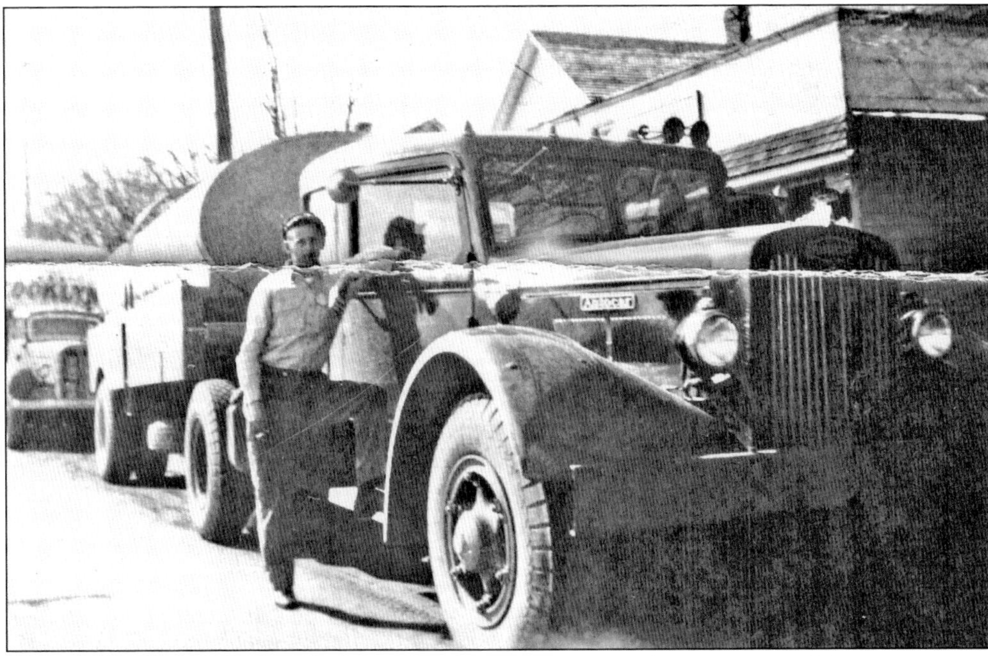

Another Cooklyn Milk Plant driver stands next to his truck in front of the Goldsboro Restaurant, a popular stopping place for drivers as they prepared to begin or end their day. (Courtesy Mary Kinnamon Jones Raughley.)

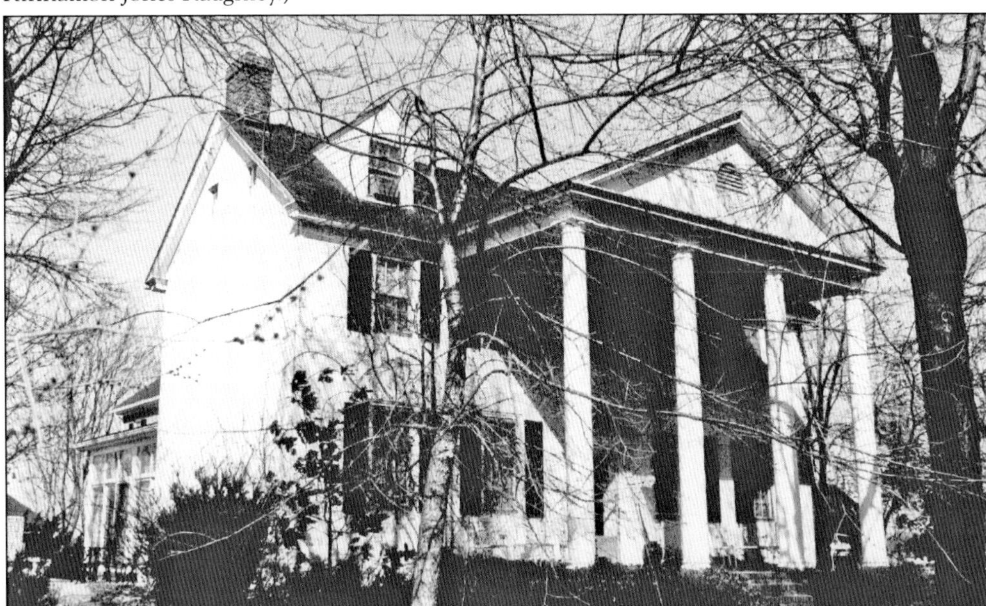

The Enterprise, built around 1840, was originally the property of the Culbreath family, and the farm was only recently named the Enterprise. The Doric portico and west extension are recent additions, dating from around the 1960s. Interior work is of the period in which it was built. This house is located on Jackson Lane, approximately one and a half miles northeast of Goldsboro. (Courtesy the Maryland Historical Trust.)

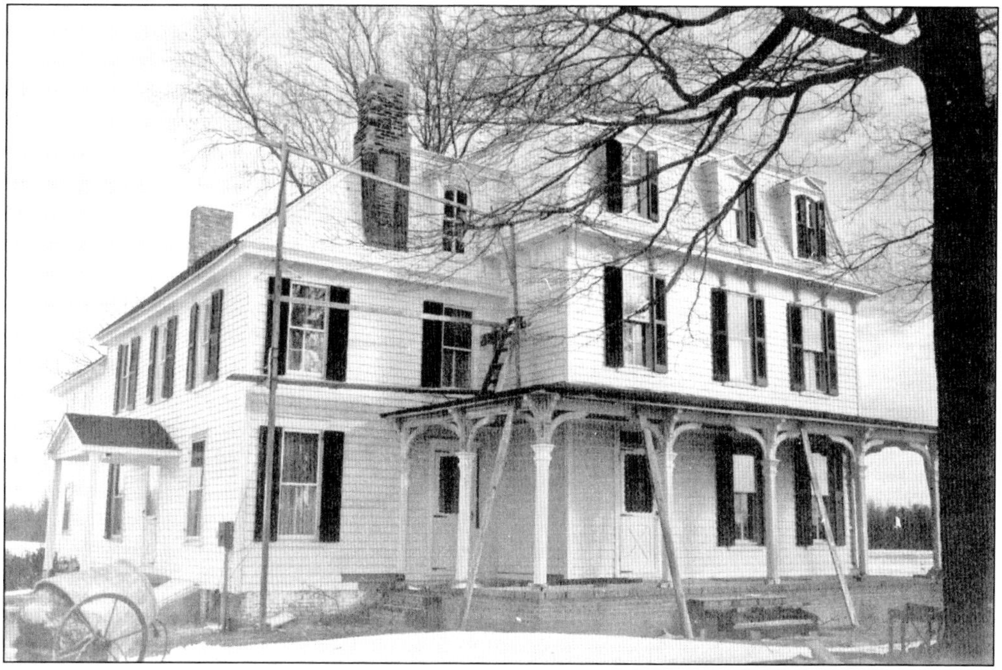

The Sherman Council house, with its mansard roof, reflects the Victorian style popular in Caroline County. Built in the late 19th century, it is located on Maryland Route 313 approximately one and a half miles south of Goldsboro on the way to Greensboro. (Courtesy the Maryland Historical Trust.)

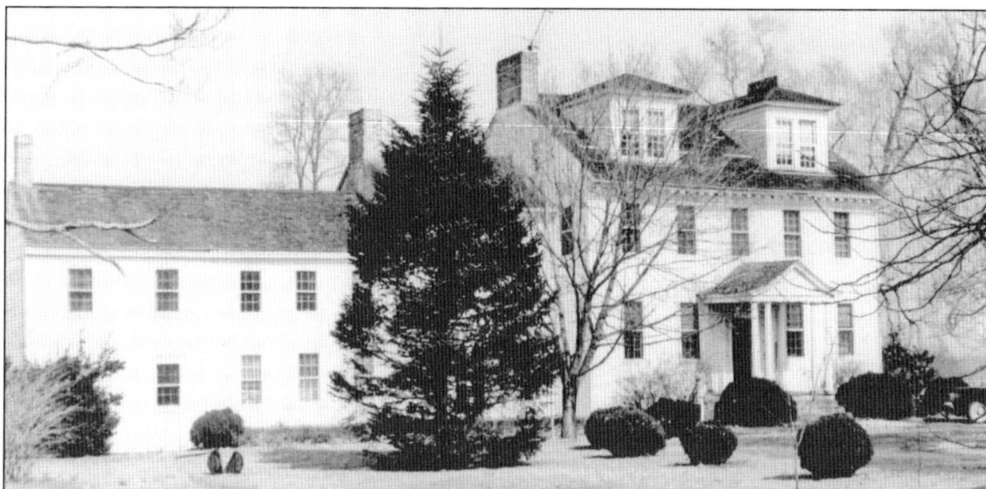

Thomas Hardcastle inherited his father Robert's wealth and property and further acquired an additional 1,268 acres of land in the area of Greensboro. Between 1778 and 1783, he built his home and named it Golden Bottom. Hardcastle served in the American Revolution in 1776 as quartermaster of the west battalion of the Caroline County troops. He was also a member of the Caroline County Committee of Safety, and after the war, he served as justice of the peace and of the county court. He married Henrietta Downes in 1756; they had two daughters and 10 sons. At some point around his death, the estate became known as Castle Hall. (Courtesy the Maryland Historical Trust.)

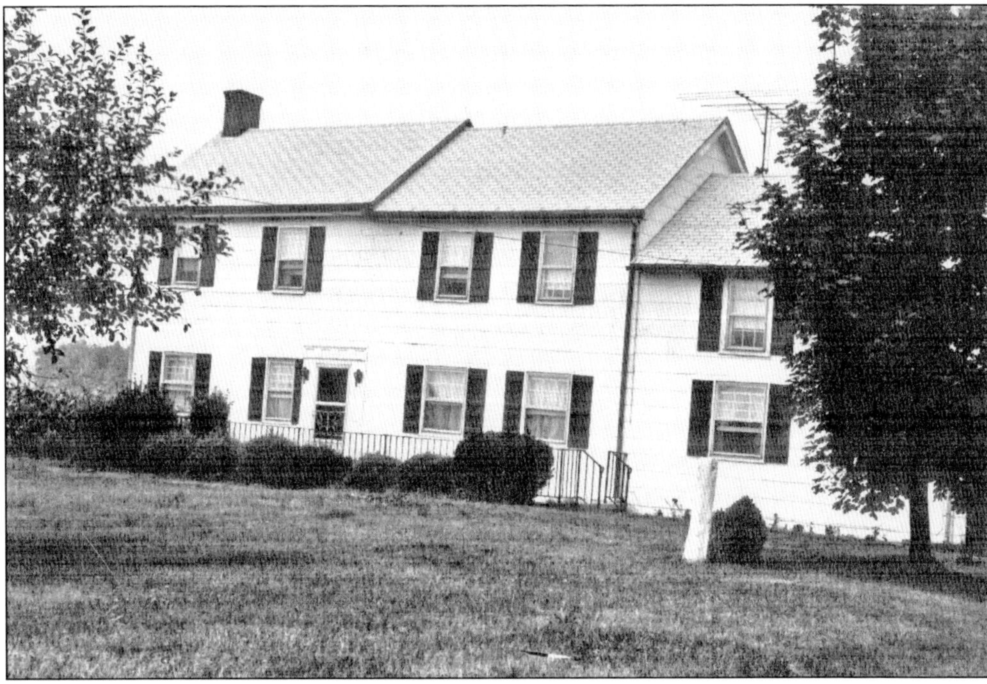

Jackson's Hardship sits between Greensboro and Goldsboro on Route 313.The original section of the house was built around 1830. It underwent extensive remodeling in the early 1960s. (Courtesy the Maryland Historical Trust.)

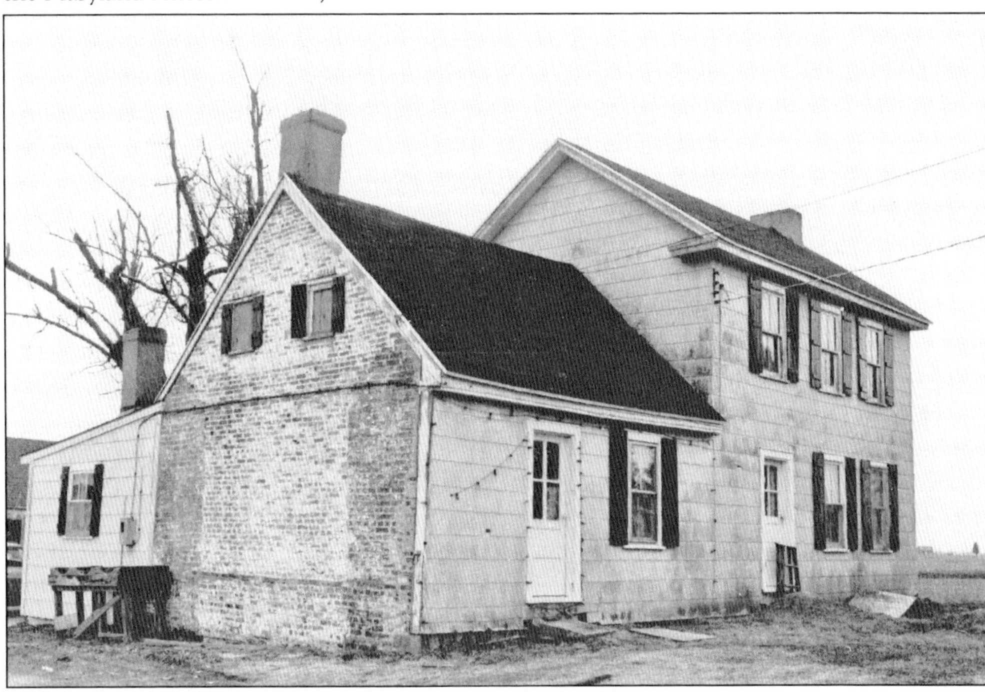

The T. Noble Jarrell house is located two miles south of Goldsboro on property known as Jackson's Hardship. The original house was built around 1800; the several additions reflect the changes that occurred as a result of growth. (Courtesy the Maryland Historical Trust.)

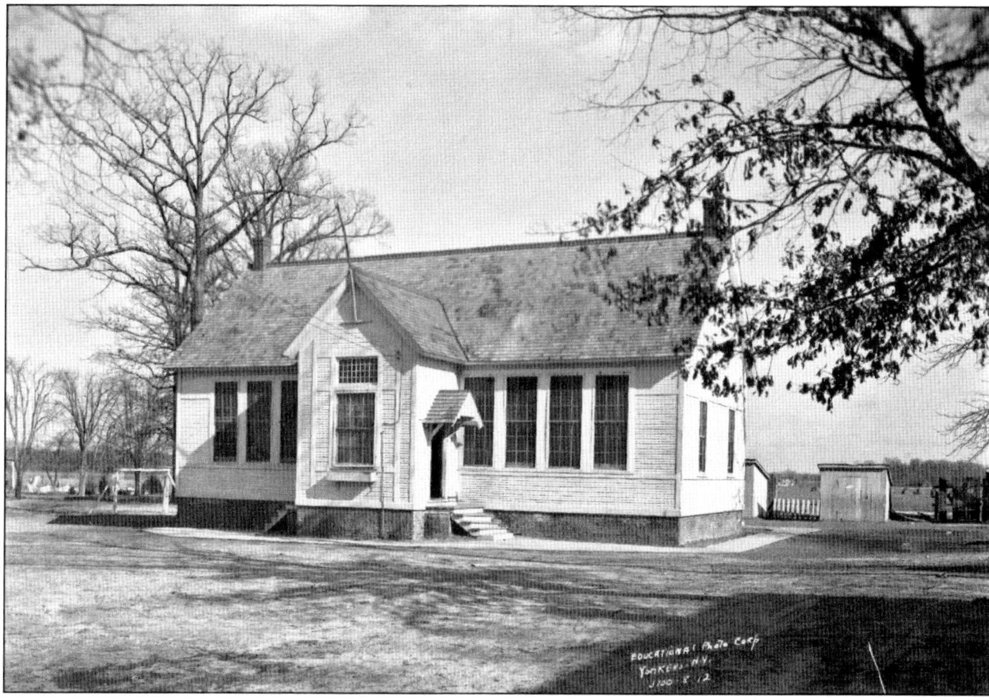

Although Goldsboro was a smaller town than Greensboro, it still had a school. This c. 1938 picture above shows the Goldsboro School, which provided educational opportunities for elementary school-age children. (Courtesy Caroline County Board of Education.)

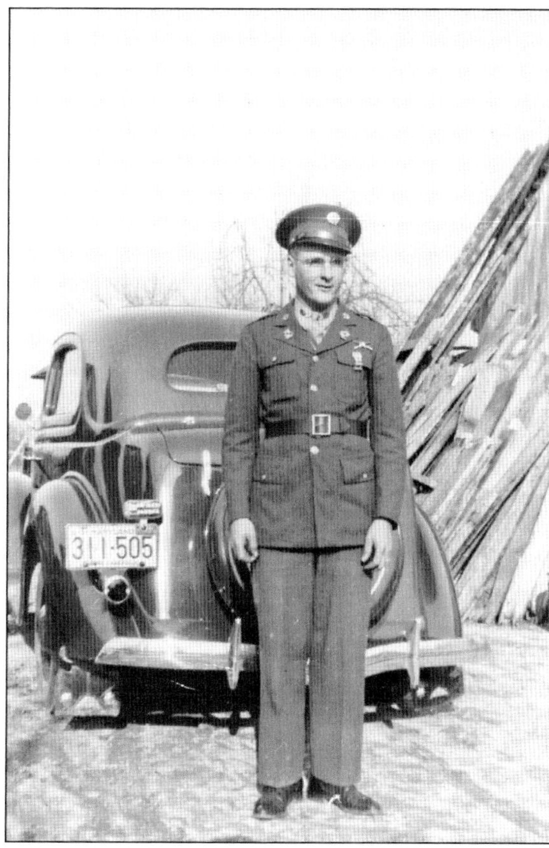

Born in Goldsboro, Hackett Kinnamon proudly served his country during World War II. (Courtesy Mary Kinnamon Jones Raughley.)